Taylor-Carlson's pen strokes mirror those of her paddle through the water...crisp, unhesitant, and smooth...a gutsy adventure around every bend. Take it from someone who was along for a few miles...this woman is the REAL DEAL.
~ Denise Goforth, river guide, *Venture West*

Cari Taylor-Carlson writes as she lives—with exuberance and spontaneity. Her colorful accounts are both entertaining and inspiring. If only we could all learn to extract as much joy from life's experiences as the author.
~ Lynne Bergschultz, Artist

In one sentence, Cari Taylor-Carlson tells you why you should read Life on the Loose. "Everything changes when you're on the edge, ready to slide into a river..." Few of us shift from Mom-in-the-kitchen to Outdoor Adventure Guide and fewer still can write about it with such grace and wisdom. Taylor-Carlson's book is an inspiration.
~ Judy (Redbird) Bridges, author, *Shut Up and Write*

Nonstop action fills this memoir, beginning with a solo canoe descent of Utah's Canyonland's wild Green River, and a successful ascent of Wyoming's Cloud Peak. Grab a good chair and settle in for a wild ride.
~ Eric Hansen, author, *Hiking Wisconsin*

Cari gives us the inside scoop on what it's like to be an adventure travel guide—quite an eye-opener. Each chapter is well paced, and her narrative arc pulls the whole book together. Best of all is her appealing voice: funny, insightful, honest, vulnerable. In short, a delightful read.
~ Carolyn Kott Washburne, Associate Professor,
English Department, University of Wisconsin-Milwaukee

A pilgrim's process of awakening the soul to life's scary and wonderful challenges. It's never too late to cross the river of no return.
~ Paul Guerin, *Venture West* guide, Mexico

In "Life on the Loose," Cari Taylor-Carlson takes you on an inspired ride though the journey of life from her experience of shifting gears from what you are "supposed" to do, in order to follow her passion against all conventional wisdom for her station in life. Her clever turn of phrase, coupled with her self-deprecating and vulnerable wit, revealing the thoughts we all have but seldom share, draws the reader in from the first sentence to the last. I find her tale particularly inspiring, not just in the activity of leading wilderness trips, which is near and dear to my heart as the Executive Director of the Urban Ecology Center in Milwaukee, but in the way she decided to do this (and do so successfully) so late in life! If she can do it, we can too! It's a great message shared in a fun and engaging style making it accessible to all.
~ Ken Leinbach, Executive Director, Urban Ecology Center, Milwaukee

Cari Taylor-Carlson was born to explore the world. Starting a tour business in her mid-forties with four children and going through a divorce? What! Only a courageous and talented person could pull that off. Cari is just that person. Not only did she have her adventures, but she introduced so many others to the beauty and wonder of the wilderness. In "Life on the Loose," Cari opens up and tells her stories of three decades as an adventure guide. From her first scouting trip paddling down the Green River in Utah—

asking herself "What am I doing here?"—to her last awe-inspiring hiking tour in Zion and Bryce and all the escapades in between, her accounts of these adventures are told with humor and wit. Her love of wilderness and adventure jumps out from every page. And her self-confidence is infectious. Those of us who were fortunate enough to sign on for Cari's adventures are eternally grateful.
~ Laura Olsen, *Hike-Inn tours*

Cari Taylor-Carlson's "Life on the Loose" is a fun, fast-moving, adventure tale. At its heart, it's a story about bravery, an autobiographical account of how a suburban housewife faced her fears to recreate herself though travel, and by creating her own outdoor adventure company. Like all great travel books, it is about both the external and internal world, capturing the wonder and beauty of those freshly encountered places, as well as how they can challenge and change the traveler who dares take the plunge. Cari does so again and again, with self-deprecating, humorous honesty, and we find ourselves captivated and rooting for her to succeed.
~ Bruce Murphy, Editor, *Urban Milwaukee.com*

"Life on the Loose" is a stunning rendition of one woman's journey, when a relationship falls apart. In the face of adversity, Taylor-Carlson maintains composure, grit, integrity, and all in the throes of arduous adventures in nature that many won't even dare to take. These stories, all vastly different, yet somehow connected, are a true testament to her fighting spirit. And written deftly with elements of grace, wit, and bravery. This is an honest book, as the reader is thrown into the wilds of the great outdoors—a transformative, lyrical experience.
~ Robert Vaughan, author, *Rift* and *Attics and Basements*

Whenever I think of hiking, backpacking, or skiing with Cari, a smile of pleasure fills my heart. Perhaps Cari was filled with anxiety when a sudden flash flood rose to our tent doors, or the ski trails were a sheet of ice, or the map and our trail weren't communicating, but we in her group were never aware of any angst on her part. Cari found a way to smile with confidence through every surprise, and to make whatever happened just be part of another wonderful trip in magnificent wild areas. Countless trips with Venture West add to my refrain, "Cari is a wonder."
~ Nancy Ball, frequent traveler with *Venture West*

Cari Taylor-Carlson is a real person who refused to allow real life heartache to defeat her spirit. I was fortunate to join her on several trips. In spite of her carefully planned agendas, I remember boarding the wrong train in Italy and fearing for my life as she encouraged me to climb onto the Navaho Knobs in Capital Reef National Park. Most of all I remember smiling a lot. Whether your idea of adventure is a walk in the woods or a hike in the Swiss Alps—beware—Taylor-Carlson's stories may encourage you to venture out beyond your comfort zone, one step at a time. Be prepared to laugh, cry, and carpe diem!
~ Carol Hebbring, frequent traveler with *Venture West*

What happens when a restless suburban mother of four listens to the voice that beckons her to travel and adventure? Why, she starts her own business as a wilderness travel guide, of course. With candor and wit, Cari Taylor-Carlson shares it all—her joys and revelations, challenges, and foibles—as she pushes herself out of her comfort zone and into the wild, with her trusting clients following close behind. This is a book about following your dreams, digging deep, and learning what you're made of.
~ Kim Suhr, Director, *Red Oak Writing*

Life on the Loose

My journey from suburban housewife
to outdoor guide

Other books by Cari Taylor-Carlson:

Milwaukee Walks: 20 Choice Walks in a Classy City

Milwaukee Eats: An Insider's Guide to Saloons, Cafes, Diners, Dives, and Neighborhood Restaurants (out of print)

The Upscale Outdoor Cookbook: Simple Recipes for Campers, Backpackers, and Short Order Cooks

The Food Lover's Guide to Milwaukee: An Insider's Guide to Ethnic Bakeries, Grocery Stores, Meat Markets, Specialty Food Shops and Cafes

Milwaukee's Best Cheap Eats
With Lynne Bergschultz: 190 Restaurants Where $15 Still Buys a Meal

Milwaukee Walks Again: 20 More Walks in a Classy City

Life on the Loose

My journey from suburban housewife to outdoor guide

Cari Taylor-Carlson

Serendipity Ink / HenschelHAUS Publishing, Inc.

Milwaukee, Wisconsin

Published by
Serendipity Ink
www. CariTaylorCarlson.com
In collaboration with HenschelHAUS Publishing, Inc.
www.henschelHAUSbooks.com
Milwaukee, Wisconsin

ISBN: 978-0-9629452-6-7
Kindle ISBN: 978-0-9629452-7-4
E-Pub ISBN: 978-0-9629452-8-1

Publisher's Cataloging-In-Publication Data
(Prepared by The Donohue Group, Inc.)

Taylor-Carlson, Cari.
Life on the loose : my journey from suburban housewife to outdoor guide / Cari
Taylor-Carlson.
pages ; cm
Issued also in Kindle and ePub formats.
ISBN: 978-0-9629452-6-7
1. Taylor-Carlson, Cari. 2. Tour guides (Persons)--Biography. 3. Housewives--
Biography. 4. Adventure travel. I. Title.
G154.7 .T39 2015   305.4379018/092

Cover design and font by Lynne Bergschultz
Front cover photo by Maureen Fitzgibbon, Annapurna One Base Camp in Nepal
Author photo: Denise Goforth

Printed in the United States of America

For my parents Buzz and Audrey Ferry,
who encouraged my adventures,

and for my children
Cathy, Linda, Wendy, and Chris,
who thrive despite their peripatetic mother.

Table of Contents

Author's Note

Some names have been changed out of respect for privacy, others because after a few hundred trips, names and faces have started to fade. Nothing in the book was invented, but in many cases, especially dialogue, I reconstructed as best I could. The stories are true.

Prologue

The woman seated next to me held her hand over her mouth. "I'm terrified," she moaned. "I feel like I can't breathe." She looked pale, pasty white, with beads of sweat on her forehead.

"You might be hyperventilating," I said. "Try to breathe into this bag and you'll feel better." She grabbed the lunch bag and took a deep breath. If only that was me. If only a bag could contain my projectile vomit.

I was too busy throwing up to speak coherently, not into a brown paper bag, but all over the deck of the *Isle Royale Queen* as we pushed through fourteen-foot waves on this five-hour journey from Copper Harbor, Michigan, to Isle Royale National Park. With the exception of one woman we named "Chatty Cathy" because she chattered nonstop to anyone who would listen, everyone on the boat had varying degrees of nausea. Fortunately, those giant waves washed away the remnants of our breakfasts, keeping the deck clear for anyone brave enough to stand.

I was the guide on the way to escort eight backpackers on a week-long trip along the Greenstone Ridge. I sat, glued to a wooden bench on the back of the boat, and asked myself, "What am I doing here?" Puking for five hours had not been my plan when I'd started this adventure travel business. This was my dream, the fantasy that carried me away from suburbia where I was an outsider, and on to adventure that would leave me fulfilled and wanting more. If this was adventure, I preferred laundry.

I ran outdoor trips for thirty years. When I started in 1982, I came up with a motto, a tag line for Venture West, my new business: "Complete Carefree Adventures." That's how I envisioned the business and the trips I planned to guide.

"*Complete*" was the easy part. I scouted new trips, arranged transportation, drove the vans, wrote, designed, and mailed six thousand yearly catalogs, answered the phone, and prayed to the weather gods.

But "*Carefree?*" A responsible guide creates a carefree experience for the customers. I had to forgo my carefree to ensure the safety and satisfaction of those customers.

Venture West had a perfect safety record, but that didn't mean there weren't close calls. I lost people: I lost Delores twice, once in Zion National Park and once in the Three Sisters Wilderness. I made wrong turns, like the time I turned left in Canyonlands and led the group six miles in the wrong direction until we were lost at sunset, four miles from the van. And I, the trusted guide, made an occasional bad judgment call, or inadvertently twisted the truth when I said, "No tick has ever been seen here," just as one dropped from a hemlock on to my shoulder.

Nor did I anticipate a steep learning curve in the guide business when I set off on a trail with my first four paying customers in 1982. That's why I've written *Life on the Loose*, not to rave about the joy of adventure travel, but to tell back stories, escapades not to be revealed until I shut down Venture West.

When I took six, eight, twelve people into a wilderness, the success and safety of the trip was up to me. It's not easy to pretend that everything will be fine when you're exposed on a rocky trail, you see lightning flashes in a black sky across a valley, and you're five miles from your campsite. When that happened in the Alaska Basin in the Tetons, rain turned to hail, sleet, and snow before we found shelter in our tents.

You will read about the challenges, the struggles, and more than a few surprises in *Life on the Loose.* There were also many glorious times. Grab your backpack and join me on the trail.

In the Beginning

Chapter One

Solo on the Green

2002 Venture West Catalog
Here's the wilderness trip you've been waiting for. The Green River in southern Utah meanders fifty-two miles from Ruby Ranch to Mineral Bottoms. The twisting, looping Green winds its way between sandstone cliffs towering fifteen hundred feet on either side.

"You're the only person on the river this week," Dirk said as he helped load my canoe. "Oh, you're traveling light. Do you have enough food, warm clothes?" His muscles bulged from hauling canoes. "Most people we put in fill the canoe."

He should know, as one of the three brothers who owned Tex's Riverways, my canoe outfitter. They launched hundreds of canoes each season. Good thing he couldn't hear my heart slam against my chest.

I had brought two duffels, stuffed with clothes, food, and gear. Six gallons of water, a Coleman stove, and those duffels didn't take up much space in an eighteen-foot aluminum canoe. It looked as empty as I felt. The breakfast cheese omelet and hash brown potatoes at the Westerner Cafe couldn't fill the scared hole in my belly.

Dirk added to my growing panic when he said in a flat voice, "You know my concern for your safety requires me to tell you what you're doing is dangerous. This is off-season." He walked to the bank where I sat in the canoe, and put his hand in the water as if to judge the current. "Ordinarily, we tell people if they run into trouble, another canoe will come along within an hour. For you, no such luck." He looked smug, as if confident in some secret knowledge of pitfalls looming ahead of me on the river.

When I planned this trip down the Green River in Utah, I'd arrived at a midlife junction. It was time to start the business I had dreamed about for many years, adventure travel guide. I loved the symbolism: launch a canoe, launch a new life. Ten, fifteen miles a day in a mild current would be about right for an experienced paddler checking out an adventure for her soon-to-be clients. I envisioned warm sunny days, sixty to seventy degrees, with a slight chill at night, spectacular canyon scenery, and around every bend, convenient campsites on sandbars. It added up to a dream wilderness trip in my favorite Western state. What could go wrong? I relished the challenge, a chance to prove to myself that I could be an intrepid adventurer.

At breakfast, a man at an adjacent table announced in a loud voice, "The dog's water froze last night. It was twenty-three when I went to bed at ten." He slung a winter jacket on a chair, gulped his coffee, and took off his gloves. "Feels nice and warm in here." He looked at me as if he could read my mind. How could he know?

In exactly thirty minutes I would leave for the river and five nights in a tent. Did I have to do this? Yes, if I wanted to reinvent myself as an outdoor guide. Thanks to lack of weather foresight and a habit of traveling light, my wardrobe included neither a fleece jacket nor long underwear. I knew better, but packed for Utah, not Montana. To my credit, I brought a rain jacket and rain pants that came in handy for warmth at night when I needed to wear everything I'd packed.

Food had been my primary concern, not my wardrobe. I had planned meals down to the cheese sauce for the Pasta Alfredo, fresh garlic, and the curry powder for the chicken. I would eat well.

As I stood by the river, "strong, confident, free" dissolved into "small, insignificant, scared." At home, the Green River was a cute little wiggly blue line on a map. Now those fifty-five miles from Ruby Ranch to Mineral Bottoms looked more like a Lewis and Clark expedition than a casual six-day outing. At least I was going downstream, not up. I should have done some research, made a plan that more closely matched the risks of this solo voyage. As an experienced outdoors person, I should have known to bring fleece, even to Utah in early November.

Would I find campsites? Did I have enough food, water, fuel, and what if my stove broke down?

Then Dirk said, "When it's time to come off the river, you'll come around a bend and see a cottonwood on the left bank. It's a big tree." He walked to the bank and started to slide the canoe into the river. "You can't miss it. Get ready to pull out there."

"That's it? You want me to watch for one tree? Anything else I should look for?" Now I felt the fear that would obsess me all day, every day, until I found that cottonwood. That fear sucked the joy out of the trip. Of course, I could miss it. Could I watch both sides of the river at the same time in a current that whipped me around every bend?

"Oh, you'll recognize the tree. It's at Mineral Bottoms, right in front of you." As he said this, his voice a monotone, he wouldn't look me in the eye, just stared at the river. I knew what he thought. This middle-aged woman is crazy. His disdain for my adventure eroded every remaining fragment of my fragile confidence. Damn Dirk. Damn the river. Damn my confident plan back in Milwaukee.

Life on the Loose

If I got myself into a jam, there was no one to lend a hand. The Green flowed through a wilderness canyon. I had choices: let go of the dream and stay the course in suburbia, or turn off the monkey-babble in my head, get in the canoe, and paddle.

"Don't worry about me. I'll be fine." He didn't ask about a cell phone. I didn't have one, but even if I did, it would have been useless in the canyon. Would I admit to Dirk that I was scared? Never. Just in case, we made a plan, because this mother of four wasn't ready to feed a turkey vulture in the desert.

"If you're more than a day late," he said, "I'll send a helicopter to search for you."

Dirk didn't know I would swim miles in the murky Green, before I'd flag down a helicopter or pay hundreds of dollars for a rescue. There would be a way out of that canyon even if I had to crawl naked and bloody over prickly pear cactus all the way. Still, it was comforting to know we had a plan.

Everything changes when you're at the edge, ready to slide into a river that will take you into the abyss, the unknown. Could I flip a switch, let go of my predictable life? A tree branch floated down-river and disappeared, and finally, tentatively, I let go of the root that bound me to the riverbank.

The current caught the bow of my canoe, and in thirty seconds, I was three hundred yards downriver. I wouldn't need to paddle, the Green would do the work. There was no turning back.

* * * * *

Labyrinth Canyon lived up to its name. The river wound back and forth making a series of S curves as it flowed into Navajo canyon walls that shuttered it like skyscrapers on Wall Street. I was a passenger, surrounded by beauty as the placid river reflected each nuance of the canyon that dwarfed my canoe. Again and again as I paddled and floated in the gentle current, I saw a wall of red rock coming at me, blocking my passage. Just when I'd think there's no way, it's a dead end, the river made a hard right or a hard left, and I coasted around the outside edge of the bend in the faster-moving current.

If only I could get the fear out of my gut, the terror that gripped my stomach every time I thought about the cottonwood tree. Dirk hadn't given any details. How big was it? How close to the river? I should have asked more questions. He said there were no other options. Did that mean the road at Mineral Bottoms was the only exit until the confluence with the Green and the Colorado? From the cottonwood, the Colorado River was fifty-five miles further downriver. Even if I got to the Colorado, there would be no jetboat ride back to Moab. The season ended on October 30. The boat would be winterized and put in a garage in Moab, and I would be on my own.

If I swept past the tree, I could climb out of the canyon, a thousand feet up to Canyonlands National Park, but there would be no trail to follow when I got there. I'd still be in the middle of nowhere. If I went too far, the canoe would be engulfed in whitewater that would take us both to a place of no return.

I paddled two-and-a-half hours on the first day. I saw desert, endless miles of sand lit by bright sunshine in a cloudless Utah sky. The river took me past a flat, beige landscape that gradually gave way to an increasingly deep, red rock canyon. The water reflected in perfect detail the rock walls and the golden tamarisks that lined its banks. That beauty was lost on me. My stomach hurt.

I looked at those walls, the map, and the walls again, and knew I had forgotten something important: how to read the brand-new, hundred-and-four-page, waterproof river map. Dirk had said something like, "Be sure you always know where you are on the map, because at the end of the day, when you get off the river, you won't be able to tell where you are. When you're out of the canoe, all the canyons look the same." He knew what he was talking about. All the canyons did look exactly the same, gaping holes, gashes in the landscape that suggested drainage, flowing water somewhere behind the weed-choked inlets that popped up on both sides of the river.

An experienced river rat would recognize the inlets and surmise the possibility of an opening that led to a campsite. Not me, I saw weeds.

The map didn't look like any map I'd ever seen. Maps have marked trails and intersections. This one looked like a book, one where each page covered a section of the Green. As always, north was at the top, but I was supposed to be heading south, or so I thought when I studied the Utah map at home. After I turned the upside-down map around and put south where it belonged, it made sense, not much, but at least the sun set in the west now, and I had a better shot at locating myself as I paddled downstream.

The first night I stumbled into Trin Alcove, a place where three canyons came together at the apex of a hairpin bend. As the canoe swished around the corner, a broad bench of sand looked like an obvious site for a tent. Canyons, waiting to be explored, opened behind the beach, but Dirk's warning played in my head. "You're the only person on the river." I played it safe, sat by the tent, and watched the water that looked like chocolate pudding slide by my temporary home.

At 5:30, it turned dark, cold, and lonely. Had I forgotten about November's short days, or chosen not to acknowledge the fourteen-hour nights? And, where was the fleece I left behind in Milwaukee? I built a fire in the required firepan and propped it between my legs for warmth. Even the songs of the canyon wrens ceased, their cheerful trill replaced by silence, while my little fire flickered and lit the rock that surrounded me. When the nighttime blues hit, exacerbated by wine, I felt the weight of the unknown, and wondered as I would every minute of every hour for the next four days, *What am I doing here?*

I had left four children at home. The oldest, Cathy, was seventeen; Linda and Wendy came in the middle; Chris at eleven was the youngest. If I started a business, I figured a couple weeks a year in the west, and three or four weekends closer to home would be overlooked, as they went about their busy lives. Maybe pride in their mother's adventures would overshadow the loss of an ordinary mom who cooked dinner every night and kept the cookie jar full.

What were they doing? Did Cathy and Linda get tickets for The Who concert? Did Wendy finish her science project for Mr. Horowitz? Did Chris go to Ricky and Ray's house for a sleep-over?

Did they miss me? Would they ever understand my need to live part of my life in wild places? I made hard choices. Safe at home, I longed for wilderness and adventure. Then when I left, I wanted to be at home with my family. I needed someone to tell me that what I was doing was okay, that I could be both a mom and an outdoor guide.

This new life was supposed to be easy; everything was supposed to fall into place, while my children unanimously expressed pride in their mom. Someone, maybe Cathy, would say, "You're way more cool than Sue's mom. She doesn't even know how to build a fire," and I would get all gooey inside and feel proud, and give everyone a hug. It never happened that way. They wanted a mom who looked like the other moms. I didn't know how to do that. Even when I dressed up in my Chico's jeans and some clunky, hip jewelry, I didn't get it right. I wanted to look stylish with cool clothes and good hair, but I hated to shop, and was too frugal to pay for a haircut at a salon.

I watched the remains of the afterglow from the sunset and turned my thoughts to the river and my new life.

I'd always been the one who organized camping trips for family and friends, the person who planned every detail because it was fun, and because no one else wanted to do it. I'm not a detail person, but when it came to outdoor adventure, I loved every step of the process. I reserved the campsites, planned the meals, bought the groceries and set up the tents. This was my playtime.

Wasn't this logical, to start a business doing what I loved? I thought so. My husband Peter said if there was profit involved, then he could understand why I did it. But, of course, he was a business-man. He had made it clear that I couldn't expect his help with laundry, cooking, cleaning, the daily chores that keep a home running. He had said, "When you make as much money as I do, I'll help you at home." This was the early eighties, before women received enough well-deserved credit for their "work" at home. His attitude reflected the thinking of most suburban husbands with stay-at-home wives.

In his world, money mattered. I'd have to show a profit to earn his respect and his permission. Money would prove that I was more that a dilettante.

I ate a Snickers bar and went to bed.

On the second day, I positioned south where it belonged, on the downriver side of the map. As I glided past Bull Hollow, Ten-Mile Canyon, and Keg Spring Bottom, I worried. Between mother-guilt and the cottonwood, nothing felt right except the current that gently pulled me down the Green as I sang "Cruising Down the

River" and "Down by the Riverside" to keep up my spirits. Maybe I was a crazed, middle-aged housewife who should have stayed home with her family. Maybe I just needed a hug.

At the end of the day, every sandbar, a potential campsite, was covered with a layer of mud that stuck to my shoes. To make it worse, a thin layer of ice coated the muck. The first time I explored one of those icy terraces, rather than lose my shoes in a sinkhole, I tiptoed onto the ice in bare feet and sank in something up to my knee. Quicksand?

I had grown up with a horror of quicksand. My mom convinced me that I would sink up to my eyeballs and die if I stepped on that allegedly treacherous sand along the shore of Lake Michigan where we spent our summers. Now I pictured myself disappearing forever in a bottomless mud bath while the canoe coasted down the Green. My family would never know what happened to their mother. I'd turn into a statistic, an unresolved death on the Green. Now there was a new worry, something else to obsess about besides finding the tree.

Only once, at Trin Alcove on that first night, did I find a site with reasonably easy river access and sand, not ice and mud. The rest of the time, I hauled the canoe across the mud or up a bank to a place where I could tie it on to something sturdy. Then I used a willow branch to floss the mud from between my toes. It wasn't all bad. After dinner, I sat in front of my green tent that faced the river, watched the golden sun light up the rocks, and felt at peace with the journey.

Each day I paddled, ate two semi-frozen Snickers bars, one after lunch, and one after dinner, and tried to quell my thumping heart. Each night, I built a small fire in the firepan, wrapped my legs around it, and sat outside until my backside got cold. By 7:30, I tucked myself inside my warm sleeping bag where, secure in the tent, sleep came slowly while I attempted to visualize the damn cottonwood. I couldn't still my mind. It wandered to sudden windstorms, quicksand, or my canoe ripped from its moorings, disappearing down the Green.

Each morning, I broke the ice in my water bottle, took a frozen towel into my sleeping bag, scrubbed my face with ice crystals, and peed in a bucket. Dirk had told me to pee in the river, but the bucket was easier, and closer. Later, I dumped the bucket in the river, so it ended in the same place. And the rest, along with kitty litter, went into a second bucket that came with me in the canoe. Or as Dirk put it, "There's a rule on the Green: no shit left behind."

After morning chores, I sat outside and waited for warmth from the sun before I could think about breakfast, or getting ready for the day. While I listened to the canyon wren, the sound of rustling leaves, and the soft gurgle of the river, the red rock canyon glowed as if lit from the inside by a giant candle.

Then it was D-Day, day five of the six-day journey. I'd gone around Bow Knot Bend, past Oak Bottom, and found Hell Roaring Canyon. I'd worried my way down the Green for four days, survived cold, lonely nights and stressful days, searched for campsites, and walked barefoot on ice. The river gave me perfect sunny days, idyllic canyon scenery, and an easy float, but where was the pleasure? Joy? Contentment?

My morning oatmeal tasted like warm sawdust. Coffee didn't perk up my spirits. I had to find that cottonwood. My mouth felt like it was full of gauze. My heart pounded. I checked the map and started down the final four miles. I scanned both sides of the river. My chest throbbed, tightened, my heartbeat matched the cadence of the second-hand ticking on my watch. I couldn't breathe. Time stopped.

I rounded a curve, paddled past an endless sandbar and then, suddenly, the obvious appeared, a detail Dirk had neglected to mention, a prominent dirt road, and that tree, a golden specimen, backlit by the late afternoon sun. The muscles in my gut unclenched as I landed the canoe, pitched the tent thirty-six hours early, and waited for the noon pickup on day six.

Relaxed, I savored the heat from the afternoon sun, the taste of strong coffee, the quiet, the woodsy smell of my tiny fire, and the silent river flowing south. I'd paddled through magnificent canyons and only occasionally noticed the details, the clean rock faces, their colors reflected in the river, and the changing contours, surprises around every bend. I could have trusted the Green to take me where I needed to be. Instead, I wasted much of the beauty, obsessed about how the trip would end.

I was about to leap into the unknown with a business full of risks. I would never know how a trip would end until it ended. I'd have to project total confidence, because future customers would depend on my guide expertise. Despite my best efforts to control every aspect of a trip, I'd have to fake it, pretend everything would be fine, and we'd be safe no matter what happened, or how scared and incompetent I felt.

I ate the last semi-frozen Snickers bar, toasted the cottonwood with a glass of wine, and slept soundly under the stars.

Chapter Two

The Doll in the Jar

Lyrics from *On the Loose*
Girl Scout National Center West (1979)

*There's a trail that I'll be hiking
Just to see where it might go.
Many places yet to visit
Many people yet to know.
For in following my dreams
I will live and I will grow
And tomorrow I'll be out there
On the loose.*

In the great room in my suburban home, under the wood-beamed cathedral ceiling, my Salvation Army leather chair fit me perfectly, like a nest, each time I curled up with *Woodswoman* by Anne LaBastille, or *The Man Who Walked Through Time* by Colin Fletcher. Would I still be sitting in that same chair at ninety, reading about other people's adventures, instead of reminiscing about my own? Or was it time to get off my duff, to start living the life I dreamed about? When I met people who traveled in wild places, backpacked, canoed, or hiked, and didn't just talk about it, but did it, I wanted to do that, too.

I used to be a fearless risk taker. At nineteen, I took a train by myself from my home in Fort Wayne, Indiana, to San Francisco, with no job, no money, no place to live, and no plan. All it took was optimism and youthful exuberance. I'd fallen madly in love with a

19

traveling salesman named Kent the previous summer in Fort Wayne who wooed me with candlelit dinners in fancy restaurants. He lived in San Francisco and promised to show me the city if I came to visit. At the time, I had completed my freshman year at the University of Wisconsin and was ready for an adventure. On the train ride across the country, my diet consisted of peanut butter and jelly sandwiches and fountain water, because I didn't have fifty cents for a soda. I did have two hundred dollars saved to get by until I found a job.

It was a close call. My roommate loaned me fifty for groceries until I landed a job waitressing at David's Delicatessen in the theater district. Nothing on the menu sounded like anything we ate back in Fort Wayne. When customers ordered corned beef on rye, I served them pastrami on pumpernickel. It all looked like sliced red meat to me. The manager fired me on my second day. To add injury to insult, my would-be "boyfriend" Kent lowered the boom. It went something like this. "You came all this way to see me? I have a girlfriend. We're getting married in September." Kent broke my nineteen-year-old heart.

I lied about my college plans to get my next job. When I said, "I've decided to drop out and stay in San Francisco," the manager hired me. From nine to five at the Federal Reserve Bank, I stuffed checks into a machine that sorted and counted them. Every afternoon, somewhere around 3:00, my eyes closed. It was nap time. No wonder: I partied and drank cheap beer every night, often until 3:00 a.m., then set the alarm for 7:00 for another dull day at the check machine.

This was a crazed time in the city. In addition to the beer parties after midnight, I drank too many straight-up martinis at Tadish Grill, ate free food at the bars to save money, called that dinner, and acquired a fondness for Irish Coffee at the Buena Vista.

I loved every minute of that summer.

* * * * *

Taking risks made me happy. Trying to be popular gave me stomach aches. In junior high in Fort Wayne, I wanted to fit in, be one of the popular seventh grade girls at Mrs. Gates Dancing School. Instead, I was a "wallflower" in an orange corduroy dress and shiny, black, patent-leather shoes. The popular girls wore puffed crinoline skirts and fancy blouses. I wore braces on my teeth and black glasses. The cute boys never looked at me when they chose dance partners for the fox trot.

I hated that orange dress. It had a fat belt and an a-line skirt that made me look like a gussied-up pumpkin. It was one of two "dancing school" dresses. The other dress, a navy-blue sheath, hugged my chubby body, letting everyone see my belly fat. Three white stripes circled my waist, setting off the worst parts of my adolescent figure.

Thanks to the same number of boys and girls in the class, I usually ended up with a dance partner, the short boy who wore a bow tie and had food stains on his white shirt. He stood in front of me, stared at the floor until the music started. Then he'd say, "Wanna dance?" He didn't want to be there either.

The boy I really wanted to dance with was Richard Johnson, but he picked the girls with cashmere sweaters and perfect teeth. His dance partners were popular. He didn't look at the girl in the orange dress with "Wallflower" stamped on her forehead.

From the first time I saw Richard Johnson when we were both in sixth grade, I thought he was perfect. We rode the school bus together, and if he sat on the seat next to me and our butts touched, I thought I would faint. He always matched his shirts with his socks and had the best wavy, blonde hair. At twelve, I wanted to marry him, but in the six years we rode the bus together, he never spoke to me.

Life on the Loose

* * * * *

When I was a kid, I did crazy stuff. At twelve, I took my eight-year-old brother Guy on a hike around a small lake in northern Michigan. We slogged through knee-deep water in a swamp, with no plan, just the childish joy that comes from freedom in an unexplored place.

Guy didn't share my enthusiasm. He cried, begged, "I want to go home," and held on to my leg with a death grip as we shoved through the weed-choked water. I didn't dare tell him that we were lost.

Some might call me a troublemaker, a problem child who needed boundaries. If we didn't know how to get home, that was okay with me. It was an adventure. That episode ended well, when my brother and I came to a lake and flagged down a fisherman. He looked at me, looked at Guy, who was still sobbing, and said, "Get in the boat and tell me where you live. I'll get you home." I always knew we'd be fine.

Lost in that swamp, I felt exhilarated; not scared, happy. I couldn't get the smile off my face. Even at twelve, something that brought a tickle of fear meant life was good.

* * * * *

After I married Peter Carlson when I was twenty-five, my risk-taking muscle started to shrink. Life no longer included the high that accompanied adventure, the frisson of fear I needed. But I had another high—the birth of our first daughter Cathy in San Francisco. That's when we decided to return to the Midwest to raise our family close to our birth families in Fort Wayne and Chicago. Peter found a job in Peoria, Illinois, where we lived for five years.

Since he had an executive position at a large manufacturing facility, the second largest corporation in town, I found myself on the board at the YWCA and the Peoria Art Guild, vice-president of my church group, and president-elect of my college sorority alumni group. I wore pleated skirts and nylons held up with a garter belt, balanced an infant on my hip, fed homemade baby food to two toddlers, and cooked meat, potatoes, and vegetables for my hardworking husband.

Being a troublemaker was more fun. Putting on nylons, looking well-groomed, going to meetings, making small talk, serving on committees, was not my plan for the rest of my life. I loved being a mom. It was the rest of it, the dressed-up matron role, I didn't like.

Nor did I play that role well. The first and only time we invited Peter's boss Stan and his wife Lou to dinner, Lou fell asleep at the dinner table.

"It must have been my fault," I said to Peter afterward. "Was I that boring?"

There I was again, the wallflower in the orange dress at Mrs. Gates Dancing School, feeling like a loser.

* * * * *

Could this be the same woman who had graduated from the University of Wisconsin with a degree in merchandising? Was this the person who took the train twice from Fort Wayne to San Francisco without a job, once for love and again after graduation for a career in fashion? Was this the woman who quit her job as a buyer in the Junior Woman's dress department at The White House, a boutique department store in San Francisco, and instead survived on coffee and cigarettes in order to pursue her passion—weekend ski outings in Squaw Valley?

Life on the Loose

The day I said to Mrs. Proudfit, the personnel manager at The White House, "I quit," and left the buyer in the fabric department without an assistant, I might have known life would be different. I cared more about freedom, excitement, and adventure than I cared about job security, cash in the bank, and health insurance. Out of a job, I had small change for groceries, so I ate a lot of hot dogs and drank cheap beer. The unemployment check paid the rent while I looked for another job, but I made sure it was one that didn't include weekend hours. There were other plans for those weekends.

* * * * *

Peter and I moved from Peoria to Milwaukee, Wisconsin, when I was in my early thirties. By this time, we had three children and a dog. We bought a home in the suburb of Whitefish Bay that met our criteria: good schools and sidewalks. We joined a tennis and swimming club where I felt self-conscious every time I went to the pool in a bathing suit that revealed my chubby legs. Small talk at parties where people ate crab-stuffed mushrooms and gossiped about celebrities didn't interest me. I failed at cocktail conversation with strangers. That life was not my dream.

My well-behaved persona hid the real me. The edge that had propelled me to take on risk when I was young had dissolved in everyday routines. After a year in Milwaukee, we had four children, Cathy, Linda, Wendy, and Chris, the same dog, two cats, a hamster named Herbie, a gerbil, and a bird named Dick.

To keep my brain alive, I replaced pleated skirts and nylons with jeans and tennis shoes and enrolled in an art history graduate program at the University of Wisconsin-Milwaukee.

Mine was a good life. Every day bustled with activities: tennis, art history classes, teaching environmental education, and being a stay-at-home mom. There was nothing to complain about. Yet, something shifted when this out-of-shape, size-fourteen housewife with four children, five bedrooms, three bathrooms, and a two-car garage noticed the first twitch of midlife angst.

I felt uncomfortable with the PTA ladies at my children's school. I bought second-hand clothes at the Salvation Army and cut my own hair. When I tried to look stylish, I looked foolish, overdressed. I quit trying to match the other suburban matrons and wore jeans with holes in the knees, grungy tee shirts, and a bulky Army Surplus jacket in the winter. I wanted to make a statement, show everyone I didn't give a damn, in a neighborhood where everyone else looked like they had stepped out of a fashion magazine when they went to the store for milk.

No one in my family complained about the way I looked, but a chance remark from my daughter Cathy hit home. "What really matters when people want to look good is their hair and their shoes." She didn't mean her mom, but when I looked in the mirror, I saw bad hair and shoes that looked like they belonged in the trash.

My marriage was going down. The harder I tried to talk with Peter about my feelings, my insecurities, the faster he ran in the opposite direction. He was no different than most men of that generation. Feelings were scary and talking about them made them real. Maybe I pushed too hard for those heart-to-hearts. Instead of drawing us closer, my need to talk about feelings wedged us apart.

One day, without any prior discussion, he came home and said, "I had a vasectomy." At that moment, I should have known the marriage was over, but I kept trying to make it work.

He wanted a conventional wife, one who didn't embarrass him by planting a wildflower garden in front of his home. He and our children wanted Kentucky blue grass, not cup plant and Joe Pye weed. The wild yard was different, like me, and they wanted me to match the other moms on the block, the marigold moms.

Guilt started to nag at me at 3:00 in the morning, when the nighttime demons arrived, and everything seemed wrong. Was I a bad wife, a bad person? Why didn't I care about the PTA or the bake sale? All the other mothers did. Instead of baking cupcakes and cookies, I wanted to walk away on a trail into a wild place. I wanted to sleep under the stars and cook breakfast over a campfire. I remembered northern Michigan and the swamp where Guy and I had been lost, and all the camping trips Peter and I had taken before children. I wanted to slice a piece of that life into my suburban life with my family. Could I have it both ways? I kept that dream to myself.

Then my marriage fell apart. It happened suddenly. We had rented a vacation home on Lake Superior in Michigan's Upper Peninsula. I went ahead a few days early with the children while Peter stayed behind to work. On Friday night, the kids and I picked a bouquet of field flowers, lit the grill for a treat—steak and burgers—and waited. Seven o'clock and still no husband. Eight o'clock. By nine o'clock, the embers had long turned cold. At 11:00, I sent the children to bed. Peter showed up after midnight and said, "I'm late. I moved out."

I shut down, retreated into a state of disbelief. On Thursday, I was married with children; on Friday at midnight, a single mom with four children ages four to ten. Devastated, I couldn't talk to anyone except my children, and only told a friend after a week because when she called, I broke down and started to sob.

That started a painful divorce that dragged on for eight long years. I cried all the time, tried to patch us back together, but he didn't love me anymore. It took eight years for me to figure out that when a marriage is over, it's over.

We had different dreams, but we never talked about them. If he had dreams beyond a successful career in finance, I don't know what they were. Whenever I asked, "What do we want together for our lives?" and talked about living in the country someday, he left the room. Maybe I scared him.

I had married a man I dated for three years, someone with good looks, charisma, and a career. I saw our future: safe, financially secure, predictable, a good life filled with laughter. I loved him, saw everything in rosy hues, and overlooked his martinis and his obsession with work. I needed someone who talked to me, and instead I married a man who slammed the door every time I wanted to have a real conversation about life, our dreams, our future.

When he walked out, I realized I had married a person I didn't know. I bought the superficial package and thought it was enough. Maybe he had, too. We were flawed when it came to making a marriage work and we knew it.

During the heat of the divorce, I drove my Volkswagen van to Door County, Wisconsin, and checked into a cheap motel in Sister Bay. I had a plan: drive to Newport Beach State Park, sit on a rock along Lake Michigan's shore, and write the class assignment for a human relations course, a requirement for my degree. If I left everything familiar behind in Milwaukee, perhaps I could clear my head and get this writing assignment done.

I took pen and notebook to the park on a misty, cloudy day in October. Close to the parking lot, the forest looked dense, dark, scary, like the time my basement light burned out while I was folding laundry and everything disappeared in the dark.

Life on the Loose

I took a few steps down the Newport trail that led from the parking lot to a series of backcountry campsites. It wasn't a narrow path. It was a former logging road, big enough for my van, but when the parking lot disappeared, I had a full-blown anxiety attack. I started to sweat, my legs wobbled, my throat filled with bile. I ran back to the "safe" parking lot and jumped in the van.

What had happened? Was I afraid to be alone in the woods in a state park? The risk-taking muscle had vanished, and in its place, shame at the fear that overwhelmed me. That was a sad epiphany.

As we were closing in on our divorce, I received the letter that changed my life. The local Girl Scout chapter had offered me a job at their National Center West in Wyoming. I agonized over the decision to leave my children for three weeks, but something compelled me, a premonition this would be a life-changing event. I wavered, then wrote a letter and said, "Thanks for thinking about me, but as I have a young family, I have to decline." I wanted to scream, to let out my frustrations before I split down the middle like an orange popsicle on a hot day. Why couldn't I be a home-maker, a good mother, and an adventurer? Did the two parts of me have to be incompatible? Was I a selfish bitch who thought only of herself?

After Peter offered to move back into our home to care for the children, I reconsidered, weighed the practical realities against the tantalizing possibilities of a Wyoming adventure, and took the job. I couldn't have known that his generous offer would change my life.

In Ten Sleep, Wyoming, I joined three other leaders to take twenty-four teenage girls on a two-week backpacking trip into the Big Horn Mountains. That first small step turned into a lunge. The leader in charge, an experienced backpacker, put me in charge of equipment. I'd never backpacked. Equipment? What equipment? I faked it, pretended to know what we needed, thought I could wing it.

"We'll take twenty-four tent stakes, twelve boxes of matches, and four gallons of fuel," I said with authority to the person at the store. The leader standing behind me—who did know what she was doing—corrected my order, and thanks to her intervention, we had what we needed on the trip.

Before we left the base camp, a high desert located in the foothills of the Big Horns, we spent several days getting to know the young women we would live with for the next two weeks. They were ages fourteen to eighteen, nervous adventurers about to start the journey of their young lives. We had one thing in common: we loved thunderstorms, the bigger and louder, the better.

The girls worried about the details:

"Can I wash my hair?"

"Will I get enough to eat?"

"Where do we go to the bathroom?'

'What! You want me to poop in the woods and bury my poop," said Alice from Texas.

"Yep, that's what the shovel is for." said Irene, the experienced backpacker, and pointed to the orange plastic trowel.

"Oh," I thought to myself. "I didn't know that."

The trip turned out to be the hardest thing I'd ever done. At age forty, I climbed my first mountain, Cloud Peak, thirty-five-hundred feet up until my legs felt like overcooked linguine and my heart tried to exit my chest.

Every night, we sat around a campfire and sang the old camp songs and a new song someone had written especially for the Girl Scout National Center West. The words to *On the Loose* burned into my psyche, especially the chorus. It became my mantra, a reference point whenever I felt discouraged.

On the loose to climb a mountain
On the loose where I am free

Life on the Loose

On the loose to live my life
The way I think my life should be.
For I only have a moment
And a whole life yet to live
I'll be lookin' for tomorrow
On the loose."

After two weeks in the wilderness, I looked in a mirror and saw a tan, fit stranger sporting a smile that split her face, someone who had carried a forty-pound pack on steep rocky trails for two weeks and loved every sweaty minute.

It was time to get off my duff and to start living the life I dreamed about. Maybe I was a selfish bitch who thought only of her own needs, but I craved adventure. It made me whole, gave me purpose, pride, and great enthusiasm for the future.

Soon after I returned home from Montana, I went shopping at the Goodwill store where I sometimes bought my clothes. On a shelf, I saw a child's doll and for some reason decided to buy it. I stuffed her in a one-quart mason jar, and placed her on my desk. She looked ugly in the jar, crushed, her distorted arms and legs tight against her body, her flattened face pressed against the glass, staring at me from her prison.

The doll was me. I could relate to her prison. I wondered if other people felt the same constraints. I couldn't talk about this with my friends or the façade would crack: the contented mother, homemaker, albeit almost divorced, but doing her best to make a happy home for her children. I needed to find a way to live that confirmed both my love for my family and my passion for wilderness adventure. Otherwise, I was just another worker drone, getting a weekly paycheck from the Audubon Center where I worked as an urban naturalist.

The public saw a happy face, but at home, I felt cranky, disagreeable. If one of the kids left dirty dishes in the sink or a peanut butter knife on the counter, I'd overreact.

"Clean up this mess," I said too many times when I came home after work. Soon my four children left the room whenever they saw me coming. They didn't like the person I had become and neither did I.

Why did I feel strong and exceptional on the inside, but ordinary and dull in my suburban life, a loser? It was as if that wallflower in the orange dress at Mrs. Gates Dancing School had returned to haunt me. Every day I looked at that contorted doll in the jar and remembered the other woman, the tough and adventurous one who had carried a forty-pound pack in the mountains.

For two years, the doll and I stared at each other. I read self-help books that promoted "Do what you love and the money will follow," or "Follow your bliss," or "Pick a color for your parachute." I read and reread a book about pathfinders because I wanted to join that club, be someone special, follow my passion. Those authors wrote about courage, taking risks, living life unafraid.

"I can take people on backpacking trips. I can fake it," I told myself. "I can be a good mom and still have adventures. I don't have to be gone all the time. Maybe once a month? Why not? My mom always said, 'Nothing ventured, nothing gained.'"

Puffed up by that happy talk, I took my shaky confidence, looked into the future, and launched Venture West.

And the forlorn doll sitting on the desk? I released her from the mason jar and returned her to Goodwill.

Chapter Three

Magic Slippers

2001 Venture West Catalog

After you arrive at the Jackson airport, we'll travel over Teton Pass to Driggs, Idaho. The next morning we pick up our packs and hike up the mountain via South Teton Creek to a site just below our destination. The next day we arrive at camp at ninety-five-hundred feet in the Alaska Basin where we spend four nights surrounded by Battleship Mountain, Buck Mountain and Mt Mead.

For the first Venture West trip, I planned a four-day backpacking adventure to Pictured Rocks National Lakeshore in Michigan. I could do this in a wilderness-like area, not too far from a road, a place to take people who knew a tiny bit less than I did. Fifty dollars paid for postage, chartreuse Ultra-brite paper, and printing for the seventy-five one-page flyers mailed to everyone I knew. I charged fifty dollars for an all-inclusive adventure, including transportation from Milwaukee to the trailhead in my Dodge Colt.

Four people signed on. I packed food, got the permits, bought tents and stoves, and rounded up all the miscellaneous equipment I learned about from the Girl Scouts. Then I planned a route and figured out how to hang food to keep it safe from bears. Four customers and I packed the car, traveled three hundred miles to Pictured Rocks, and set off down the trail.

Life on the Loose

* * * * *

Two years later, I had a business, or to be honest, I had the glimmer of the possibility of a profitable business. But did I look like a guide? Did I have the casual, weathered nonchalance necessary to look the part? I wanted strangers to see me from afar and say, "She must be a guide," as I sauntered into an outdoor store, reduced to a size ten, wearing slightly worn Levis, a torn tee from Kathmandu, and dusty hiking boots. Sales people would recognize me and say, "Hey, two people asked about your Montana trip today."

I would smile and say, "Early snowstorm. We were trapped for three days. Great trip."

In Wilson, Wyoming, I saw someone wearing clunky unfashionable shoes, but he had "The Look": slender, mountain-fit, scruffy jeans, and a tee that said "just do it." He asked the clerk at the general store, "Do you have any medium beeners?" He dropped his well-worn backpack on the counter, glanced in my direction, and disappeared down an aisle.

What is a beener? Dare I ask? A pink flush crept up my face. His sunburned, rugged face, muscled arms, and grimy backpack advertised mountain charisma. He came back to the front of the store holding something metal and said, "I'm taking a client to the top of the Grand in three days, an old guy, must be fifty at least." Okay, he meant carabineers, gadgets used by rock climbers. I knew something about mountaineering, though I had no idea what to do with a beener. And the fifty part, I was dangerously close.

He looked like someone who would exercise before breakfast, climb the Grand Teton before noon, live in an energy-efficient house with solar panels, and eat low on the food chain. His shoes were light brown, soft suede slip-ons, shaped like fat Idaho potatoes with drawstring closures. Worn with faded jeans and a ripped tee, they pulled his outfit together, the way an Oriental rug organizes a room.

Self-conscious in my tan Gap chinos, hot pink Ralph Lauren tee, and new Merrill Gore-tex hiking boots, my look screamed suburban couture. I hoped he didn't notice that my face matched my tee. There I stood, about to hike solo, nine miles up the South Teton Trail to the Alaska Basin to scout trails for a backpacking trip for Venture West, yet too intimidated to start a conversation with an attractive mountain man.

Was I still the gawky teenager at Mrs. Gates Dancing School, waiting for Richard Johnson to notice me? No, darn it, I was a guide, strong, fearless, intrepid, about to have an adventure in the mountains.

I wanted his shoes. They completed the "mountain man" look. After visiting every camping store in Jackson Wyoming, I found them at Teton Mountaineering. They were designed for adventure, but not what the salesperson at the store meant when he said, "You'll love them. They'll be good for shoveling snow in Milwaukee." That would not happen. They were my statement shoes. I would never wear them with anything from the Gap or a pink tee. I had a new look.

I also had a foothold in my new business, a mailing list from press releases sent to newspapers and magazines, speaking engagements at every Rotary Club in the Milwaukee area, and a booth at the Milwaukee Sports Show. I needed those shoes, "The Look," to build confidence and to impress my future customers.

* * * * *

Later that summer, the shoes and I had our first adventure, a climbing incident near Jackson, Wyoming. I'd come a day ahead of a

Venture West group to set up tents and buy food for a camping/ hiking trip in the Tetons. After I organized the campsite, I joined my friend Kim for a hike up Blacktail Butte. "We'll follow the trail to the top," he said. "It's pretty easy. There's a great view of the whole Teton range from there." He pointed across the valley, "You can see my house."

"Looks pretty steep to me. If this is such a great hike, where is everyone?" I stepped into the shade. Between the sun and the thin mountain air, it felt like ninety, not my favorite kind of day for a hike. I was already hot and sweaty from setting up six tents and organizing food for my group, who would arrive the next morning.

Kim looked around as if he hadn't noticed the empty parking lot. "Don't worry. Only the locals know about it. They're at work." He was a seasoned climber, but he didn't look at my feet, nor did he ask if I'd ever climbed.

"You think I can do this?" My brand-new shoes pinched my feet. "Statement shoes," I muttered to myself. "Don't be a fool. You wanted this. Now do it."

Kim started up the trail, looked back to see if I was coming. "Oh, Cari, it's easy. Look, you can see the trail. See how it zigzags to the top." I did see something that might have been a trail, until it disappeared behind a rock and didn't come out again.

"Right, I see it," I lied.

We started up a gravel path, me in my potato shoes, and Kim in sturdy hiking boots. If he'd mentioned climbing, scrambling, two thousand feet up a boulder field, with terrifying rest stops on six-inch-wide ledges, maybe I'd have changed into real boots, or better yet, waited in the car. I trusted the sturdy, albeit slippery, rubber soles on the potato shoes, and trudged upward.

"I don't like this," I called up to Kim. "Don't get so far ahead of me."

36

Magic Slippers

If I quit, Kim would think I was a sissy. He knew I came to guide. This was my time to practice stoic, strong, the "can do" attitude I'd need when things went wrong. Admit I was scared? Never. There must have been a fine view behind me, but I couldn't take my eyes off the trail or I'd topple backwards and land in the parking lot.

Kim danced up the trail and disappeared. Then it ended. Instead of a civilized trail, a series of narrow rock shelves like vertical stepping stones stopped me cold. My feet didn't fit. The shoes had round toes, not designed for climbing. I put the ball of my right foot on the rock and felt like a ballerina balanced on one toe, except I have flat feet and bad balance.

The man in the store had been right. The shoes were meant for shoveling snow in Milwaukee.

My knees shook. My legs felt like jelly. Crumbly rocks broke from every handhold. Sweat ran down my face. My glasses slipped so far down my nose that I could barely see the rock I was supposed to grab. The mountain-chic shoes felt like bedroom slippers on ice.

"Come on, Cari. You can do it" came from above. I took baby steps across a ledge as narrow as a gymnast's balance beam.

"Don't look down. You might lose your balance." Kim didn't sound concerned.

"There's no room for my feet. You're damned right I'll lose my balance." I grabbed a tree root and tried to slide sideways to get a better foothold. "Don't worry, I won't look down." I clung to the edge. "Kim, wherever you are, I quit." I started to cry.

He climbed down to my perch, as if he were coming down the front steps on my porch, and pointed to a series of ledges. "Put your right foot here, your left foot there, then, slide over here." I followed, using his instructions for every step, until the terrifying toeholds led to the top. I flopped in the gravel on my stomach and sobbed tears of relief.

Life on the Loose

When I could speak, I croaked, "Nice view." Okay, I had wanted adventure when I left behind the predictable life in suburbia. This must be it, hard but good.

A raven's call broke the silence. In a vertical wilderness, looking across the valley at the snow-capped Teton Range, I felt calm, peaceful, and alive. "Thank you," I said.

Kim smiled, pointed to the other trail to the top, a gentle hike with normal switchbacks, unlike the mountaineering route we took. "Do you want go down the other way?" It was my turn to smile.

I needed that success. I'd just quit my job at the Schlitz Audubon Center to focus on the guiding business. I had no money except family maintenance from Peter and an occasional freelance writing gig. Because I had given up the weekly paycheck, I needed to grow the Venture West business to support myself and my children.

Blind optimism kept me going during the early years when Venture West barely broke even. The kids and I ate a lot of peanut butter sandwiches while I hoped things would improve. Since I had grown up with frugal parents, I knew how to cut corners and make do with pennies and dimes, not dollars. No regrets. I should have known when I quit my day job, poverty and peanut butter would be part of the package.

* * * * *

The following summer, the shoes and I traveled to the Alaska Basin in the Tetons, where they received a baptism, prolonged immersion in South Teton Creek, a raging torrent that separated my group from our destination.

This time I was the guide, charged with the responsibility of keeping nine backpackers safe and happy on an eight-day trip. On the way to the Basin, we came to a crossing. Thigh-deep water crashed over boulders and cascaded down the mountain. This was a place to sit on the bank and marvel at the force of the water. It was not a good place to cross. The year I had scouted the trip, the creek was barely a foot deep. I had walked across it in bare feet.

I smiled. "You have two choices. You can inch across the log that juts over the creek on your butt, or walk across the boulders, holding on to me." I used my cheerful voice, kept a smile pasted on my face.

Nancy, the first to speak said, "I'm going on my butt." She scowled at me, as if this was my fault.

"That's fine," I said. "Go very, very slowly."

Janet stared at the churning water. "Me, too. I'm not getting my boots wet. I didn't bring any other shoes. You didn't tell us to bring extra shoes for water." She followed Nancy to the log. "Good luck," she called to the group, still lined up on the bank.

"Okay, that's one way to do it." I hoped they didn't rip their pants on the log "Everyone else, take off your boots, and put on your camp shoes. They'll protect your feet." I unlaced my boots and tied them together. "Hang your boots over your shoulder. You want to keep them dry."

Lucy stuck her walking stick in between the rocks to see how deep the water was close to the edge. "It's three feet deep here. That means it will be really deep in the middle."

"You'll be fine. Hold tight to my hand and I'll get you across."

I didn't like this any better than they did. It looked dangerous, fast, deep, and cold. I'd have to stand thigh-deep in water that had been snow less than an hour ago, and stand there as long as it took to get six people, one at a time, across to safety. This was just the first day.

"Oh, shit," I said to myself. "This guiding thing can be a pain in the ass."

Life on the Loose

Everyone looked at me for reassurance. This was a time to practice false bravado as if I had a choice. "You can do it. I'll hold your hand in the water." I looked at the group. No one would look at me. They stared at their feet. "Before you start, undo your hip belt, so you can slip out of your pack in case you fall." I tried empathy. "I know this is scary. Sorry, we have no choice." Still no one looked at me. They stared at the churning water.

This was a lot to ask of beginning backpackers.

I put on the potato shoes and waded into the creek. I didn't want to be there. A confident guide doesn't get a stomachache the first time something happens that doesn't fit the ideal backcountry journey. Was this my dream? Would some stupid, unanticipated challenge always show up? Like a responsible guide, I had scouted that trail, checked it for possible problems, and found none. Now I knew what it was like to be a guide when things go wrong. There is a learning curve to this business, and it sucks.

Why weren't we safe in camp with tents up and everyone happy? Low, dark clouds on the horizon, a potential storm, added the possibility of hypothermia. What if someone fell, or had a panic attack? Sandy and Jane kept looking at the sky. Without a word, they put on rain jackets.

"I hear thunder," Nancy said. "There's a storm coming."

"We have to get out of here. Let's go." I waded into the creek and held out my hand to grab Sharon, the first to cross. One at a time, six backpackers stumbled over boulders in the icy water. Lucy slipped, but I caught her. Everyone stayed upright and dry. Nancy and Janet struggled on the log and ripped their pants. My feet and legs went numb. The potato shoes with their flimsy soles stuck like barnacles on the slippery rocks.

Ten minutes later we found a place to camp, put up the tents, and settled in just before the storm hit.

Magic Slippers

* * * * *

Then the shoes met the Green River in Utah. Instead of my struggle with ice-covered sandbars when I had scouted the trip, I found a gentle river, one with campsites shaded by cottonwood trees around every bend. It was an ideal place for inexperienced paddlers to enjoy a leisurely, fifty-five mile float through Labyrinth Canyon from Ruby Ranch to Mineral Bottoms. When afternoon shadows lengthened and it was time to come off the river, campsites appeared like *Brigadoon*, perfect in every detail: sand, shade, a river view, a side canyon to explore, and a scenic tent site, as if a part of a master plan to execute a perfect river voyage.

For three years, the Green gave me an easy wilderness float, until the year a spring melt left a twenty-four inch layer of silt and clay-like muck on top of the formerly pristine sandbars. That's when my co-guide and I felt like draft horses hauling beer wagons, not canoes.

On this trip, as on all wilderness trips, I had a co-guide. I had met Tom on a backpacking trip to Isle Royale and we became friends. A competent outdoors person, he was a strong partner and co-guided several trips.

At each campsite, we shoved and pulled the canoes across mud flats, then dragged them up six-foot embankments to campsites. When we jumped in and sank into mud three feet deep, we made sure we could grab a canoe, just in case we landed in quicksand under the spring slop.

When I felt myself going down, I'd yell, "Tom, hold on to me. I'm sinking."

He laughed at my fear of quicksand. He always said, "Don't panic. I'll be there is a minute," and then he waited until my knees went under before he grabbed a hand. We worked well together; our humor balanced the grunt work, kept us sane.

This wasn't ordinary mud—it was clay, the kind that hardened on our legs and had to be removed in chunks with fingernails. At night, if I felt too tired to scrape it off, I slid into my sleeping bag, and hoped it would fall off by itself. Getting muddy up to my butt was part of doing business. It was my day job, getting clients out of their canoes, keeping them out of mud and quicksand, keeping them clean, and keeping a smile on their faces. I loved the challenge, the struggle, and the satisfaction of a guide job well done. They had paid for the trip; they didn't have to do the hard work.

Once everyone settled into camp, Tom and I pitched tents, tied down the canoes, and prepared dinner. This was not my former life at the club—tennis in a white tutu and drinks by the pool.

The potato shoes survived the first muddy year on the Green. I took them every morning to the river, scraped the mud off the outside with my fingernails, and used a spoon to dig it out from the inside. Every day, when it came time to unload the canoes, I jumped in the muck, and the whole thing started all over again.

The second year, the shoes started to stiffen in the night. After their daily bath, they were no longer "soft suede slip-ons," but no matter how bedraggled they looked, I could still jam my feet into them. I had a look—not the "beener seeker" look from the store in Wyoming—but the Charlie Brown Pigpen look. No matter how hard I tried to stay clean, that mud stuck to my legs.

The end came on the third muddy trip down the Green. On the first overnight in Trin-Alcove canyon, we found the usual slop separating us from camp. After we jumped in, hauled canoes, and made dinner, I set the shoes out to dry. The next morning, they had stiffened, like concrete. I took them to the river, soaked them, scrubbed them, but the suede refused to soften. Like their owner, they had aged.

Everyone followed me to the river while I worked on them, perhaps because I had told them about their history, the mountain man in Wilson, the climb with Kim, and my desire to acquire "The Look." Often people hold on to a talisman to keep them safe, or to bring them good luck. I wore mine on my feet.

"We have to have a burial," I said to the group standing silently on the riverbank. "They're dead."

I filled them with rocks and flung them into the turgid river. The shoes floated for a second before they disappeared into the brown water. They left a tiny ripple that spread in circles to where we stood at the edge. On the Green, it's customary for paddlers to leave a small donation for the river gods, especially a river that has treated them kindly.

I'd had four wonderful trips down the Green. Visions of canyons reflected in still waters flooded my mind as I watched the ripple from the shoes spread and disappear. There would be many more trips for me on the river. It had become my sacred place, a respite where I found peace and strength when life turned rocky.

This ceremonial gesture, in my case leaving the shoes behind, didn't violate the integrity of the river, but instead showed respect.

Something more important than a broken-down pair of potato shoes sank that morning. We had shared many adventures. I would never be slender or mountain fit, nor would I walk into a store and say, "Do you have beeners?"

I didn't need a makeover. I'd earned my stripes. And the Wilderness Guide Look? That fantasy sank with the shoes.

Chapter Four

Dangerous Crossings

1996 Venture West Catalog
From Sonoran desert canyons to subalpine mountain peaks, the Gila Wilderness in New Mexico is a world of contrasts and diversity. This fierce and beautiful landscape will delight you as you explore many dramatically different sections of the Wilderness Area.

"I'll take the convertible," I said to the clerk at Budget Rent-A-Car. "I'm on vacation." I couldn't stop smiling at the prospect of an adventure in Mexico.

I'd flown from Milwaukee to El Paso, Texas, on the way to Copper Canyon, the Barranca del Cobre, in Northern Mexico. With twenty canyons carved by six rivers, it sounded like it might be a challenging Venture West trip, and if not, a place worth a visit.

In the early years of the business, I traveled to many places, usually solo, looking for potential trips. Not all of them worked out. I had high standards, and that included my preference to hike where there were no bugs, cool temperatures, and low humidity. Trips scouted that didn't make the roster included Sedona, too hot and crowded; St. Johns in the Virgin Islands, too hot, humid, and buggy, Wales, too much bus travel to trailheads, and Big Bend, an oven.

Life on the Loose

From the beginning, I tramped every trail before I brought a group. It was part of the job, to give customers the best possible hikes on every trip.

* * * * *

I needed to get out of Milwaukee. Our divorce was not going well. Peter had moved back into our home on a temporary basis, but without a long-term commitment from either of us. I wanted to keep the marriage together for the sake of our four children. However, living together after a year-long trial separation turned out to be harder than we anticipated. There were arguments and tears after too many glasses of wine.

He drank too much. Four nights out of five during the week, the children and I waited to eat dinner while he sat in a bar with his drinking buddy, John. Many times, I had to leave the house because I couldn't stand the stress of the wait. I'd walk to Lake Michigan, two blocks from our home, and sit on the bluff. Then I would walk home, slowly, and pray that when I turned the corner, his car would be in the driveway.

I hated the drinking. The tears and the fights were not good for the children, but we were swept along with a shared fantasy that somehow things would get better. Actually it was my fantasy that the marriage could be healed. He had stopped loving me years ago, but I was too stubborn or blind to face the truth. He was the love of my life and I was determined not to let him go.

I didn't want a divorce, but couldn't fix the marriage by myself. Every time I initiated a conversation about his drinking, or asked, "Why are you always late for dinner?" he left the room. Often, the conversation deteriorated to "Why didn't you pick up my cleaning yesterday?" or "Did you forget to clean the litter box, again?" During our unsuccessful reconciliation, I cried constantly. My plugged nose from the tears led to non-stop sinus infections. When I look back at those years, my life could be distilled into one word: *miserable.*

I was the home economics/merchandising major who had married the Stanford MBA. It looked like a perfect match, the businessman married to the homemaker. It didn't work out that way. The homemaker dreamed of adventure, wilderness, a partner to share her dream, someone to tramp beside her on paths that led to mountain vistas and secluded hideaways. The businessman thought only of his work.

When our second daughter Linda was born in Peoria, Illinois, I had a hard birth and a fifteen-month-old toddler at home. On the day I came home from the hospital with the baby, Peter dropped us off and went back to work. That's what men did in the sixties. Later that day, when I called him in tears because I had started to bleed, he said, "Call a neighbor. I'm at work." Without questioning that inappropriate response, I called a neighbor. That was the first of many times when I should have seen the obvious: the marriage was doomed.

It was complicated. Despite the pain, the arguments, the drinking, exacerbated by my stubborn refusal to acknowledge the truth, I hesitated to initiate a divorce, afraid I'd lose my freedom. As a stay-at-home mom, I could guide a few trips each year and still keep the home running. At that time, divorce looked like a black hole. Could I keep the business? Would I have to get a nine-to-five job? Change and the unknown had always frightened me. It was easier to run away to my tent and think about divorce another day. A week in Mexico sounded like a good idea. I could clear my head while life at home would temporarily fade as physical challenges replaced mental anguish.

Life on the Loose

* * * * *

On that sunny March morning, I headed south on a twelve-lane highway filled with bumper-to-bumper traffic. After I crossed the Rio Grande, I sped past an official-looking building with a busy parking lot and a barricade across half the highway. Several miles later, I came to another gate, this time a bar across the road like the ones at railroad crossings, but it stayed in place, blocking me.

An official gentleman in a gray uniform tapped on my window and said, "You need a permit to cross the border, lady. Go back eighteen miles." He pulled a pack of cigarettes from his shirt pocket and struck a pose I'd seen many times in Mexico. Chest out, hip cocked, he looked like a cowboy who needed a horse. "You'll see a building on your right. They'll help you there." He lit the cigarette and waited for me to leave. A permit? Had I missed something?

I turned around, found the official border crossing, the one I had sped past, and pulled into a parking lot bigger than a football field, adjacent to a square, red brick building. Inside, bureaucrats in uniforms looked bored. Each sported a belly, a mustache, and a cigarette. No one returned my smile; they took their jobs seriously.

The man behind the counter got right to the point. He said in English, "I need your passport, driver's license, and a check for $137.50 to insure the car in Mexico."

He wants my passport! No way. When I didn't respond, he shrugged and repeated slowly, as if he thought I was an idiot American traveler, "Lady, I need your passport, your driver's license, and a check."

What if he kept the passport, or the license, or both? Oh, well, he runs this show, not me. Complaining wasn't going to get me on the road again. "Fine. Here's the passport. Here's the license. I'll write a check." I returned to the parking lot, and waited for permission to continue.

Soon I would be on my carefree way, wind rustling my hair, heading for the canyon and an adventure. I could almost taste a warm gordita filled with beans and cheese in a lovely garden filled with blooming jacaranda. While I waited, sitting on the fender of the rental car, two Mexican businessmen in suits and ties walked away from their black Mercedes and approached me. They introduced themselves as Pedro and Roberto.

"Where are you heading?" Pedro, the younger one, asked. He wore a bright orange tie with a gray suit, a good-looking businessman with flair. He stood close to the convertible, looking me over, first my face, then my clunky hiking boots.

"I'm going to Chihuahua, then heading west to Creel and the Copper Canyon to do some hiking." Their smiles disappeared and a funny look crossed their faces, followed by a long pause. Had I said something wrong? Roberto moved closer to me.

"Is that your car?" He eyed the red convertible. He looked like a banker in his charcoal suit and maroon-colored tie, someone trustworthy.

I moved away, trying to look casual, unconcerned, but my heart raced. "Did you know that road is dangerous for a woman? There are bandits everywhere." Robert looked grim. He stared at me and clenched his fist, as if to emphasize his point. "They stand in the middle until you stop, force you off the road, take your passport, your driver's license, your credit cards, your money, and very likely your car." Pedro nodded, motioning toward the car with its top down. "You don't want to drive in Mexico in that car," Roberto said. "It's like waving a red flag in front of a bull."

"Oh." I couldn't think of anything else to say. Something about the look that passed between them told me they knew what they were talking about.

Life on the Loose

While they continued the conversation in Spanish, I considered the options. I saw myself stranded, standing alongside the road in my black lace underwear, flashing my thumb at passing cars. I saw myself—no passport, no money, no credit cards, no brain. What would Budget Rent-a-Car say? What would my children say? What if I died? My husband wouldn't say anything. Or if he did, he'd say, "I told you so. You should have known better. Should have stayed home."

He didn't have my adventure gene. We had traveled together, had good times on the road with the family, but we never did anything spontaneous. He wanted to know where we were going and how we would get there. Like most people, he didn't like surprises. I was the one who didn't want a set-in-stone plan. I liked to get up and go on the spur of the moment. "It's a beautiful day," I'd say. "It's Saturday. Let's take a picnic to Bradford Beach with the kids." It was always the same. He had to go to work, or cut the grass, or wash the car.

We were oil and water. I drove him crazy. I wanted spontaneity; I wanted to play; he wanted to work.

He also didn't like to camp. When we went with the family, I was the planner, the one who dragged him, kicking and screaming, to the campsite. Once we got there, he was fine. Every time we went, I felt like Mother Courage, dragging him behind me. He did not share my enthusiasm for wilderness. Sometimes, I wondered if he secretly liked to camp but wouldn't admit it, because camping was my passion.

Roberto and Pedro stood by my car, waiting for me to decide.

I'm brave, but not stupid. "I think this is not a good idea. Maybe you can help me turn around." I looked at those twelve lanes filled with bumper-to-bumper traffic. I needed more than a little help. I needed a miracle.

"Follow us," Pedro said. "We'll get you turned around. Stay as close as you can to our car."

Roberto added, "Don't lose us, or you'll be in trouble."

"Wait! Gotta go get my stuff. They've got my passport."

I raced back to the building, heart pounding. I hoped I could find the right clerk. There had already been too much drama and I still had to get out of Mexico. After waiting fifteen minutes in line, the same beefy clerk returned the passport and the driver's license—but kept the check.

Once back in the car, I clutched the steering wheel with a death grip. Pedro's black Mercedes sliced through six lanes of oncoming traffic. Horns and obscenities came from every direction. People yelled, "Fuck you, go home gringo, stupid American," waved their hands, screeched their brakes, tried to avoid me, as the Mercedes and the convertible pushed through the traffic. Car after car skidded to a stop inches from my Budget rental.

In the middle of that chaotic jam, I made a U-turn in a twelve-lane highway. When Pedro waved me on, I waved back, shouted "Thanks!" gunned the engine, honked the horn, and sped away.

What next? I had a car, a map, and a back seat full of camping gear. I'd heard good things about Big Bend National Park in southwest Texas from people who like hot, dry deserts. Why not? I don't like heat, but I could hike there as well as Copper Canyon, without risking my life to get there.

I headed east, then south, until my eyes started closing. Since the highway was not lined with McDonald's or even a gas station, I couldn't get caffeine. I slapped my face, turned up the tunes, and drove.

Camping alongside this road wasn't an option, as it's rumored Texans don't look favorably on strangers who make themselves at home on their range. In the past, I've pulled off the road, set up my sleeping bag next to the car, and made myself comfortable for a few hours. The three-foot ribbon of grass between the barbed wire and the road didn't look especially hospitable. Besides, if I slept on the shoulder, I would be road kill if a semi passed too close in the dark.

About midnight, I came to Marathon, the only town on the map that looked big enough to have more than a gas station, a bar, and a restaurant. One hotel and one motel displayed bright red "No Vacancy" signs. Tired and crabby, I banged on the door of the motel. An elderly woman with curlers in her hair opened the door. "Can I help you?" she asked in a scratchy voice. "We don't have any rooms left. Didn't you see the sign?"

"I know you're full. Could I please sleep in the parking lot?" I begged. This day had to end.

She smiled and pulled her chenille robe down to cover her spindly, blue-veined legs.

"What a good idea." She looked out at the half-empty parking lot. "There's plenty of room. Feel free to use the motel bathroom, the one with an outside entrance."

As I spread my down sleeping bag on the pavement and prepared to sleep, she returned with a caveat and a roll of toilet paper.

"Honey," she said, "If you use my toilet paper, you'll have to pay for it." I handed her a dollar and went to bed.

The next morning, surrounded by the stink of wet goose down feathers, I felt great appreciation for my soft, dry, Percale sheets back home. The heavy dew that soaked my sleeping bag also brought the southwestern Texas desert to life. Everywhere I hiked during the following week, tiny flowers popped up like Wisconsin daffodils in April, springing from the sandy soil in a landscape where wildflowers were a rarity. I didn't know their names; I didn't care. They decorated the desert with shades of blue, pink, yellow, little soft colored dots underfoot everywhere. A night on concrete in a parking lot in a smelly, wet bag was a small price to pay for that unexpected beauty.

* * * * *

The campgrounds at Big Bend National Park said "No Vacancy." What had I expected? Spring break college students spilled out from every campsite. I found a private RV campground where the owner sent me to the back forty. Normally I turn up my snobby tent-camper's nose at those places, but I'd run out of choices.

I found a place at least a mile from the motor homes where I felt smug, secure in my piece of wild desert. I didn't want to be close to the official campground, where people sat in air-conditioned boxes, drinking something cold, and watching the 6:00 news.

In the outback, I saw dagger yucca with white flowers as big as tennis balls and prickly pear cactus decorated with tiny yellow blossoms. The Merlot tasted especially good that night under a star-studded Texas sky.

There was one frayed edge to perfection: something snored.

The next morning, I said to the locals sitting outside the campground store, "There's something out there making a disgusting racket. It sounds like a drunk in an echo chamber." I knew right away I should have kept my mouth shut. Everyone sitting on the porch stared at me, as if I'd just arrived from Pluto. An uncomfortable silence followed my faux pas, as if no one knew what to say.

An old man with a beat-up hat that covered his eyes chuckled and said, "Little lady, that was a javalina. It looks like a wild pig, smells like a skunk, and snores like a drunk." I heard snickers when I turned my back to buy potato chips and a Milky Way.

"Yer not from around here, are ya?" An elderly woman in a rocking chair half stood up and said, "If ya got some time, there's a café in La Linda with real Mexican food. Sits by the river, ya know, the Rio Grande." She hobbled to where I stood, "I can tell yer not a regular tourist. Yer kinda fancy." She must have seen my red Budget convertible.

My face matched the car as I headed west toward the café and some good food. I pictured a place off the tourist trail, with fresh salsa served at fewer than four tables. A cold soda with a slice of lime and homemade chips smothered with refried beans would complete this paradise. Some mariachi music would be nice, too. I'd traveled in Mexico many times. A food snob, I knew the difference between canned beans and beans cooked on a stove over a wood fire. I wanted the latter.

The gas gauge pointed to empty, but the warning light hadn't blinked. If La Linda had a café, it would have a gas station.

After several miles, about fifty more than I expected, I came to the Rio Grande. A one-way wooden bridge led across the river to a stop sign and an open gate. No one came out of the tin shed; the gate stayed open. I glanced at the stop sign and kept going.

La Linda barely qualified as a town. Half a dozen deserted buildings alongside a dirt road and one stray dog greeted me in an unlikely place for an Amoco station. The only other car in town sat on concrete blocks. The gas gauge blinked red. I'd only run out of gas once in my life, and that was on a hill in San Francisco in a Volkswagen that had a spare tank.

A U-turn took me back to the river and two uniformed Mexican guards with their hands on their guns. Now there was a gate and it was down, blocking my trip back across the river. What had happened? Where were they when I drove through the gate the first time? Was I supposed to stop? They knew I'd be back; La Linda didn't offer much in the way of tourist attractions.

I remembered the friendly warning from Roberto, "There are bandits everywhere." These guards were not English-speaking, reasonable, gun-slinging Texans protecting their grazing rights. They were skinny kids, barely old enough to shave, with guns pointed at my belly. They didn't speak English; I didn't speak Spanish.

One of them motioned me to get out of the car. When I did, my legs buckled. I grabbed the door handle. Surely they heard my heart pound, saw my lower lip quiver. I started to cry. I hate that. It happens when I get scared.

I remembered my solo trip down Green River and the raw fear I felt when I worried about finding the cottonwood. That trip had a happy ending. Things will work out. They won't shoot me, will they?

I pointed to the gas tank, made some hand motions to panto- mime empty. They kept their guns aimed at my gut.

"No gas," I said. They remained silent, stared at me, guns still pointed. I unscrewed the gas cap, and stuck a finger in to show them something was wrong. No response.

We stood there, the three of us, looking at each other, the language barrier a wall between us. I couldn't look at the gun. No one had ever pointed a revolver at me. Maybe it was a toy? Not a chance. These were guards, with bullets. I, the salsa-seeking tourist, was at their mercy.

Without a word, one of them slowly, deliberately, walked to the gate, released the bar, and glared, while the other stood by, his gun now aimed at my left foot.

Still, no one spoke. I prayed the car would start. Why would it? It had been out of gas for ten miles. I turned the key and a miracle happened. It sputtered, coughed, and started.

"*Gracias,*" I called out the window as I drove through the open gate, crossed the Rio Grande, blew my nose, turned left at the first dirt road, and headed up a hill. How did that little red convertible chug up that hill on an empty gas tank? Another miracle.

At the top, I found The Outdoor Café, the elusive paradise where three small wooden tables overlooked the river. An elderly gentleman wearing denim overalls and an undershirt came out of a wooden shed and asked, "Can I help you? Are you all right?" He had a kind face, looked like my grandfather, who always gave me big hugs and a piece of candy.

"I'm out of gas." Tears started to run down my cheeks, again.

"Don't worry, little woman. I'll take care of you." He chuckled as he disappeared into a shed, returned with a five-gallon gas container, siphoned a portion into my tank, and led me to a table in the shade where I gulped a frosty mug of freshly squeezed orange juice and munched on store-bought chips dipped in Paul Newman's Pineapple Salsa. High above the Rio Grande, I enjoyed a view of that troublesome river. Some boundaries we don't cross with impunity.

I thought about the adventure that faced me at home, the leap from married to single mom with four children. That would be the hard crossing, the one that would temporarily bankrupt my emotional energy. I would think about that crossing another day.

Chapter Five

I Should Have Stayed Home

Comment from 1996 post-trip evaluation:
"Your enthusiasm and matter-of-factness for the unexpected did a lot to ease our worries."

My friend Jean and I left San Cristobal, in the state of Chiapas in Mexico, in the dark on an early morning bus, headed for Palenque, the Mayan ruins, and a private guided trek into the jungle.

It was an ordinary day—cool, crisp, breezy, my kind of weather. I was there scouting, hoping to put together a trip to San Cristobal and the surrounding villages where indigenous people create a fascinating variety of crafts. Jean came up with the plan to go to Palenque after she spent a day fighting *la tourista*.

With nothing to do, she combed my *Lonely Planet Guide* for a new adventure. "I'm bored," she said. "A day in bed and I need to get out of here." She pointed to a page in the book. "Look at this jungle thing. It could be fun." Then she added, because she knew my opinion on heat and humidity, "You'll have something different for Venture West, a guided trek in the jungle. I'll bring *Off* because it might be buggy."

I didn't really want to do this. Heat, humidity, and bugs, are the hated triumvirate of discomfort that I always tried to avoid.

At the time, the business was going well. The *Chicago Tribune* had printed a press release and two hundred people responded with requests for catalogs. I could be interested in a new Venture West trip to Mexico, especially one with a private guide and an overnight in the jungle. "Okay, let's do it."

At the first stop in Ocosingo, we grabbed warm coffee at the bus station. "This better be good, Jean. We could be having breakfast in the garden at Hotel Paraiso right now, drinking hot coffee, while we listen to the birds."

We brought our cardboard cups with us on the crowded, air-conditioned, first-class Mercedes Benz, Cristobal Colon bus, and drank coffee while *Born on the 4th of July* blared from mounted television screens. "The noise is making me motion sick. I think I'm going to puke. Should we ask the driver to turn it down?" I've always had a delicate stomach.

"Cari, look at him. He's happy, listening to the radio, singing romantic ballads. He's probably got a hot date in Palenque." He was a looker, about thirty, with slicked back black hair. "Dump the coffee. That should settle your stomach."

"Forget it. I'll look at the scenery."

This spectacular drive over the mountains in Chiapas, where villages cling to the forested sides of steep slopes, looked like the Himalayas in Nepal where I'd traveled many times on foot, not in a first-class luxury bus. Tiny farms dotted the edges of cultivated fields where corn grew in perfect lines. The landscape looked like the view from an airplane. From a window seat, I could see three thousand feet down into a valley carved by dozens of centuries of erosion, and tried not to think about the narrow road. Where was the shoulder, the margin of safety between the bus and the drop-off?

I started to tell Jean, who doesn't like heights, about the wheels of the bus, and the edge of the road, and the drop-off, but she didn't want to know. When I said, "You won't believe how close we are. . ." she got up to go to the bathroom in the back of the bus.

"Not a good idea," I said. "The last time I used that bathroom, the door flew open while I was trapped on the toilet."

Jean sat down. "I'll wait."

We sped over ridge after ridge, climbing to a summit, then another and another, while I sat, white-knuckled, trying not to look down. I thought about a time in the early eighties when I'd had a close call with a Volkswagen van. A gust of wind caught me on an icy freeway, and spun the van sideways. I got an ambulance ride to the hospital, lost a couple of teeth, and gained new respect for the unexpected. Fortune had smiled on me that time. The truck driver who called the ambulance had said, "I didn't think anyone would come out of that van alive."

After that close call, I never felt comfortable when I sensed I was in a vehicle that might lose control.

Our bus was close to the edge, too close. All we could do was trust our driver, who appeared attentive as sang along with the radio.

"Wow! Look at that," Jean said, after sneaking a glance at the scenery. "It's at least ten thousand feet down to that village."

We noted a turnoff to Agua Azul ("blue water"), where several taxi drivers stood on a dusty road while they waited for people who needed a ride to that popular swimming hole. "Look, Jean, there's the road to Miso-Ha." I pointed to the map in my *Lonely Planet Guide.* "We're almost there."

By this time, from our seat directly behind the driver, we knew he was driving too fast on this two-lane road.

"Cari, there's barely room for two cars to pass. I wish he'd slow down."

"I know. He's paying more attention to his damn music than he is to the road." I noticed he steered with one hand so he could drink his coffee while we careened down the mountain. I gripped the armrest between Jean and me as if holding tight would help if we slid off the road.

"I like his tunes. Love those ranchero songs. Makes me horny." Jean's words hung in the air.

The bus pulled into the left lane, what there was of it, to pass a small pick-up truck carrying farm workers. As we pulled alongside, the driver of the pick-up swung left at exactly the same moment to pass a third vehicle, a slow-moving truck. Our bus was in the way. The driver of the little truck didn't see us. I wondered later, did he look? Our side-view mirrors collided, screeching like fingernails on a blackboard.

"Oh, my god, Jean, we're too close to that truck."

The top-heavy bus jerked sideways, and pitched down the mountain.

"Here we go," I thought as I flew out of my seat. That's all I remember.

Later, an Italian woman who had been on the bus would tell me the bus rolled over four times. I don't remember that, nor do I know how I landed outside the bus, fifty feet further down the mountain. I felt a crushing impact but no pain. My left hip slammed into the ground in a shrubby area next to a jagged stump. Even in a semi-conscious state, I saw that stump and wondered, "What if...?"

I tried to sit up. Nothing. I tried again. Still nothing. When I tried to roll over, my stomach muscles didn't work. Was I paralyzed? I was dead weight, in a thicket, halfway down a mountain in Mexico. The middle of my body felt mushy, like Jell-O. Too scared to cry, I didn't think about internal injuries, paralysis, broken neck. I felt relief. I was alive.

What had happened? How had I ended up on my back, unable to move, down a steep mountain in a country where I didn't speak the language?

I'll never know how I flew out of that bus, from the seat behind the driver, without leaving any blood. I must have shot down the steps and out the door like a cannonball. I missed the stump by inches, the one that would have snapped my backbone like a day-old Thanksgiving wishbone.

"Help me, help me!" I screamed from the bushes. Dozens of Mexicans scrambled down the steep slippery mountain to help other passengers. I heard sobbing, but no one heard me. And, because I couldn't sit up, no one saw me.

I felt the *Lonely Planet Guide* press against my ribs, the book I'd stuck in my jacket pocket right before we left for Palenque. I loved that book, bought in the early nineties. I had filled it with notes about restaurants, hotels, and tidbits about my favorite places. It was an old friend, one I would never see again, along with my camera, and my Salvation Army Patagonia jacket, the one that had become my daily uniform in Mexico.

Six men came to rescue me. They must have fanned out from the bus to see if they had missed anyone. They brought something metal that looked like a piece of the bus, maybe a fender, rolled me onto it, and carried it up the mountain. At the top, they lifted me over their heads, chanted "*Uno, dos, tres,*" and muscled the makeshift stretcher onto the road.

A second team carried me to a wooden bus shelter across the highway and rolled me on to the pavement. That's when the first pain shot through my body. It felt as if a giant vise had wrapped around my midsection and squeezed until every rib pulsed with sharp vibrations that took my breath away. I started to cry. Pinned to the concrete, unable to move even a hand, my body throbbed.

61

"Jean, Jean, are you here? Where are you?" I called, desperate for someone to tell me what happened.

Was Jean dead? Had anyone died? What happened to the driver and the other people in the front of the bus?

"I'm here, but I can't see anything." Jean, temporarily blinded from blood that flowed from a deep cut over her eye, lay somewhere close to me, but I couldn't see her.

Then someone said, "An ambulance will come from Palenque. It just left the hospital and will be here in an hour and fifteen minutes."

Many people stopped to take the injured by car and truck to the hospital in Palenque, but no one touched me. They assumed I was paralyzed, as I lay helpless on the pavement while everyone stepped around me.

Always the optimist, I trusted safety and relief would soon be mine in an American-style hospital, one with glistening floors and a ready team of E.R. specialists in white coats, attending to my broken body.

Hours passed. I must have drifted in and out of consciousness. I heard someone say in English, "The ambulance left. They took three people, and it's not coming back," I heard the same woman say, "Two backpackers died. They put the bodies in the ambulance along with the driver." She paused. "He's dead too."

She walked over to where I lay on the pavement. "I'm from Italy. I speak English." She put her hand on my arm as if to reassure me. "I think I can help you." She looked at the cars and trucks stopped along the highway. "Someone will take you to the hospital in Palenque in a pick-up truck. If you want, I'll come with you."

I started to cry again.

"I found your friend," she said. "She can come, too."

I wanted to say thank you, but I was crying too hard. "I can't breathe. What's wrong with me? I can't move." She sat down next to me, took my hand. "It will be okay. You'll be in the hospital soon."

We waited, maybe five minutes, maybe five hours.

Sometime later, six men carried me to a pick-up truck, again on that fender, and set me on the floor in the back end. I remember that the truck was rusty and red. It needed a muffler. My Italian friend said, "Jean's here, too. You're going to be okay." She squeezed my hand. "I'm here. Try to relax."

I begged Jean to hold my other hand, but she didn't hear me. "Someone please touch me," I sobbed. The Italian woman hugged me as best she could. She was my angel. This was a time to be strong, but I wasn't. I couldn't worry about Jean, or the blood running down her face, or the backpackers who died, I just felt my pain. I only thought about myself. Maybe that's what people do when they're badly hurt.

Then I got a cramp in my leg, a ball of muscle in my right calf. I screamed, "It hurts. Shit. Someone squeeze my leg." I felt a hand on the muscle, now a knot of pain bigger than a ping pong ball. "Oh, that's better, thank you." It wasn't. I screamed until it released.

I wanted to get the *Lonely Planet* out of my pocket, it jammed against my ribs, but I didn't ask because I didn't know where the Italian woman was, and I didn't know how to say it in Spanish. When the truck turned on to a bumpy road that ended at the hospital in Palenque, I wanted to die, the pain was so intense. My whole body throbbed, pain shot through my pelvis, and the worst part—I was completely helpless.

At the hospital, nurses strapped me to a board and deserted me in the middle of a noisy emergency room crowded with injured passengers from the accident. It was oddly quiet except for the sounds of people sobbing. No one paid attention to me. The cramp came back in my leg. Everyone who looked like he or she might be a medical professional ignored me until the cramp grew to the size of a baseball. I grabbed a nurse by her sleeve. She shook off my hand, kept going.

Desperate for relief, I screamed at everyone who came close hollering, "*Tengo dolor*, I have pain," over and over. "I'm going to choke. I can't breathe. Give me water." Someone handed me a wad of damp gauze.

A nurse said in English, "Suck."

"Damn it. I said water, not cotton. *Tengo dolor*." I knew what that meant from my limited Spanish, and they should have known about my pain. Finally, a doctor gave me morphine to shut me up.

Now I know why they refused to give me water, but at the time I didn't think about the possibility of serious injuries, rib pierced lungs, or pelvis fragments lodged in my spleen. I wanted water, and to hell with internal injuries. If I choked on vomit, so be it.

Then my Italian friend came back. "They can't keep you here, because your injuries are serious, and the hospital isn't set up for long-term patients. You have to go to another hospital in Villahermosa."

My mind danced around the possibilities. Would I ever hike again? What did she mean, "long-term patients?" Maybe I can guide canoe trips. Am I paralyzed? Is this the life I dreamed about while I washed dishes and polished floors? What if I can't walk? The voice in my head churned out images too scary to contemplate. I saw myself in a wheelchair, on a ramp into my home, while my children whispered, trying to hide their pity for their formerly adventuresome mother. Was life as I knew it over? I had been blessed, and now, did it turn on that proverbial dime?

"Do you know where Jean is?" I asked my Italian friend.

"She's in another room, but they told me she can come with you to the hospital. An ambulance will be here in two hours." I can still see her brown eyes filled with compassion. She gripped my hand while we waited. When the ambulance came, she said, "I have to go now. My friends are injured, too." I never saw her again.

Two young men in white jackets carried Jean and me on stretchers to the ambulance and loaded us into the back, where we lay on wooden shelves with just enough space in-between for the attendant. It was another bumpy ride from hell. The pain-dulling morphine had worn off. I cried all the way from Palenque to Villahermosa.

At 11:30 p.m., we arrived at Hospital del Sureste, my home for the next thirty days. Just like my fantasy, there were doctors waiting for me. After several x-rays, the doctor told me I had a crushed pelvis and nine broken ribs. Twelve hours had passed since the accident.

They gave me excellent care in that small Seventh Day Adventist hospital. Three doctors who spoke a little English attended to my injuries—one for the pelvis, one for the ribs, and one for the fluid that had gathered in my lungs. They assured me I would walk again. Every morning they came to my single room to monitor my progress. They talked to me, encouraged me, gave me courage to keep optimism alive, and put a smile on my face.

I loved the docs—their visits gave me something to look forward to while I lay helpless on a hard mattress. An intern, Sonia, said, "We don't have the latest equipment, so we have to talk to the patients and use our brains instead." Maybe that's why they spent so much time with me.

She was right about the equipment. My bed had a hand crank, and the air conditioner rattled several times a day until someone stood on a chair and banged on it. That someone wasn't a nurse.

They refused to touch it. If an orderly came into the room, I'd ask him to stand on a chair and slap it until it shut up.

After three days, it was time to say goodbye to Jean. With a broken foot and a shoulder injury, she could go home. She wanted to go home. So did I. Because she didn't have MedVac insurance, she paid $20,000 for the flight on a private medical jet with her Visa card. And unlike me, with my busted bones, she could be moved. I was stuck.

The day she went home, a nurse brought her to my room in a wheelchair to say good- bye. She looked awful, pale, weak, sick, a pathetic invalid with bad hair.

"You look great," I lied. "Have a safe journey." I felt betrayed, jealous. We were in this together. She left me behind.

I would have made the same choice.

If I needed a nurse to crank the bed, or wanted pain pills, I had to reach for a phone on a bedside table, balance it on my stomach, dial 3943, and say, "*Necessito personna ayudarme por favor.*" If I dropped the phone, my lifeline to the nurses and doctors, no one would hear me calling, because they kept my door closed. If I died, no one would find the corpse until an attendant brought the next meal.

My son Chris and daughter Linda each came to stay for two weeks. Their loving presence saved my life and my sanity.

Chris came for the first two weeks. He brought the bed pan when I needed it, cranked the bed up and down, dumped the bad food I couldn't eat, and talked with me for hours each day. I felt like the luckiest person in the world that I had a son who loved his mom enough to spend two weeks hanging out in her hospital room in Villahermosa. There was nothing for him to do there. The city was hot, humid, buggy, boring. He never complained.

With Linda came the leg lifts. I didn't understand the medical reasons for that torture, but Linda and the doctor assured me they were necessary if I wanted to hike, or backpack, or even saunter more than a mile in the city.

She was my cheerleader. In the beginning, I couldn't lift either leg off the bed. She would say, "Go, Mom. You can do it. Just a little more. One more inch." And so it went. I whined and moaned and said I couldn't do it, and she kept the encouragement coming, until I could raise both legs over my head.

She saved my life. Without her patience and kindness, I would not have tried to lift my legs off the sheet and never over my head.

After the daily ordeal, she went to a nearby grocery store, and rewarded me with an ice cream sandwich, the highlight of my day.

I received dozens of calls from friends. Every time one came in, and someone mumbled something in awkward Spanish, a nurse automatically put the call through to my room. I learned that many people cared about me. Their loving support helped me heal.

For entertainment, the nurses showed me how to work the television, a recent addition to my solitary room. Seventy channels in Spanish bored me, but I looked forward to the daily bullfights, if that said anything about the programs in Villahermosa.

Every morning, the doctors came to tell me how I was doing. They fed me meds for pain, for fluid in my lungs, for my stomach, and calcium for my bones.

"You must be patient," the pelvis doc told me, "In eight weeks, you will be healed and walking again." He lied. It was more like eight months.

Everyone was generous with their time, including the head dietitian, who came daily to ask, "Do you like the food?" or "Is there anything special you would like?" I can only hope whoever emptied the trash didn't tell her about the food deposited after every meal in the wastebasket. Someone did tell her about the time I made a joke, saying to one of the aides in Spanish, "I wouldn't feed this to my dog." Shame on me. I felt like an ugly American when the chef came to my room to apologize and said, "Tell me what you want. We can make it for you."

The problem was that the hospital food was vegan. To their credit, they fed me fruit three times a day. That's fine for people who like sour green apples and purple grapes filled with seeds. I don't. I wanted salt and pepper, butter, cheese, sour cream, cream cheese, and even healthful cottage cheese. I craved milk and vanilla ice cream. I'm a Wisconsin girl. Where was my dairy?

After three weeks, the rib doctor said, "When you can sit in a wheelchair for two hours, you can go home." I couldn't sit in their wheelchair, circa 1930, for five minutes until someone put two pillows under my butt and one behind my back. How did he think anyone could sit in that thing for two hours?

"You have to sit in an airplane for four hours. You must show me you can travel." It took a week to get used to that rock-hard chair, and after four long weeks in that hospital, he agreed to release me.

Many misunderstood conversations between the staff and my pre-school Spanish kept us laughing up to the last night, when a dozen nurses and aides came to my room, closed the door, set up a boom box, and played a CD of their favorite Mexican tunes including my favorite, *The Road to Guanajuato*. They sang, danced, and hugged me. I wanted to jump out of bed and dance with them. These beautiful Mexican, women filled with vitality showed boundless compassion for the only American in their hospital. The music was a gift, the party a fond farewell.

I learned later that the bus company had a contract with the hospital. This arrangement covered all the costs of my thirty-day hospitalization, or a hundred dollars per day, according to intern Sonia.

Back home in Milwaukee, many friends, including Jean, suggested MedVac insurance for future trips. If I'd had internal injuries, this might have been a different story, but my broken bones healed in Hospital del Sureste. To those doctors and nurses I was a person, not a room number or a problem, charted on a computer, hurriedly bathed, and fed three meals a day. I loved their personal attention, and because they spent endless hours talking with me, I knew they cared about me.

I gained a friend in the thirty days I lay on my back, Nurse Caroline, who brought me barbequed chicken or *pollo asada* from her mother's kitchen, undoubtedly the best meal, the only edible meal, in the hospital. Despite my limited Spanish, we didn't need words. We spoke with smiles and hugs.

This was not the adventure I had envisioned. I'm an impatient person who was forced to practice the art of patience, or, in a friend's words, "Cari, it's time to be a little Buddha."

I won't add San Cristobal, or Palenque, or that jungle trek to the Venture West trip roster, but someday I'll return. When I told this to my-ninety-four-year-old mother, she said, "Are you crazy? You would get on another Mexican bus?"

Chapter Six

Hitched

1988 Venture West Catalog
Escape the winter blahs and bask in the sunshine on the beach at Cinnamon Bay on St John Island in the Virgin Islands. The trip includes snorkeling in several diverse locations, educational programs, a day sail through the islands, an island tour by jeep, an historic bus tour, and time to relax.

When I look back at a life filled with adventure, there were no risks I wouldn't take again. Those were the best of times, the ones I remember, like the time on the Green River when my mouth felt like cotton and my heart slammed my chest. That's when I felt alive, when my body tingled and adrenalin flooded my brain. Whenever I hitched, I felt some of that same rush, and loved it until the time I found myself stranded in Charlotte Amalie in the Virgin Islands.

I used to think people who were afraid to hitch missed the possibility of adventure, the suspense, the edge that accompanied a thumbs-up ride. A hitch offered me the chance to leap into the unknown, vulnerable as a fly approaching a spider web. I never discussed this in front of my children, or my conservative-minded friends who would have given me the look, the raised eyebrow, the blank stare, the silence that spoke of disdain.

Life on the Loose

* * * * *

My first hitch happened in Michigan when I was eighteen and I took my six-year-old brother Bruce on a hike in the woods on a cloudy day. We followed a stream called Shalda's Creek, a meandering trickle through a maple-beech forest close to Leland in northern Michigan. I didn't know where we were going, or where we would end up. I didn't care. We were having an adventure, and I, the absolute leader and dictator, was on a mission.

We followed the stream, sometimes walking in the water, occasionally swimming through deep pools, and when a log blocked our way, we pushed through the underbrush alongside the creek. Bruce, his arms and legs covered with mosquitoes, wanted to go home. We were both bleeding from scratches. I was having fun. He wasn't. "Stop crying," I said, showing no empathy for poor Bruce, an hour into the trek, his arms and legs now covered with red welts from bites. "I know what I'm doing. We can get out of here."

We came out of the woods at Highway 22, four miles from where we started. There were no stores or gas stations, no phones, just a road that didn't go where we lived.

"We're safe," I said to my sad little brother, who by this time had stopped crying. "We'll get a ride. I'll stick up my thumb."

I walked to the middle of the highway and looked both ways. There were no cars in sight. "Someone will pick us up, and take us home."

An elderly couple, who said later they were headed for dinner in Leland, passed us, then stopped and backed up. After I admitted we were lost, the woman hugged Bruce, opened the back door of the Pontiac, and soon we were safe at home with Mom and Dad. I would do it again, but the next time, I would leave Bruce at home. I loved every scary minute—just like the time I took my brother Guy into a swamp and a fisherman rescued us. In both situations, I thrived on the adrenalin rush.

* * * * *

When I scouted a trip in Switzerland, my friend, Denise, and I hitched often—when we missed the bus, or didn't want to wait, or didn't know where we were, or landed in a place where there was no bus service. It worked every time. We met lovely people from Holland, England, Australia, and a few locals.

When we needed a ride after a hike around Lac du Moiry in the Valais Canton, because there was no bus service to the lake in June, I approached the best-looking man in the parking lot. Tall, slender, about fifty, he wore a black fleece jacket and pressed jeans. "Do you speak English?" always the first question in this French-speaking valley.

When he answered, "*Un peu*, a little," I followed with, "We need a ride to Grimmitz to catch a bus back to our hotel. We're stuck." To get there we had hitched a ride from Grimmitz to the lake. "Do you think you could give us a lift?"

"Oh, yes, I would like very much to do that, but let me check with my wife." After a brief conversation, he motioned us to come to his Mercedes convertible, and off we went down the mountain. 'My name is Rudy and this is my wife, Lotte. Do you like wine?"

Denise gasped. I felt her elbow in my ribs. With admirable restraint, we answered in unison from the back seat, "Yes, we like wine."

He didn't miss a beat. "Would you like to come to our home? I helped a friend harvest his vineyard and he gave me some of his wine. I think you'll like it." Lotte turned and smiled at us from the front seat. She said something in French we didn't understand. Everyone smiled and nodded.

Denise whispered in the back seat, "Good job, Cari. I think we just got lucky."

After a stop for bread and a hair-raising drive up a mountain road barely wide enough for one car at a time, we arrived at their traditional Swiss log home, perched on the side of the mountain. Lotte went inside for a few minutes and returned with a tray. She said something in French and pointed to a delicious spread she had set out for two strangers.

We sat at a long wooden picnic table and drank Fondant, the white wine Rudy had helped his friend harvest. We snacked on local cheese, crusty bread, and special dried meats from the area as we watched the sun set across the valley.

Rudy spoke a little English, Denise spoke a little French, Lotte and I nodded. We all used body language. When it came time to leave, after espresso and cake, Rudy said, "You don't need to take the bus. I will drive you to your hotel."

* * * * *

In the Virgin Islands on St. Thomas, I had a free afternoon before my friends arrived and we left for St. John and another scouting trip for Venture West. While I sat in the garden reading the guide book, the hotel owner, Larry, said, "Why don't you catch a bus to Charlotte Amalie. It's the biggest city on the island."

"Okay. Maybe I can get a close-up look at a cruise ship." I could also do some sightseeing or shopping, though I'm not a shopper. There was nothing else to do.

Larry said, "I'll give you a lift down to the road, and show you where you can catch a bus." That's when I should have asked a couple of questions about Charlotte Amalie and the bus service.

As Larry drove a mile down a narrow road from the Mirador Hotel to the bus stop, I noted the impossibility of walking back to the hotel. Cars barely squeezed past each other, thanks to a thousand foot drop-off on one side and a stone wall on the other. This was not a walker-friendly road.

At the bottom of the hill, we came to a two-lane highway where I caught an open-air bus, a perfect transport for this tropical island. After a few miles, I jumped off at a harbor lined with hotels, and saw a cruise ship bigger than two city blocks. I frittered away the afternoon, window shopping, people watching, and then enjoyed a leisurely dinner in an Italian *al fresco* restaurant. After a couple glasses of Chianti Classico, the soft evening air enveloped me in a cocoon of warm sultry loveliness. By the time I finished, all the lights in downtown Charlotte Amalie had been turned off. The city had gone to sleep.

Across the highway at a bus stop, I waited for the next bus, the one that would come at any minute and take me back to the hotel. A brief, St. Thomas-style thunderstorm came and went, the moon rose, my clothes dripped, and still there was no sign of a bus. Thankful for the warm night, I didn't have to add cold and shivering to my growing anxiety.

Through the mist and the wet hair that hung in my eyes, I saw a beat-up, rusted-out station wagon pull up to the curb next to me. Someone said, "You look like you need a ride!" I couldn't see the driver's face clearly, but he had Bob Marley dreadlocks and a cigarette, or a little cigar, something brown hanging from his lip. This did not look promising. It was that hanging thing that scared me, but the rest of the picture didn't look good either.

Life on the Loose

I was not getting in that car. I remembered the narrow road up to the Mirador, the one no sane person would navigate on foot, and said, "No problem. I'm waiting for a bus. I'm sure one will be along soon." My strong woman pose, shoulders straight, big smile, arms relaxed, direct eye contact, didn't fool him.

I thought about something my mom told me when I lived in San Francisco in the 1960s. "Your dad and I never worried about you. No matter what happened, you always landed on your feet." I don't know what she might have based that on, but I wondered what she would think if she could have seen me, standing in downtown Charlotte Amalie, without a clue how to get back to my hotel.

The Bob Marley look-alike laughed. "Lady, there are no more buses tonight. They quit running at 9:00." He took the little brown thing from his mouth. "You want a ride or not? Where you stayin'? Jump in."

My body stiffened. That's when I learned what real terror feels like. I couldn't move. My knees wobbled and my feet glued themselves to the sidewalk.

"I'll give you a lift," he said as he reached over and opened the door for me.

"I'm staying at the Mirador." My voice quivered. "Do all the buses quit early here?"

He didn't answer, just smiled and motioned me to climb in. I crawled in the front seat, grabbed the door handle on the passenger side, and got ready to jump out if he tried to touch me. What was I afraid of, that he would rape and rob me, leaving my comatose body by the side of the highway? My brain churned out terrifying images, desperate scenarios. I clung to the door. What if I jumped? Who would save me? At least I had a plan.

"Wanna hit? I've got some good stuff wit' me." He had a nice smile.

"No thanks, but thanks for asking." I scrunched closer to the door.

"Wanna see my tattoo? I just got this yesterday." He shoved his bare arm in front of me. A female body part on his bicep rippled as he flexed the muscle.

"Oh, that's nice." I didn't offer to show him the large tattoo on my chest.

"What you do for a livin'? What you doin' here?" He smiled again. He had good teeth.

"I'm an outdoor guide on the way to St. John to put a trip together. I'll be checking the hikes, and looking for things to do with a group."

"Do you need a driver? I can be yer guide. I know my way around." If I overlooked the joint, the dreadlocks, the strange tattoo on his arm, he was just another Islander, happy to chat with an outsider. But I never let go of that door handle. What if he went past the turnoff to the hotel? No matter how fast he drove, I would jump.

When he turned left, and started up the familiar road, I let go of the handle, and relaxed into the ripped seat. I could breathe again. At the Mirador, he refused the $20 bill I held out and instead thanked me for my good company. In the light from the parking lot, I could see he was a good-looking guy, tall, slim, dressed in jeans and dark blue shirt that could have come from L. L. Bean. Then, I could ask the question. "Is that thing in your mouth a joint?"

When he stopped laughing, he said, "No, lady, it's an old cigarette, you know, the one that doesn't have a filter. Don't they have them in yer country?"

What was I afraid of? If I had glanced in the rear view mirror, I would have seen a middle-aged, suburban housewife with scraggly wet hair wearing baggy jeans and a pink tee that read, "Life's uncertain. Eat dessert first."

Chapter Seven

Scammed in Sedona

1997 Venture West Catalog
**Diversity and destination will always be two
parts of the scouting process. Each day hike
must present a landscape that's different from
every other day and it must have a worthwhile
destination.**

W henever I scouted a new trip, there was no guarantee it
would make the Venture West roster. I burned up a lot
of time and money on trips that never happened for a
variety of reasons, mainly heat, humidity, and bugs, in that order.
Sedona was a different case: too many tourists and too many hikers
clogged the trails. Nevertheless, my friend Denise and I had an
adventure in Sedona.

I planned to meet Denise near the baggage carousel in Terminal
#2 in the Phoenix airport at 6:30 p.m. She was coming from Peoria,
Illinois, on Northwest while I flew Continental from Milwaukee. We
would pick up a rental car and zip out of town.

The trip started to unravel when the Northwest carousel
emptied out and there was no sign of Denise. I found a pay phone
and called her cell phone four times, leaving increasingly anxious
"Where the hell are you?" messages. At 10:00 p.m. I left the final,
"I'm going to the closest Motel 6," followed by several unprintable
words.

Life on the Loose

At the end of my rant, she answered. "We just landed. We left Peoria four hours late." I knew what she was thinking: *Get a cell phone, Cari.* This was an ongoing discussion between us every time we traveled together. "I missed the connection in Chicago. As soon as I get my bags, I'll be there."

"Great. Let's get the hell out of Phoenix."

We were headed for Oak Creek Canyon, a couple hours north of Sedona, and hopefully, an idyllic campsite. Fantasies of a warm, humid breeze curling my straight hair had come easily on a blustery March day in Milwaukee. Now it was April in Arizona and we had high expectations for perfect camping weather.

At 11:00 p.m., we left the airport. After we picked up soda and tuna sandwiches at a gas station, our moods lifted as we anticipated a restful week camping and hiking.

We found a sleazy motel about seventy-five miles down the highway, where we ate the greasy gas station sandwiches and retired at 2:00 a.m.

* * * * *

I didn't feel good about this trip. My son Chris would go to his first high school prom while I camped in Arizona. Once again, a hard choice filled me with guilt. How could I have life both ways, or be two places at the same time? An insistent voice in my head ran the same tape over and over, "You are a narcissist, Cari. Stay at home where you belong. You're selfish." I couldn't stop myself. An insatiable passion pushed me away from a conventional life and led me always to my tent.

It eased some of the guilt to know one parent would be there for Chris. After the divorce, Peter moved back into our home when I traveled for Venture West. This was a good arrangement for all of us, as he was not interested in the traditional one-night-a-week-and-one-weekend-a-month visitation. Without my travel, the children would have seen their father only occasionally.

In the first four years of the business, I traveled infrequently, just three or four weekends a year, and those were good times for Peter to spend with the children, who were ages ten, eleven, fifteen, and sixteen. In 1986, after the divorce was final, I guided the first trip in the West, a ten-day backpacking trip in Oregon, but by that time, Chris, the youngest, was fourteen, and at twenty, Cathy was the oldest. They were far from self-sufficient, but they no longer needed me to keep the cookie jar full.

* * * * *

When Denise and I got to Sedona the next morning, the thermostat in our Ford Escort told us the outside air temperature was seventy degrees Fahrenheit, perfect spring weather. "Let's stay here," I said when we stopped for gas. "Feel that warm breeze. Who needs to camp?"

"No way. I didn't haul my camping gear so we could stay in town. I'm ready to live outdoors for a week." Denise jumped in the driver's seat, ready to take charge of the final push to an idyllic campsite. I could see it, nestled in an old-growth forest next to a bouncy creek, a cozy site with space for two tents, and perfectly spaced trees where I could hang my hammock.

As we drove north up Oak Creek Canyon on that breezy, sunny morning, the temperature gauge in the car started to drop, to sixty, fifty, settling at forty-five. We saw less and less sun as we traveled up the canyon. By the time we pulled into Pine Flat Campground alongside Oak Creek, the old-growth forest had swallowed the remaining sun, adding to the chill.

"I'm cold," Denise said as she dumped our camping gear on the picnic table.

"Me too, but the highway keeps going up. It's not going to get any warmer." I pulled out my fleece jacket and put on a hat. "Feels like snow. You're the one who wanted to camp. Remember?" She was right. It was cold, damp cold, the kind that settles in your bones and stays until you get to a warm place.

"I'm not having fun," she said as she scooped a jacket, a wool hat, and winter gloves from her duffel. "Let's get moving. Damn, it's cold." She put on her jacket and hat and glared at me. "You told me Arizona would be warm in April. Remember?"

"We could have stayed in town." She was right. Arizona was supposed to be warm in April.

Maybe I should have checked temperatures in the canyon instead of Sedona.

"Drop it, Cari, I'll pretend it's warm. Maybe it's not really forty-five. "

We pitched the tents and set out to hike a section of Oak Creek Canyon on the West Fork Trail. According to our guidebook, it was one of the premier hikes in the area. After twenty minutes on the trail, I knew it was a bust. There was no drama, red rocks, canyons, sweeping mesas, everything we'd been promised in Sedona. All we saw was the little creek and the rocks we stepped on to cross. "If this is one of the best hikes around here," I muttered, "we're in trouble. This trail sucks."

Denise laughed, kept walking ahead of me.

"Where are the cascades and waterfalls we read about in the guidebook?" To make it worse, we soaked our boots and socks crossing the stream several times, balanced on logs or rocks, or simply wading. "Loser hike," I said. "This is not my idea of a beautiful canyon. Let's try again tomorrow."

When I scouted a new Venture West trip, the goal was find six- to eight-mile hikes, each different from the others, each special. I looked for vistas, waterfalls, cascading creeks, canyons, mesas, and, in the spring, wildflowers. I always found the good ones, but there were many false starts because when it came to an eight-mile hike, I was fussy.

We returned to camp at dark, where I dressed for Pinot by the creek: five layers of clothing on top, three on my legs including rain pants even though there was no sign of rain, a wool hat, a hood, and winter gloves. We tried. We sat in camp chairs, nestled between boulders next to the creek, and shivered, our delicate Pinot inappropriately chilled.

"It's too cold to cook." I picked up my chair and headed for the car. "Let's go find a restaurant. We don't have to suffer."

"So, Cari, what are we waiting for? Let's get out of here and eat in a warm room." Denise, ahead of me with her camp chair, ran to the car and jumped in. "Let someone else cook," she called from the front seat.

We found a restaurant about five miles further up the canyon and lingered over a delicious trout dinner with wine, dessert, and coffee.

After a long, cold night, I woke up fantasizing about the fresh-ground Columbian coffee I would make in my French press. After I cracked the ice in the water bottle, I lit my backpacking stove with its butane fuel canister and waited. First a tiny flame, then nothing.

Denise shook it. "Cari, the fuel is frozen solid. What next?" She shook it harder. "Now we can't even have coffee."

She walked back to her tent. "I'm getting in my bag where it's warm. Let me know when you're ready to go out to breakfast."

"Wait. We can take the stove in the car and crank up the heat. If we can defrost the fuel, I'll cook breakfast in the car." I wanted my coffee.

Denise called back from inside her tent, "Let me know. I'll bring my mug."

I got in the car, started the engine, turned the heat on high, and waited. After several minutes I took off my jacket, hat, gloves, and scarf, and shook the butane. It jiggled. Breakfast would follow.

I balanced a bowl on my legs, beat the eggs for cheese omelets, cooked them on the backpacking stove carefully set on top of *50 Hikes in Arizona*, and served breakfast on the dashboard, just above the steering wheel. I was not going to let winter in April in Arizona interfere with coffee, cheese omelets, sausage, English muffins with orange marmalade, and fresh fruit.

For the next three days we hiked, explored the canyons, and marveled at the landscape, a mix of pine trees, the famous red rocks, and small creeks.

"Too bad the trails are so crowded," I said. "I'm tired of people passing us every time we stop to look at something." That's how it was: no excessive heat, no energy-sapping humidity, no biting bugs, too many people. I added crowded trails to my list of issues that led to Venture West scouting rejects.

On the fifth day, we came out of the canyon for gas. We pulled into the first place we saw, a Chevron station in the center of Sedona. It was warm and sunny in town, unlike our campsite. I took off my winter jacket and went inside for directions to a coffee shop.

"I'm looking for a cafe. Can you tell me how to find one from here?" I said to a nice-looking man about fifty wearing a plaid shirt and jeans standing by the Tourist Information Center. He had a good haircut, a friendly smile, and a clipboard.

He paused, looked down at my hiking boots before he answered. "Sure. There's one up Highway 89 about half a mile, but, by the way, where are you staying tonight?"

"We're camped up Oak Creek Canyon at Pine Flat. It's beautiful, but the warm sun down here sure feels good."

"How would you like to stay in a luxury lodge for $39.95 and get $50 to spend in town? No cost to you. It's free money." He moved closer. "We pay you $10 to stay with us." He paused and wrote something on the clipboard. "You want to get out of the cold? You'll have a window facing the red rocks, coffee in bed, a private patio, a dream room, and it's free."

He had hit a nerve. Breaking ice for morning coffee, cooking omelets between my legs, fun the first four times but . . . a luxury lodge, now that sounded like something we could do. I had finished my job for Venture West. Sedona would not make the cut. It was time to relax and treat ourselves.

He pointed to a man buying gas. "Look at him. He's filling his tank with our money." Gas was $3.11 a gallon that day in Sedona, a dollar more than a gallon in Milwaukee.

"That sounds too good. What's the catch?"

"All you have to do is come to the time-share presentation. It takes ninety minutes." From the corner of my eye, I saw Denise move toward the door. "You have to stay to the end, because if you leave early, we'll put $189.95 on your credit card. That's the retail price for the room."

Denise and I looked at each other. "We want time to think about it," she said. "We'll come back later." She opened the door and started to leave, whispering something about "no free lunch," but all I could think about were those cold nights and scrambled eggs in my lap. Mr. Plaid Shirt knew I was hooked. Denise would be a hard sell. He stepped in front of us, blocked the door.

"I'll be gone in fifteen minutes," he countered. "Then there's no deal. How about we think about it right now?"

"What do you think?" I looked at Denise, who was halfway out the door. I felt myself slide toward "yes."

"I don't know. What do you think?" Denise sounded tentative. "We can have someone else make breakfast."

"Let's do it. Sounds like a deal."

We signed some papers, grabbed our vouchers worth $50, and drove to the Sedona Vacation Club. Our oversized room, with two king-size beds lost in its vast space, opened on to a grassy patio with two deck chairs facing the famous red rocks. That's what we had come to see, those cleverly marketed rock formations. Too bad I couldn't pull a trip out of Sedona. Those rocks were lovely.

The next morning, showered and well caffeinated, we arrived at 9:00 a.m. for the ninety-minute presentation. We got Lisa, a perfectly coiffed older woman with purple eye shadow and heavy mascara. Anorexic skinny, with dyed jet-black hair and thick make-up on stretched skin that forced her mouth into an odd grimace, she had a face that had seen the knife.

Denise nudged me, "This will be interesting."

"Good morning. How are you on this lovely Sedona morning?" Lisa said as she walked toward us. She had desperation in her eyes; her smile looked forced as if she knew this would be a waste of her time.

"We're fine. How are you?" The social patter ended as she covertly glanced at our jeans and boots. She wore a red pantsuit and pointy black heels.

"Have you ever been to a time-share presentation?" she asked. Apparently "no" was not the answer she wanted, because she followed it with an antagonistic "Why not?" She glanced at our feet again. I hoped I'd cleaned the scrambled eggs off my boots.

She sized us up, looked at me, and asked, "Are you two mother and daughter?" That hurt. Denise and I have been good friends for many years, traveled together often. I thought of her as my contemporary, not a daughter. Did she look young—or did I look old?

We followed Lisa into a large, sunny room with windows that faced a courtyard filled with flowers and manicured shrubs. Several well-dressed couples wearing colorful Bermuda shorts and sandals sat at nearby tables. They sipped coffee and appeared to listen to sales reps giving the same pitch we were about to hear.

We sat across the table from Lisa like obedient children. I felt my brain grow numb as she nattered on. "It's a great investment, you can't lose, it will grow exponentially, blah blah blah." I perked up when she said, "Do you want to stay in a castle in Ireland, or a tree house in Costa Rica? If you buy a time-share today, you own one week a year, free."

"One week? Is that all?" Denise wasn't buying the routine.

"Well, yes, but you can purchase two additional weeks anywhere in the world for less than $700 a week."

Lisa turned to me, "Your eyes are glazing over." I stifled a yawn, crossed and uncrossed my legs for the tenth time.

"You might be right. I'm feeling a little bored." I glanced at my watch. We'd been there the full ninety minutes and we were still sitting at a table. We had to stay to the end. It was time to get out of there.

"What do you think, Denise? Should we go look at one?" We were stuck. We could look at the condos or pay full retail for our room.

Denise shrugged and excused herself to go to the restroom. Lisa put her made-up face so close to mine I could see the gold fillings in her teeth. Her black eyes bored into my face until I could almost feel blisters rising from the heat. I flinched, and pushed my chair back from the table.

"Why are you spending an hour-and-a-half on a beautiful day doing something that's of no interest to you?"

When I didn't respond, she answered the question herself.

"I know. The only reason you are here is because you and your friend wanted a cheap room."

She was right. They had offered us a free room and we took it. Why not? My eyes had glazed over. We were trapped on a perfect hiking day.

When Denise returned, Lisa led us outside where we found flowers and shrubs sheltering units in cocoon-like privacy. The grounds looked like a well-tended botanical garden, an extravagant oasis that felt far from the nearby highway traffic. We liked the condos with their burnt orange décor and immaculate interior.

"This is beautiful. I could live here for a week every year." At that point, I thought it wise to toss out a remark to soften our tour guide.

Lisa turned to me and grabbed my arm, "You are humoring me. You don't like this at all. Why are you wasting my time?"

What? We were not trailer trash, riff-raff with egg on our boots. "Denise, what do you think?" She shrugged. "You said you like it. I'd rather hike."

I slipped around the corner and motioned her to follow. "I'm desperate to get out of here. I'll buy one and think about it later."

"Are you nuts? Okay, then we can split, get the hell out of here. You can always cancel it tomorrow."

Lisa came around the corner looking for us. "What are you two whispering about?"

Her voice went soft, like velvet. "Cari, I think you want to talk about this. What do you think?" Her manicured hand on my arm gave me goosebumps. "You look like you'll fit in here."

She was a good liar. I can be a good liar, too.

"I'm interested in the one-bedroom studio, the one at the end with the red flowers by the front door. I want to buy it."

Instantly, we were best friends. She relaxed her grip on my arm and pulled out some papers, the ones with the prices. I picked the low-end $10,000 studio condo. That price meant one week a year for $10,000. Was I nuts? When I hinted that I was an independently wealthy heiress, Lisa glowed with victory. Denise remained silent.

Back inside the main salon where we started this fiasco, Lisa handed me a dream catcher. Apparently she didn't know most people view them as a place to rid oneself of bad dreams, not collect good dreams. "This is for you, because we made your dream come true." This was a dream all right, a nightmare.

A man in a gray suit wearing a nametag that said Eric, ILX Resorts, sat down with us, popped a bottle of champagne, and took my credit card for the $2,000 deposit. After forty-five minutes, he returned with a dozen papers waiting for my signature.

At 1:30 p.m., we escaped, four-and-a-half hours after it started. I turned to Denise, "Isn't that the dumbest thing I've ever done?"

"Let's get out of here."

She smiled.

"I came to scout a trip, not to buy a time-share. I have to get out of this thing. I don't even like Sedona."

After a short hike, we returned to camp and made a plan. When I signed the papers, Lisa had agreed to a twenty-four hour cooling-off period. If we went back in the morning, I could wriggle out of the contract. I've always been impetuous and decisive, but overly cautious and frugal with money. Maybe I was seduced by the gardens, the red rocks, and my burning need to get out of there. This was a high price to pay, albeit temporarily, for an overnight in a luxury suite. We did enjoy the room, the view, and the high-thread-count sheets on the king-size beds.

Why did I react that way? Did I feel diminished because Lisa looked at me as if I was trailer-trash, or because she insulted me with the mother/daughter suggestion? She saw two women in jeans who didn't belong in her world, yet she carried on with the spiel. I gave her high marks for perseverance. When she looked down her nose at me, I felt like the chubby girl in the orange dress at Mrs. Gates Dancing School, again. Would I always be the outsider, the one with an empty dance card?

At 9:00 a.m. the following day, I signed more papers, returned the ridiculous dream catcher, and chuckled when the same ILX man named Eric, wearing the same gray suit and the same red tie, said, "Looks like we were right."

Lisa was nowhere in sight.

In the end, no one was fooled. We had all wasted a spring morning.

We spent our vouchers for gas at the Chevron station. When we went inside to pay, an older woman stepped away from the Tourist Information Center and handed me a map and two brochures. "Welcome to Sedona. By the way, where are you staying tonight?"

Mistakes Were Made

Chapter Eight

Lost in Snow

1984 Venture West Catalog
**Many women have expressed a desire to learn
about backpacking and to share that experience
with other women. They have also requested a
winter camping adventure. We'll escape the city and the
February blahs and camp at Newport Beach State
Park. I don't promise perfect snow but there will be
twenty-five-hundred acres to explore and no other
campers will intrude on our privacy.**

I used to dream about winter camping. It sounded romantic,
quiet, peaceful, something only the intrepid would attempt. I
saw my Venture West group, sitting around a fire, toasty warm,
unfazed by the January wind whistling in the trees. After we cross-
country skied all day, dinner would magically appear and everyone
would be laughing, joking, feeling smug. Someone would say, "I
wonder what the rest of the world is doing?" I would stir the
fire and pour a shot of Bailey's Irish Crème into everyone's hot
chocolate.

However, there was a missing detail: short winter days.
Afternoon darkness at 5:00 didn't factor into the planning the year I
ran a winter trip the second week in January.

I listened to everyone who said, "Oh, please take me winter
camping. That's something I've always wanted to do." These were

friends. When they talked about camping in the snow, it was on a sunny winter day, never on a cold, snowy, icy day when anyone with a brain would stay indoors with a good book. They had no intention of doing it; they wanted to talk about it. In the eighties, many people I knew wanted to camp in the snow, or so they said.

Easily persuaded, I replied to the wanna-be winter campers, "Fine. Sure. I'll do it." I should have known better or done a bit of research on the travails of winter camping. We would be trapped in the cold, sitting in the dark, at the same time most people are thinking about what to have for dinner or watching the *CBS Evening News*.

This was the second year of Venture West, when I ran women-only trips. Right before my divorce became final, and for three years afterwards, I went through an anti-male phase, hence the brief reign of women's trips. I was hurt, deceived, disillusioned by the end of our marriage, and turned my pain into a mistrust of the entire male species. By doing this, I eliminated half my potential market and the good times generated by men in co-ed groups. This was short-lived. I soon changed my mind when I moved on after the painful divorce, and included men on the trips.

* * * * *

On January 15, four women and their gear piled into my red Dodge Aries station wagon for my first and last winter camping trip, and set off for Newport Beach State Park by Lake Michigan in Door County, Wisconsin. We were a mismatched group: two Marys, a Penny, and an Irene.

From the start, the group had nothing in common. Mary M. was surly, quiet; Mary G. sold insurance; Penny and Irene were successful businesswomen looking for adventure-lite.

Lost in Snow

We had barely pulled on to Interstate 43 heading north when Mary M. said, "Can you pull over? I think I'm going to throw up." I'd never met her; she had worked part-time at a YWCA camp, a beefy, unhealthy-looking woman about twenty-five with a blotchy red face. Perhaps I should have turned around after the third time she asked me to stop so she could puke, but I kept driving north as she left her breakfast and lunch outside the car.

I had to keep driving. Everyone, including sick Mary, had paid for the trip. I couldn't go back, refund all the money they put up in good faith for this camping adventure, and say "Sorry, this just won't work. Mary seems to be too ill to continue." That would have been my preference but I had the integrity of Venture West to consider. This was starting to feel like a possible trip from hell.

* * * * *

The year before, my guide career had almost crashed on a camping trip in the Smoky Mountains. The first night, I took the group of ten on an after-dinner hike. My co-guide Mary Eloranta and I assumed they would savor the mystery and the danger as they hiked in the dark a mile-and-a-half to Laurel Falls.

Mary liked to toss out a unique challenge as much as I did, but I forgot about the drop-off on the left side of the trail close to the falls. When we got to that part of the trail, everyone plastered themselves against the rock wall on the right. Not one of them wanted to carry on. One woman sprained her ankle when she stepped on a rock on the way down. No one cared about the waterfall, except Mary and I. We loved our moonlit adventure.

The next day, rain turned to snow on a long, challenging hike to Ramsey Cascades. Afterwards, a woman who wore jeans on the twenty-six-hundred-foot hike up the mountain, verbally attacked

95

me in front of the group. She said, "Cari doesn't know what she is doing. It's her fault I'm wet and cold."

"My fault? Did you read the letter I sent, the one that said, 'Jeans are not a good choice for hiking'?" She glared at me and said nothing. I kept going. "Jeans get wet and stay wet and they suck the heat from your body."

I was both devastated and surprised at my reaction to her nastiness. Maybe I was partly to blame, but when she criticized me in front of the group, I fell apart. I left the group, went to the woods, sat on a stump, and sobbed. Mary took over while I pulled myself together. That's when I knew I would need a thicker skin for the guide business.

* * * * *

Newport Beach isn't a drive-in campground. It's sixteen campsites with tables, fire rings, and latrines, each site located at least two miles from the parking lot. The Wisconsin State Park system calls it a "wilderness campground." Everything must be carried into the campsite: clothes, sleeping bags, mattresses, tents, stoves, pots, fuel, and food.

We planned to camp at #2, two miles from the parking lot. That's a long two miles when you're schlepping the aforementioned stuff and have to make two round trips. The ice on the trail didn't help, nor did the elongated sighs coming from Mary M, whose grim mouth and slumped shoulders suggested a mental and physical wreck. Why not? She'd thrown up three times already. She could barely move, and given her condition, who could blame her if she felt sour? An offer of chocolate didn't bring a smile, nor did my cheery encouragement.

"You'll feel better soon. At least you got it out of your system." What a dumb thing to say to someone who was sick and still had to carry her backpack for two miles so she could camp in the snow.

Our camp in the woods would be a lovely site in May when wildflowers bloomed, but in January, it had about as much charm as a county dump. The snow had melted and refrozen, leaving bare spots and icy patches hidden under what snow was left. My winter camping fantasy evaporated when I saw what we were in for. We kicked and pounded the remaining snow into submission to make platforms for our tents. Mary M. sat on a stump and watched.

I noticed the obvious. There was no firewood, a few sticks, but no logs to make a real fire. If there was one thing we needed, it was a fire to dispel the gloom that settled after we put up the tents and imagined the long night ahead.

Always the perky guide, I said, "Let's all walk back to the parking lot. I saw a wood pile covered with a tarp." I didn't want to make another round trip, but we needed a fire. What else was there do before dinner? "If everyone carries one log, we can build a big fire to keep us warm when the sun goes down."

Penny rolled her eyes, "Are you kidding? Four more miles?" She was right. We would hike two miles to get the wood and two miles back to our tents. Another slog!

I nattered on, "Walking will warm you up. It beats sitting around here."

Big sigh from Mary G. "I'm in. What the hell?" She was about fifty with a sense of humor. She would be fine, but she would be exhausted from the additional hike to the parking lot. The extra trip for wood added up to ten miles for the afternoon, an impressive distance on icy, rutted trails.

"Me, too," said Penny and Irene, both in their forties, fit, slender outdoors people dressed in North Face and Patagonia. They could afford the best; they were businesswomen. My winter gear came from Goodwill and the Salvation Army.

Everyone except sick Mary set off down the trail. "I'll be fine. I'll get in my sleeping bag and wait for you." She disappeared into her tent, no doubt relieved to be left behind. "See you soon."

Without the slow one, we picked up the pace and the group mood lifted. It felt good to hike quickly along the now familiar path that ended by the parking lot next to the dry wood. When we got there, everyone took two logs, enough for fires for both nights.

"Let's get going," I said. "I know a shortcut. We'll follow the shoreline and cut off almost a mile." I felt certain this would be the shortest route back to camp. "It will be more scenic, and besides, we all want to get this over with. What do you think?"

Everyone nodded, silent in the ebbing afternoon light in the woods. "We'll be off the trail, just so you know." We still had some daylight left, maybe an hour until dark and barely a mile back to camp if we followed the lakeshore. I wasn't wearing a watch. I had left my flashlight behind with sick Mary.

Penny spoke first. "Sure, as long as you know the way." When the others looked like they agreed, I set off in the direction of Lake Michigan, three campers lined up behind me. We beat our way through the brush and headed for the lake and the shoreline, but without the sun, it was hard to orient ourselves. We were definitely not on a trail. Mary G. slipped and fell first. Irene tripped on a bush and lost her balance.

"Cari, slow down. We can barely see you."

I heard panic in Irene's voice. "We can't see the ice. Someone's going to get hurt."

"I'm scared," Mary whispered.

"It's okay. We're at the lake now." So far, so good, I said under my breath. "We have to follow the shoreline. Stay in a line behind me."

That's when I remembered the six foot drop-off. "Don't get close to the edge." I hoped no one thought about a flashlight, asked me to turn mine on.

The sky continued to darken as we made our way along the edge. The woods don't slide gradually into night when there's a solid cloud cover, they turn black, as if the show ended but someone forgot to turn on the house lights. That darkness is oppressive, frightening.

"Cari, I can barely see my hand in front of my face. I can't see where I'm going," Mary G. called from somewhere behind me.

"I'm here. Follow me. Stay together." I waited for everyone to catch up. "Concentrate on your feet. That will help your balance." What I needed was a rope to tie us together.

"This is dangerous, Cari. We should have stayed on the trail," Penny called from right behind me. She almost stepped on my heels, sounding pissed, as well she should.

The route would have been tricky in full daylight when we could see the drop-off. We had to keep going because we had left sick Mary in her tent. Another guide lesson learned the hard way! Never separate the group.

Penny, Mary G., Irene, and I walked slowly, teeth chattering. Fear made us cold, sapped our already-drained energy.

Did my voice hide my desperation? "Let's head away from the lake. We're not going to find the trail if we keep going like this." We were lost in the woods, in the dark, in January. "When we find it, we can follow it back to our camp." Why did I think we could follow the shore back to camp? Our site was at least one hundred yards inland. There was no way of finding #2 in the dark from the lake.

We beat our way through the underbrush. I prayed we could keep going in a straight line, because people lost in the woods tend to walk in circles.

I saw an opening in the trees, packed snow, footprints, and maybe—the path. We forced our way through thickets, climbed over downed trees, and bumbled through the dark.

"I found it!" I yelled. "Stay close. Now we have to find #2." I could take no credit for stumbling on to the trail. I just got lucky. "Look for anything that might lead to our camp."

"If we can't see our boots, how will we see a sign?" Irene spoke the truth. So far no one had questioned me about a flashlight. Thank God!

Through the darkness I glimpsed something man-made, about waist high. As we came closer we saw # 2 shimmering in the dark. The marker for the camp site had been painted glow-in-the-dark-white by someone clearly prescient. We were home. No one said anything. Where were the cheers? Were they cold, scared, or disgusted with their guide? Most likely the latter, and with good reason.

"Where was your flashlight?" Penny asked. The others looked at me, their grim faces expressing the anger and mistrust I had earned.

"You scared us," Irene said, and glared at me.

"I'm sorry. I wanted a fire." This was not the time to downplay my role in the fiasco. I told the truth. "I didn't pay attention to the time and didn't bring my flashlight. That was stupid."

I smiled at the survivors, Mary G, Penny, and Irene. They still looked grim.

As they headed for their tents, I wanted to get in mine, bury myself in my sleeping bag, and not come out until morning.

Instead I called to sick Mary, "How are you doing? We made it."

"Feeling much better. I'll be right out." Her face appeared in the door to her tent. "I found some twigs and got everything ready for a fire. All we need is your wood and a match."

"Great. Let's get a fire going and I'll cook dinner. Anyone want hot chocolate with a shot of Bailey's?"

I should have known there would be a learning curve to the guiding business, and it started with common sense. No one goes into the woods in late afternoon without a watch and a flashlight. And what was the point of camping in January when days were cold and short, and the only place to feel good was stuffed in a sleeping bag?

Chapter Nine

Lost Canyon

1995 Venture West Catalog
**Join Cari Taylor-Carlson to explore the magnificent
Needles section of Canyonlands National Park.
You'll see an array of geological wonders,
lush canyons, Indian ruins, rock art panels, and
the autumn desert in bloom. Who can ask for more?
Three hiking days in the park will showcase three
sections of the Needles including a hike around
Squaw Canyon Loop.**

After the winter camping debacle, I took great care in predicting, as much as possible, just how weather would impact the success of the trips. Summer trips ended—too many hot days no matter where we were. After we unexpectedly endured ninety-five degree heat for five days in the Tetons in August, there were no more June to August hikes in the western mountains. I ran many trips to Utah in November when I could count on sixty-degree days and cool nights, my kind of weather.

* * * * *

The first time I took a Venture West group to Canyonlands National Park in Utah, we stopped mid-afternoon at a trail intersection for a photo. This was a joke, a group shot, with everyone pointing in a different direction. We posed in front of a post with arrows that pointed to four trails. If we hadn't been having so much fun, or if the day had been rainy or hot, or if the sign had pointed in three directions, not four, maybe I'd have been more observant. Maybe. One arrow led to Big Spring Canyon, one pointed to Druid Arch, one circled back to Squaw Flat Campground, and one pointed to Lost Canyon. I oriented the map to be certain that we would continue on the correct trail, the one that led back to the campground, and turned right instead of left.

This was the last leg of a well-marked loop from Squaw Flat Campground to Big Spring Canyon via Squaw Canyon. On the map, the loop looked elliptical, egg-shaped, and measured eight miles, not including side trips to scenic overlooks. When we came to that junction, we'd walked more than halfway, about six miles, with two to go. There was no hurry. We had hours to savor the canyons and mesas before the sun set and the evening's chill set in.

We found the multiple trail choices humorous, especially the arrow that pointed to Lost Canyon. "How do you lose a canyon?" Susan asked. Everyone laughed. She liked to make jokes.

I looked at the group: six women, ready for adventure, a potpourri of ages from middle thirties to mid-seventies. There were two Susans, one a light-hearted blonde who turned everything into a joke and the other, a Susie, a chunky first-grade teacher, always leading the pack. I worried about Fran, who said her legs were weak, and Jane, who didn't like heights. Mary, another teacher, had long legs, but moved in slow motion, and Grace, somewhere in her mid-seventies, was a sport who plodded at the end of the line.

I knew this hike would challenge them. My guide philosophy included the premise that when I challenged people, they pushed harder. They always thanked me—later. Many hikers in their post-trip evaluations raved about their accomplishments and gave me credit for enthusiasm and encouraging words.

"Maybe it's the hikers who get lost," Mary said. "Cari knows where we're going."

"I'm glad we're not going to Lost Canyon," Grace added. "I don't like the sound of it. I'll follow Cari."

"We're not going to Lost Canyon. Trust me." I picked up my day pack and set out on a brisk pace. "I know where we're going."

Of course, I knew where we were going. I could read a map, follow directions.

This was early in my guide career. I felt proud that I could do this, take a group of strangers, turn them into friends, and lead them to new places. I loved hearing someone express trust in my guide expertise.

* * * * *

The business was off to a good start. After several articles had been written about me in local publications, people started to know who I was, and recognized the name Venture West. As a contributing editor for *Wisconsin Silent Sports*, I gained credibility and customers as I wrote about camping and backpacking. I couldn't afford to pay for ads in magazines, so I grabbed any free publicity I could generate. I would have stood on my head on Wisconsin Avenue in downtown Milwaukee if I thought it would attract new customers.

Things weren't going well at home. No matter how I tried to please my soon-to-be ex-husband, I failed. This was during the time when he expected silence every morning for twenty minutes while he meditated. He blamed me every the phone rang for one of our teenagers, said it disturbed his concentration. He complained about my vegetarian dinners, dust, occasional breakfast dishes, blah, blah,

blah. It was hard to be perfect when petty judgments haunted me. It felt like he carried a list of my transgressions in his head, a permanent record of my imperfections.

I'd lived with my failures and struggled to hold on to the marriage, and to keep the family together, but our twenty-year marriage would end in three months. It was time to dry my tears, pull myself together, and move on.

Sometimes I wondered if Venture West trips were my escape from problems at home. The trips were addictive, especially when everything went well, the group bonded, and I had the illusion of several instant best friends. I felt happy, high on adventure, the people, and the wilderness. When the trip ended, my new best friends went back to their lives. Many took more Venture West trips, some disappeared.

At home, when I told friends and family about my adventures, they listened for about five minute before they changed the subject. They had their lives; these were my adventures. For a few days, I felt sad until I planned the next trip and then, life was good again. At the end of each season, I started planning trips for the following year. That way I wasn't too far away from a trip and the new friends, albeit temporary, I would make on the trail.

* * * * *

I looked forward to the trips I ran in Utah, especially Canyonlands National Park. It's wild, rugged, and a place that deserves respect. Hikes into primitive areas—and that includes most of the park—challenge even the most intrepid hikers. Many trails are marked with cairns-piles of small rocks perched on slickrock, smooth rock surfaces with no distinguishing features. There was no other way to mark those trails.

Without the cairns, one would quickly become disoriented. It's prudent to always have the next one in sight. Sometimes there is no trail, only a jumble of boulders to scramble over in hopes of locating the next cairn. Often, trails cross areas where the rock slopes downward, and the only way to stay upright on that slanted rock is to stand straight up and trust the boots. People who pause run the risk of losing their balance and sliding a hundred or more feet to a rocky landing.

Early in the hike, we had to cross one of those slopes. I went first to demonstrate the importance of moving quickly. "See how fast I walked. That's what you have to do." I needed twenty quick steps to cross to a level place.

I looked back at the group, lined up as if going to their execution. This was dangerous. I didn't want to do it again. "I know you're scared. Do what I do, move quickly, trust your boots, and you'll be fine." I spoke slowly, clearly. "Whatever you do, don't stop in the middle."

One at a time, everyone except Jane followed my lead. She sat on the edge and stared at the soles of her boots.

"They're fine," I said. "They got you this far. Come on across."

A chorus of, "You can do it" came from the survivors.

She started slowly, her face a tight mask of fear. Halfway across she looked down, stopped, leaned into the wall, and said, "I can't. My legs are shaking." She hugged the wall with her body. "I'm going to fall."

"Don't move. I'm coming." I inched toward her. "Hold out your hand and I'll take you across." I don't know who was more terrified, Jane, glued to the wall, or me, praying my boots would stick, twice. I thought my knees would buckle. I didn't want to be there either. My boots are trustworthy up to a point, but I didn't want to find out what would happen if she started to slide and pulled me down with her. Why hadn't she listened? I had said, "Don't stop in the middle." I hate it when people don't listen. Sometimes they could get hurt. This was one of those times.

She grabbed my hand in a death grip. Together, we made it to safety.

I knew that section of trail was coming. I'd checked it out on a previous visit, and despite that stretch of scary rock, I brought the group, because it was a spectacular loop. I should have asked if anyone was afraid of heights. It's hard to trust your boots when you're terrified.

We had a group hug and started out again.

Our serpentine trail wandered in and out of small canyons, up and over slickrock mesas and along dry riverbeds. The route was strenuous, challenging, but we were distracted by the scenery, canyons, mesas and strange rock formations. We all forgot how hard we were working.

I started to feel a tingle of fear creep up my neck each time we scrambled out of a canyon and climbed up on to a high mesa. Where was the end of the loop? Something was wrong. When my watch read 4:30, it was time to see the parking lot. How long could it take to hike two miles? I do that in the city in thirty minutes.

The shadows lengthened and the sun disappeared behind a wall. I put on a jacket and suggested the others do the same. My watch showed we'd hiked three hours since the joke photo. Unless we were crawling, we could travel more than two miles in three hours, and we'd been moving right along. We needed to pick up the pace. I had to do the impossible: motivate exhausted hikers to walk faster.

Even Susie, a strong, albeit overweight, hiker, wasn't keeping up, but when she said, "Cari, please slow down. I'm beat," we were in trouble. She was the fastest hiker, the leader of the pack. Grace had fallen behind.

Fran sat on a log. "I'm not sure I can go anymore. My legs are shaking."

"We have to keep going. It's too late to turn back." This was not a good time to tell them we were lost. They were already stumbling on the rocky trail from exhaustion and stress.

"Let's take a break. If you eat something and drink some water, you'll feel better." I looked at the map again, hoping to see a trail I'd missed. It didn't make sense. We should have been at the campground two hours ago.

Now the sun was down. I checked the watch again. We hadn't seen another person for four hours. Was there no end to this trail? Where was everyone? We weren't heading toward Squaw Campground. Where were we? The map was useless. Now I wasn't even sure where we'd been.

I stepped in front of the group and picked up the pace, but no one followed my lead. An interminably slow woman I called Pokey Patsy stepped in line behind me, taking baby steps, while the rest, including Grace, fell in line behind her. They liked her pace better than mine. Mentally, I tugged, tried to pull them along, but like balky mules, they did it their way. I marched to John Phillip Sousa while they lingered to the strains of a dirge. I couldn't blame them. My legs were tired, too.

About the time the sun disappeared, I noticed vegetation and a willow tree that suggested water. Around a bend, I saw cottonwood, tamarisk, and, oh, my God, a pick-up truck. Where were we?

It was quiet in the desert. The breeze that had kept us cool in the afternoon sun felt like a winter gale on our sweaty tee shirts. Even the canyon wrens had ceased their cheery trill.

Life on the Loose

In that silent instant, I knew that they knew that I didn't know where we were.

I studied the map again, looking for water and found it. The map told the story.

"Remember Lost Canyon? We passed it two hours ago." I hesitated to go on. Tell them the truth, Cari. "This is Peekaboo Spring." What I didn't say was that we had walked seven miles in the wrong direction.

A family of four—Mom, Dad, and two teenagers—were sitting down to hamburgers and corn on the cob at a picnic table by that pick-up truck. "Where are you headed?" Dad asked.

"We started on the loop trail from Squaw Campground, but I apparently made a wrong turn because here we are. Is this Peekaboo Spring?" I tried to sound unconcerned. Their burgers sure smelled good.

"You're right. This is a backcountry campsite for people who drive in."

"Oh, great. So, what's the shortest way back to the campground? We're kind of running out of time." At that point, I figured a mile, maybe two, and we'd be on the way back to our bed and breakfast. "I guess you all came in on a road."

The Dad picked a piece of corn out of his teeth. "It's a long walk back to a main road. You'd better get started."

He stood up, put out a cigarette lying on the table, and pointed to the rutted four wheel drive road. "That's the only way out of here. Follow it to Cave Spring Road." He tapped another cigarette from a pack in his pocket, fiddled with a match, lit the cigarette, took a deep drag, and said, "Maybe you can get a ride to your car from there. I don't think you can make it before dark."

"About how far?" This was an answer I didn't want to hear.

Someone whispered behind me, "I'm scared."

"I'd say more or less six miles. I'm not sure. It's a good long ways, I know that." He sat down, picked up his beer, and gave his wife a look that said, "I'm not taking them nowhere. They can figure it out." She sat at the table with her back to me, never saying a word.

My mind raced to possible scenarios. I do that when I get into tight places. What was the worst possible thing that could happen? We couldn't walk six miles in the dark. At best, we had thirty minutes of light left. I had Grace who was exhausted, albeit a great sport who would never complain, and Pokey Patsy, whose deliberate baby steps kept the rest of the group moving like molasses in January.

It didn't have to be a death march. We could sleep in the desert. We'd be cold and miserable, but we'd get up in the morning and walk out. That's the bottom line—survival. Someday it might make a good story. I had to stay calm, set an example for the group. It's a guide's job to prevent panic. A positive attitude is mandatory in a survival situation.

"Thanks for the info. We'll be on our way."

Susan stepped away from the group and whispered something to Fran. I turned to the others. No one had spoken since we arrived at Peekaboo Spring. "We have to pick up the pace. We have a long walk." I didn't want to know what they were thinking. I didn't tell them we might sleep under the stars-that wouldn't help, they were already scared. If there was a crisis, I could go back to the family for help.

We set out down the road in single file. Every time I looked back, Grace had fallen further behind. We couldn't walk faster. The light was gone. It was moonless dark in the desert. My head lamp gave meager comfort. Fran stumbled, shouted, "Wait." We kept moving.

Half an hour later, I heard a rumble in the distance. It wasn't thunder. It was the sweet sound of an engine. The Dad pulled up next to us and said, "Climb in the back of the truck and I'll give you a ride to your car."

In a nanosecond, a cold, miserable night in the desert turned into an adventure. Everyone made jokes about our plight as if unexpected rescues happened all the time. What were we worried about anyhow?

What I was worried about? Only after we were saved did I let myself think about the "what-ifs." What if that family hadn't been there? What if a storm had come in? What if someone had an anxiety attack or sprained an ankle or broken a bone? What if someone got hypothermia? This was the desert in November. The night before, there had been a freeze.

In the end, Grace saved the day. As we scrambled into the truck, Dad said quietly to me, "I watched the older woman trying to keep up and decided you needed help."

"Thank you," I said "You are very kind. And you're right, we were in trouble."

This was a wake-up call to a freshman guide: stay focused, orient the map, check it three times, and check it again.

I looked back at the group, everyone laughing and talking at the same time. It was a good story.

Chapter Ten

Wrong Turns

1994 Venture West Catalog
1994 will be the tenth year for this woman's backpacking adventure in the Three Sisters Wilderness Area in Oregon. Since we alternate travel with backpacks and day hikes, you'll enjoy four layover days. There's time for swimming, relaxation, camaraderie, and contemplation. This is an unusual and beautiful area and we love returning each year.

I felt a twinge of envy standing next to Delores, thinking her slender attractiveness made me look pudgy. She was in her twenties, a tall, shapely brunette with long legs, a woman men notice. It didn't help that she had stylish camping clothes, a Patagonia fleece jacket, and a challenging job running a non-profit. I was conscious of my straight, thin, mousey brown hair, thick waist, and chunky legs with those damned varicose veins.

On a hike in Zion National Park, the group stayed together while Delores charged ahead. At the first lookout, I found her chatting with two twenty-something, good-looking guys who were also headed to the famed vista at the East Rim.

"See you at the top." Delores waved and turned back to her new friends. No one paid much attention when the three of them passed us and charged ahead, as they were young, muscular, fast hikers.

For the rest of us, the hike to the East Rim was an arduous, four-mile trek up twenty-five-hundred feet to the famous viewpoint. When we came to the rim, we sprawled on the rocks, soaking up the sunshine and the vista. We needed to gather strength for the long trek down. Everyone took off their boots and laid socks out to dry on this ninety-degree afternoon.

We rested for an hour then started back to the parking lot, where I expected to find Delores and her new guy friends waiting. They were not there. Where was Delores? She had a map like everyone else and heard the instructions I gave at the start of the hike. "We are here. Follow this trail to the rim." I pointed to the map to be certain everyone understood the plan. "Wait at intersections for the group to gather. I'll bring up the rear on the way down, as usual." They were supposed to bring a map on every hike, as I had handed them maps at the orientation before dinner on the first day.

I didn't ask groups to stay together. We went at our own pace. They could go ahead. I didn't care. They were adults hiking on well-marked trails, not kids, in uncharted terrain. They could read a trail map in a national park. If I were part of a guided group, that's what I would want. That way participants could choose to hike on their own or with the group.

We waited by the van until it was too dark to hike, then headed back to camp without the happy wanderer. I cursed Delores silently, but kept my anger under wraps in front of the group. Her disappearance wasn't going to goad me into unprofessional behavior.

Maybe I could have contacted a ranger, started a search, but she wasn't in that kind of trouble. She wasn't alone; I just didn't know where she was. Did it occur to her that I might worry? Not everyone is a team player, a hard lesson every guide must learn, and accept.

Back at camp, I chopped onion, garlic, and ginger in the dark for chicken curry. I stirred the pot on the Coleman stove and muttered to myself about irresponsible customers. Everyone disappeared into their tents, leaving me alone while I made the curry, holding a flashlight with my teeth because my headlamp had blown a bulb. I felt crabby, out of sorts with the group, and most of all, Delores. I said many unprintable words under my breath as I stirred. Okay, they were tired; so was I. The guide job wasn't all fun and games. Sometimes I had to work.

We ate dinner close to the fire for warmth. A couple of people asked about Delores, but no one seemed concerned. They were exhausted, more interested in sleep than crisis management. She was my problem.

At 7:30 the next morning, a car pulled into our campsite. Delores jumped out. "Bye, guys. See you around." She blew a kiss to the driver. "It was fun."

Then she saw my face. I tried to look calm, but steam was rising from the top of my head and my glare would have scared anyone who dared look me in the eye.

"What's the big deal?" Did my body language give away suppressed fury? "We made a wrong turn when we came down that steep part, you know, the part where there's big rocks on the trail and you have to climb down on your butt."

"We were worried. You could have waited." How dare she be unconcerned? I would never take her on another trip.

"I followed the guys. They had a map." And where was her map? Time to keep my mouth shut. "I lost mine. I didn't know where we were. Took us a long time to get down."

"And you didn't see our van in the parking lot?" I started cracking the eggs for breakfast.

"Okay, I did, but you weren't there, so I went to their camp, somewhere outside the park." Well, how nice for you Delores. Did she have no sense of responsibility to the group? "It was a great spot. We sat on a rock and watched the sun set. "

She was oblivious, unrepentant, smiling at her memories.

I wanted to stuff her in a jar and leave her there. That's when I remembered she had paid for this trip. Instead, I said in a pleasant, controlled voice, "We waited in the parking lot until dark. Do not do that again." What I wanted to say was, "You're a thoughtless, irresponsible, self-centered bitch."

No matter how much I loved what I did, how much fun we had on the trips, Venture West was a business, and I was responsible for everyone's safe return. Once in a while, someone checked his or her common sense at the trailhead. That brought up the liability issue, the one hidden in the back of my brain. If I thought about all the things that could go wrong, I would stay home in that cozy leather chair in the great room in Whitefish Bay. I would still be the doll in the jar. What if they had raped Delores? If I didn't contact a ranger when she went missing, was I guilty of negligence?

Liability insurance did not cover negligence, whatever that meant, because negligence was a gray area, yet to be defined in the adventure travel industry. No one—my lawyer, my insurance agent, or my accountant—ever gave me a definite answer regarding the negligence issue. There were times, and they made good stories, when I was guilty, like the time we were lost in the snow, or when we turned the wrong way at the Lost Canyon Trail in Canyonlands. No thanks to my guide expertise or lack of, those stories had happy endings.

To protect myself and Venture West from potential claims, everyone who took a trip signed a liability release and a health form. The release might not stand up against a smart lawyer in a courtroom, but it meant I could sleep at night. I also incorporated Venture West to add another layer of protection. The health form provided insurance information and emergency phone numbers, as well as any health issues I needed to know about in case of illness or injury in the wilderness.

So I relented, took Delores on another trip because Venture West was a business, albeit not a very profitable one. I needed the money. I refused to tell anyone about my revenue situation be cause I was ashamed, had an image to maintain, and didn't want people to know I was not a perfect example of a successful busi- nesswoman. That wasn't quite true. I had followed my dream, built a business, and traveled the world. I just didn't make piles of money.

This time, I took Delores on a backpacking trip. No surprise, I lost her in the Three Sisters Wilderness in Oregon. Again, she wandered off, alone. Nights in the mountains in August that year were cold, in the low thirties. When the group got ready for the hike, I said to Delores, "Don't forget to pack a sweater. The after- noons cool down fast."

"I'm good," she said and disappeared into her tent.

When we set off for the hike, she refused to bring warm clothes in her backpack for the afternoon chill. In fact, she refused to bring her pack. She took a one-quart water bottle, no food, and no flashlight. I should have insisted, but again, she was an adult, capable of following directions.

She hiked in front, kept a brisk pace, always around the next bend, not completely out of sight. By the time I missed her, she was gone. I couldn't chase her. Her legs were twice as long as mine. Since the trails in the mountains had signposts at every intersec- tion, I refused to worry. She could read.

Life on the Loose

We returned to a deserted camp. No Delores. This looked familiar. I cooked pasta, made small talk with the group, and felt panic churning in my stomach when the sun set and still, no Delores.

"Don't worry," I said to Janet who fretted about Delores' safety. "When she did this in Zion, she showed up the next morning, unconcerned."

"But Cari, this is different. We're twenty miles from help with no one to call to go looking for her." She was right. This time we were in a wilderness, in the dark, and a chill had settled into our camp. "We're in the mountains. What are you going to do?" Janet walked to her tent and peered in as if she thought she might find Delores hiding in her sleeping bag.

"Nothing. If she doesn't show up before dark, she'll have to spend a night in the woods." I sounded brave, but that was a bluff. I couldn't let my fear show in front of the group. "If she made a wrong turn, she could be miles from here. Remember how fast she walked and how quickly she disappeared in front of us?"

Ann, my co-guide, added, "She's right. We can't go out in the dark looking for someone when we have no idea where to start looking." I smiled at her, glad for the back-up.

"I have an exit plan," I said, "but we have to wait until morning. I'll hike out to the road and find someone to take us to the ranger station. They'll send people to look for her. For now, we have to wait. It will be a long night for Delores. I know you're worried. So am I."

No one wanted to go to sleep, so we sat around a candle, shivering in the dark.

An hour later, she showed up.

"I missed the turn. The trail started going down and that didn't feel right, so I turned around, but I went a long ways before I came to a road and figured out I was going the wrong direction."

Janet handed her a sweater. Delores grabbed it and kept talking. "I got really scared because I didn't know where I was. I ran out of water, and I'm hungry and cold. I'm sorry." Her voice shaky, she stood in front of us, close to the candle as if she needed to draw warmth from its flame.

"The road is five miles in the wrong direction. Where was your map?" I barely contained my rage at her stupidity. Words flew out of my mouth in staccato rhythm as I glared at her.

"Guess I didn't bring it with me. I couldn't find it." She shrugged.

"That sounds familiar, like Zion." It was time for me to shut up or I would say something I would regret. Maybe I already had.

"We saved some spaghetti for you. And I have some extra chocolate. That will make you feel better," Kristy said. She was the protective mother, the person who worried about everyone all the time.

I should have shown some sympathy for Delores, but I didn't. Sometimes the guide business can be a downer. If people listened to instructions, or, better yet, followed them, life in the wilderness would be easy, safe. It wasn't her liability on the line, it was mine. The protective guide says, "The group has to stay together." The flexible guide, me, the one everyone likes because I'm flexible, says, "Go at your own pace, don't get too far ahead, but please wait for me at intersections." I needed to be both.

* * * * *

The intersection instructions came from an experience with my own family in the Smoky Mountains. My four children, their twelve-year-old friend, and I headed for Andrews Bald, a meadow and a vista high in the mountains. As always, the young ones raced ahead, mindful of the destination, while I meandered, savoring the journey. We left the Bald together, but that was short-lived. "Meet you in the parking lot," I called to the departing group of five. "See you later."

Since they were ahead of me, they should have finished before me. When I arrived, there was no sign of them. Cari, do not panic, stay calm; they will be here any second. The worst of it was not only had I lost my own children, I had lost their friend.

What would her mother say? She had trusted me to take her daughter to the mountains, and I lost her on the first day. Why didn't I tell them to stay with me? How would I explain? "I'm sorry about your daughter when she broke her leg and had to be carried out. She'll be fine when she recovers from pneumonia. She should be out of intensive care soon."

I couldn't block the scary thoughts that bombarded me. They were young—the oldest twelve, the youngest seven—and they were alone, in the mountains on a rocky trail soon to be dark and cold. Why didn't I tell them to stay with me, or to meet at the trail intersection?

When a ranger pulled into the parking lot, I raced to the car and said, "Help. I lost five children." The ranger rolled down his window, but stayed in his car. "They were ahead of me on the trail back from the Bald, but they didn't come out. They're gone."

"Were they far ahead of you?" He didn't look concerned, as if people lose five children in the wilderness every day.

"I don't know where they are. They can't be in the mountains in the dark." I started to cry. "Can you get someone to go look for them?" By the time I finished , I was sobbing.

He patted my hand, put an arm around my shoulder, and said, "I'll call for help. We can start a rescue. You wait here." He pulled out a walkie-talkie and said something in a low voice. "We'll find them. It will be okay. I know you're scared."

Scared? I was hysterical.

Just then they came up the trail, wearing big smiles. "We were lost," my oldest daughter Cathy said. "We turned the wrong way, but when we kept going down, Linda said, 'I think this is the wrong trail. We're supposed to go up, not down.'"

They weren't worried. I didn't see any red eyes or tear-stained faces. "Mom, are you crying? We're here. It's okay."

I could barely speak, "Were you scared?"

I knew the answer.

"No, it was an adventure."

* * * * *

That's the reason I told every group, "Wait for me at the junction," no matter how obvious the trail markers. That reduced the possibility of wrong turns and put my mind at ease.

In spite of my good intentions, things went wrong. I wanted to do a good job, gain the respect of my customers. I wanted to wander in a wilderness and earn a living doing what I loved. I would take responsibility for what happened but, despite my careful plans, mistakes were made.

* * * * *

In Montana, I was the person who missed the turn. I had a map, knew where we were headed, and where we were supposed to end up. We followed a faint trail in a field in the Spanish Peaks Wilderness Area. This was a cross-country stroll, an eight-mile saunter in open country with views of mountains around every bend. At the third creek crossing, I had planned to turn right onto an animal path that followed the stream and led back to the highway in the valley. This wasn't a marked trail, but an alternative to six more miles to get back to the van.

I had stopped counting creeks after two. Big mistake! I remembered Dick saying, "Look at the frogs. There are so many." We crowded around, marveled at the unusual sight of dozens of frogs sunning themselves on the bank of a small creek. Was I distracted? Apparently.

An hour later, it dawned on me that we'd crossed stream number three at the frog place. The terrain had leveled out and now we were in a dry meadow. I didn't want to confess until people started asking questions.

"Are we almost there?" from Nate. "I'm getting tired." He had stopped to put on a hat and a rain jacket. "Wish I had a sweater."

He was right. It was getting dark; the mist had turned into a light, persistent rain.

"Did we miss a turn?" Amy asked. "I'm cold."

"I thought we were looking for a creek." said Dick, the person who had pointed out the frogs. "You didn't tell us we'd still be on the trail when it got dark." He sounded angry, had a sharp edge in his voice. "Were we supposed to turn where we took off our boots and waded? Was it the place where we saw the frogs?"

I couldn't fake it, not with the map in my hand. "You're right. We passed the turn at the frog place." Time to confess. "I'm sorry. Guess I missed the trail at the third creek, that is, if I'd been counting."

"So, Cari, what are we going to do now? I should have stayed with Dave." Jean had left her husband back at the ranch to rest for the strenuous hike planned for the following day.

"I know where we are, but we have a longer hike. Let's get going so we get there before dark." I didn't tell them how far because I didn't know exactly where we were. Yes, I had a map, a one-inch square cut from a large Forest Service map, but it was short on details. Our trail was a fine dotted line that meant a seldom-hiked route, not an official trail. I had picked it because of the views of the peaks and because it was relatively flat. Eventually, we would come to a jeep trail that led back to our cozy cabins at the 320 Ranch if I could find the turn in the dark.

The rain turned to sleet and the sleet turned into snow.

"Cari," Amy said. "We're miserable." She spoke for the group.

Anne and Jean, both over sixty, lagged behind, while LouAnn could barely walk after too many miles in tight boots. The snow and the muck on the trail slowed our pace until we were hiking in total darkness on a moonless night.

Things had spiraled out of hand. Everyone, including me, was cold, tired, cranky, and stumbling on the rutted trail.

"Dick, you're a strong hiker. You stay in front and I'll bring up the rear. I want everyone to stay close together."

Anyone could wander off the trail in the dark. I dropped behind LouAnn, who said as she passed me, "My blisters are raw from these damned boots." I fell in line behind her.

Suddenly, a figure came out of the mist from the other direction. "Are we close to the road that goes to the 320 Ranch?" I asked, thrilled to see someone who might tell me where we were.

"You are almost there," he said. "I just came from the ranch. I'm headed the other way to my car. Ugly out here, isn't it?"

"I hope you have a strong flashlight." Dick whispered as he passed me.

"We should have started earlier." Amy's face had disappeared under her hat.

"All we have to do is find the jeep road." My cheerful optimism fell flat. This forced march was not my plan for a leisurely hike.

Life on the Loose

We marched through snow and sleet until the beam from my headlamp lit the small sign that marked the turn down the road to the ranch. I wasn't going to miss that one.

"Look! We made it. Here's the way back to our cozy cabins. Thanks for being good sports." I kept my professional demeanor, unwilling to discuss my stupidity. That would come later when everyone was warm and fed. Then it would be a good story, something to joke about, but not yet.

"Right, Cari. Next time, count the creeks." Amy turned away and started down the muddy trail.

She had a right to be angry. I would apologize at dinner. Standing in the sleet and snow wasn't the time.

"Maybe I shouldn't have pointed out the frogs." Dick turned around and looked back at the trail, now invisible in the dark.

"It wasn't your fault. I missed the turn."

"You're right," he said, and followed Amy down the road. "I'm ready for a hot shower and a stiff drink."

"Amen," I said under my breath. "ASAP."

I missed a turn, but no excuses, I had a map. No one's perfect. Anyone can miss a turn—that is, anyone except the guide.

Chapter Eleven

A Close Call

2001 Venture West Catalog
In springtime we travel to Smoky Mountains National Park for gentle mountain vistas, wild rivers, and the April wildflower display. Five day hikes include the largest stand of old growth trees in the park, cascades, waterfalls, miles of streamside scenery, and a path through a forest carpeted with thousands of tiny blooms.

The year I took six women to the top of Mount Le Conte and back on the same day, I lost them. Would I ever learn?

There's a reason they're called the Smoky Mountains. The first time I looked out from the top of Mount Le Conte in the national park, the mountains peeked out from under the mist, soft gray layers that obscured and softened each peak. When they glowed at sunset, before the woods turned black and the trails disappeared, they came alive as if someone had lit a rose-colored lantern underneath them. From a distance, they looked spongy, like gentle giants, asleep under fleece blankets.

Seven women had signed up for a camping and hiking trip in the mountains. Six made it to the top. At first glance, they were fit, adventurous, optimistic, can-do people, my kind of hikers. Marty and Carole, in their forties, were long-legged runners and exuded confidence. Julie and Sandy, younger, over thirty, had not hiked in the mountains, but were young and full of "let's do it." Barbara and Eileen, good friends from Chicago and experienced hikers in their fifties, carried a few extra pounds, but from experience, would know to slow down and keep a steady pace. Lucy looked like a weak link, sixty-two, dressed in camp for an evening on the town in tight black pants, a silk blouse, and gold jewelry.

The night before the trip started, I met the group in Gatlinburg, Tennessee. That night, I had my usual anxiety dream. This dream would repeat itself, with variations, before every trip for thirty years. Loss of control was the theme, usually in a school setting. I'd lose my locker or my books. I'd forget where I was supposed to be or where my classes were held. I'd fail every exam because I forgot to study. Or the best one: I'd come to school in my lacy underpants and bra.

It's no surprise these dreams added to my pre-trip jitters. Things could go wrong, and sometimes they did.

On day one in the mountains, I gave the group the pre-climb challenge, an eight-mile, round trip up the Laurel Falls trail to an abandoned fire tower with a splendid view of the mountains. We climbed fifteen hundred feet, not a gut-buster, but a moderately strenuous hike for Midwestern flatlanders. When anyone comes to the mountains from Wisconsin or Illinois or Indiana, even a minor elevation gain feels like a challenge, especially when legs start to collapse, like al dente spaghetti, on the first day.

Back at camp, I checked with the group. "How are your legs? Anyone tired?" Mine felt like Jell-O. It's a guide's job to be Iron Woman, strong yet willing to show compassionate for others' pain.

Marty, a slender yoga instructor, replied, "Cari, that was fantastic. I loved it." She jumped up and gave me a hug. "It was a good challenge. Can we do it again tomorrow?"

Carole, a slender emergency room nurse, agreed. "It felt like a warm-up. I loved the view. Let's go somewhere where we can see more great views." She looked at the rest of the group. "How about climbing a mountain?" They had youth and fitness to propel them up the mountain. I was in my fifties, stoic and hubris kept me going.

"I've always wanted to climb up and back down Le Conte in one day. It's a tough hike, but you all look strong." I paused to check for body language. Barbara, no longer smiling, moved away from the others. "We'll climb forty-five hundred feet on one trail and come down on a different trail. We can do it. Agree?"

"I want to climb a mountain," Lucy said. "It will be a huge challenge for me. I've dreamed of doing this." I hoped she had something better suited for the trail than her glitzy camp outfit.

"This is one of those challenges that will give you bragging rights. You can tell your friends, 'I can do anything. I climbed Mount Le Conte.'"

I wanted to empower them, give them more than good camp food and a series of hikes in the mountains. If they met a physical challenge, they could take that glow home along with a basket full of new self-esteem. That was my goal. The money they paid for the adventure would be well spent.

"We'll get an early start. Get your day pack ready tonight." I emphasized "early start" or we'd never get down before dark. "We'll make a fast getaway in the morning. April days are short."

I knew these women could go up and back in a day; they were strong, committed, optimistic hikers. A good attitude goes a long way when the legs start to give out. People in their nineties have climbed Le Conte, and so did a five-year old. A man in his seventies carried a two-year old to the top in a backpack. We could do it.

I planned to hike up the Rainbow Falls Trail and return on the Bullhead. Both trails started from the same parking lot and measured about the same length, eight miles. We could rest at Rainbow Falls, a popular destination for day hikes, then enjoy the vistas from Bullhead on the way down.

We started at 8:00 a.m. with eleven hours until dark. That left time to rest at the top before the hike back to the parking lot.

The first three hours went well. Rainbow Falls is three-and-a-half-miles up, an easy fifteen hundred feet from the trail head. Marty and Carole led, barely breaking a sweat, while Julie and Sandy poked behind looking at flowers and mosses. Barbara and Eileen chatted as Lucy fell behind.

At the falls, we sat on rocks, ate chocolate and nuts, and congratulated ourselves on our fitness. With four miles to go and three thousand feet to climb, we couldn't linger on this sunny, sixty-degree day.

"Time to move on," I said after five minutes. "We have a long trek ahead of us. Got to keep moving." Everyone stood up except Lucy. "I'll hang back with Lucy and meet you at the top. See you later. Have fun."

"Cari, I'm not going to make it. My legs are weak. They're too tired from yesterday. I can't climb anymore." Lucy didn't move from her seat on the rock.

I knew she would be trouble when she showed up in those tight pants. Did she think this is a style show? I want to think people can do more, push harder, because that's what I do. I keep moving even when my legs throb and I'm pooped. Can I force someone who is out of shape to do something she thinks she can't do? I could try.

"Let's rest for five more minutes and see if you feel better." She had to get up. I could not leave her behind.

"That won't help. I'm beat." She stared at her feet, wouldn't look at me. "My legs hurt, and I don't have any energy left."

"Maybe if you drink some water you'll feel better." I took a swallow from my bottle to set an example.

Sometimes all it takes is a drink of water to restore a person's energy. I hoped that was the case for Lucy. After a long pause, she said, "I'm sorry. I can't keep going." She hadn't moved from the rock. "What do you want me to do?"

It was too late to catch the group, to tell them we needed to turn back. They were gone, thanks to my, "See you later." I had to leave her behind, yet I knew a responsible wilderness guide would never leave someone alone on a hike. What else could I do?

She stood up, looked at the trail that led to the van. Her lower lip twitched as if she was going to cry.

"You start back while I meet the others at the top. We'll come back this way and pick you up on the way down." I hugged her. "Walk slowly, carefully. Don't trip." That was the best I could do, not an ideal solution, but the only one available given the circumstances.

"I can go by myself," she said. "I'm not scared because we've seen other people on the trail. You go." Her shaky voice didn't match her brave words." I'll see you when you come back. I'll be fine." Her hands shook as she put her water bottle back in her pack and started down the trail.

Now the problem was—where were the other hikers and how could I catch them?

* * * * *

I found them at the top, laughing, talking, having a fine afternoon. Jackets and sweaters off, they sprawled on the rocks facing south where layers of peaks stretched to infinity and multiple shades of green danced in the late afternoon sun. I envied their carefree joy.

All I could think about was Lucy. What if she startled a bear? What if she tripped and fell? What if her legs gave out and she couldn't walk anymore, or she twisted an ankle? The possibilities played in my head while I chatted with the rest of the group.

I noticed Barbara smoking and moved upwind. A former smoker myself, I found the smell of cigarette smoke offensive and avoided people and situations where there would be smoking.

After a few minutes I said, "It's time to go. We need to leave time to get back before dark."

"We found the other trail" Marty said. "It starts over here. This will be a great walk down." She pointed to the sign for the Bullhead Trail. "Look at the view, and we haven't even started!"

"We have to go back on the Rainbow Trail." I said. "I left Lucy at Rainbow Falls. Told her we'd find her on the way back." I knew that would not be a popular decision.

"What if we go down Bullhead and you go down Rainbow and we meet in the parking lot. It's eight miles either way," Ellen said. "We'll get there at the same time."

"I don't want to split the group." Now I was in trouble. "We need to stay together."

Then Barbara said, "You said we're strong hikers. Why can't we go down Bullhead without you?"

"I don't want to split the group." They were right, Bullhead had been the plan.

"What if the six of us promise to stay together and you go down Rainbow and pick up Lucy?" These women were not going to give up.

"Okay. Promise you'll stay together." I didn't want to do this; splitting the group was irresponsible, but by then it was too late. "I'll meet you at the bottom. Now, get going. It gets dark when the mist rolls in."

Damn. Adventure travel guides are supposed to be assertive, strong leaders who don't give in when they know what needs to be done to insure the safety of the group. Angry, frustrated, disgusted with my wishy-washy leadership, I walked as fast as I could, hoping to find Lucy before she got to the parking lot. I had visions of a helicopter rescue, headlines in the Knoxville paper. "Eight women from Venture West, a Milwaukee organization, were rescued in the Smokies. This was a costly rescue, the result of poor guide judgment." My business ruined, I would crawl home to find an office job, one where I didn't have to be the boss.

I tried not to trip over roots and rocks as I raced down the mountain. By the time I got to Rainbow Falls, dusk had extinguished the remaining light. I still had three-and-a- half miles on a bumpy trail. The mountains no longer felt friendly. Rainbow Falls took on an ominous tone. The peaks disappeared in the mist. My exhausted legs felt like loose rubber bands.

I could run down the mountain, but what about the group on Bullhead? Would they notice the waning light and walk faster, but not too fast? No doubt they had admired the sunset from the trail, oblivious to the darkening woods and the distance to safety. They had maps but no sense of the timing of an eight-mile hike downhill on rugged terrain. Neither did I!

I picked up the pace, using a small flashlight to find the way. Now I was the person at risk for a broken ankle or a bad fall. Half walking, half running, I stumbled into the parking lot where Lucy stood, waiting.

"I was getting really worried. Where is everyone?" Her voice broke and she started to cry. "I've been here for a really long time."

"I came as fast as I could. I'm sooooo sorry you were scared."

I wanted to cry. Couldn't. Had to keep up a brave front.

"Are the others okay?" She sat down on the pavement, blew her nose and zipped her jacket. "It's getting cold."

"They'll be here soon. We left at the same time."

"I'm sure someone has a flashlight," Lucy said. "I forgot mine."

Had I reminded them to pack a flashlight? I had told them to always bring one at the orientation three days ago.

What had I been thinking? Sixteen miles and forty-five hundred feet elevation gain in a day is for twenty-year old fitness freaks who want to test their limits, not seven women out for a leisurely day hike. What had I done? Where was my brain?

I sat on the pavement next to Lucy. There were no other cars in the lot, no one to send to town to call a park ranger. We waited.

"Do you hear something?" she whispered. "I hear voices."

"I do, too. Can't tell where they're coming from." We peered into the night. Vague forms appeared across the parking lot, laughing, talking.

Laughing? How dare they laugh? I could barely speak. It was them. "Where have you been? How did you find the trail? Did anyone have a flashlight?" Now I was the teary one.

Marty told the story. "Barbara saved us. We walked slowly, enjoyed the views, hung out at the pretty places, and never thought about the time. Then it got dark. We couldn't even see our feet. We came to a place where the trail went two ways. We couldn't read the sign. Barbara remembered her cigarette lighter. When she flicked it, we saw an arrow pointing to the parking lot. I'm not sure we took the right trail, but who cares? We're here."

Everyone talked at once. Nervous chatter and laughter swirled around me. I felt like an island in the eye of a hurricane, calm, steady, relieved.

I had allowed six women to hike eight miles down a mountain without a guide, left a solo hiker alone in the mountains, and misjudged the time we needed to hike sixteen miles. This had not been my best day.

We returned to camp where I cooked pasta primavera and suggested that everyone go to bed early.

I thought about my disdain for Barbara, the smoker on Mount Le Conte. Sometimes help comes from an unexpected place.

Chapter Twelve

Corned Beef on Rye

1996 Venture West Catalog
Five nights lodging at the 320 Ranch in the Gallatin River Valley in Montana means comfort, privacy, and delicious breakfasts in their western-style dining room. In the Spanish Peaks Wilderness Area we'll hike to Lava Lake surrounded by rocky peaks and climb Cinnamon Mountain for a three-sixty view. Every day we hike high in the "Peaks" and each day will bring new vistas and magnificent scenery in this pristine wilderness area.

C owboy Bruce radiated confidence as he trotted up the trail. He looked like a cross between John Wayne and the Marlboro Man. "Where you all headed?" he asked as we cleared a space to make room for him and his magnificent stallion. He was sexy, muscular, dressed in black with a silver buckle on his belt and silver stitching on his Stetson. Even his boots were black.

My group of ten was taking a break in the morning sun on a hike in northwest Yellowstone. Relaxed, we leaned against rocks and munched M&Ms, raisins, and peanuts. We didn't have a specific destination on the hike, just a plan for lunch, close to running water.

"We're hiking up the Daly Creek Trail, taking it easy." I smiled at this handsome cowboy who had appeared from somewhere in the trees.

Life on the Loose

It was hard not to stare at the man in black. Jean and Betty pulled out cameras to sneak a fast photo when he looked away from where they sat close to the trail.

"That's a good walk," he said. "I'm here tracking a grizzly." Ten people stopped chewing and looked at our visitor. "Just saw him, 'bout ten minutes ago, a male, hangin' out in the marsh down by the creek. He's a big bruiser."

"Oh, that's a surprise. The book says we won't find the griz here." Didn't I know better than to believe everything I read in a guidebook? "It said if there was one nearby, the Park Service would have closed the trail." I paused, thought I'd better tell the cowboy what the guidebook really said. "Well, the book didn't exactly say 'close the trail.' It mentioned bears, showed some drawings of tracks, and said sightings were unlikely." I'd read it, discarded the outside chance that my group would encounter a bear, and put the thought out of my head.

I had done it again: buried my head in the sand and decided bad things won't happen to me. We had no business hiking in griz country, but darn, I loved the gentle incline on the Daly Creek Trail. It was easy, scenic, and followed a sweet, little stream.

"Oh," said the quintessential cowboy from a safe perch on his stallion, "Your guidebook was wrong. This is a Problem Bear Management Area."

"What's that?" Dave, a professor at the University of Wisconsin, asked the obvious question. A wrong answer would destroy my plan for our week in Yellowstone and the Gallatin Canyon Area.

The cowboy looked at me. "Oh, that Bear Management thing, it's just a fancy term for the place where the Park Service relocates problem bears. You know, like the ones that bother people and get into garbage in the campgrounds." He paused, looked at my group of ten. "How old is your guide book anyhow?"

That's how we learned that we sat in the middle of a hotbed for habituated bears, bears that are used to people, the most dangerous bears in the park. Why hadn't I checked the copyright date when I bought the guidebook? Just because a woman who owned a lodge at Big Sky wrote a book about hikes didn't guarantee that she knew anything about the Problem Bear Management Area.

The man in black walked his horse closer to me and said in a quiet voice, "Thought you should know about the griz. My name's Bruce, by the way."

"My name is Cari. I'm the guide, you know, the leader, the one supposed to keep this group safe from bears." I wanted the group to disappear. I was single. He was a hunk. Always figured I'd meet the man of my dreams somewhere on a trail in the west. Used to tell friends I'd sit by a trailhead in Montana and wait for Mr. Right.

It never happened. Even if I perched at a trailhead and waited, what were the chances Mr. Right would magically appear? Oh, well. A person can dream. Finally divorced, I enjoyed my fantasies about finding an ideal relationship with a man who shared my passion for wild places.

"Well, thanks for the update. We'll make a lot of noise." And unlike the Le Conte hike in the Smokies, I would keep the group together. "We're a big group, that's good."

"You all stay safe now." With a wave and a tip of his black-and-silver Stetson, Bruce trotted down the trail, our trail, the one that led to lunch by a creek.

This was a problem. Of course, people are afraid of bears, especially the griz. I am, too, but after many years in the West and several bear encounters, my fears had dissolved into an edgy wariness, tempered by knowing, or hoping, that the bear had other priorities, like a berry bush for its afternoon snack. At least Bruce hadn't said "sow with cubs." Nevertheless, newcomers to bear country have heard horror stories about bear attacks, stories that grew in magnitude as they circulated, stories that kept people out of areas where bear sightings occurred. However, when there's an attack, there's often food involved: a bologna sandwich, a bag of beef sticks, or corned beef on rye.

After Bruce left, the group remained unnaturally quiet until Dave said, "Cari, I think we should turn around. I know you." Dave and his wife Jean had taken many Venture West trips. "You want to keep going, but we're scared." He was right. I did want to keep going.

This wasn't the time to chatter on about how the odds were we wouldn't see anything more exciting than a red squirrel or a marmot, and how the bear wanted to avoid us more than we wanted to stay away from it, or how lovely was the day and the hike and the anticipated lunch by the stream. This was a time to turn around, to use common sense for once, and to find a different hike. We trudged back down the trail, disappointed that our lovely day hike had ended too soon.

Two days later, I made a plan to watch elk at twilight. This was early September, the season when bull elk rubbed off the velvet covering on their antlers to reveal them as props for attracting females. To the girls, the antlers were shiny sex symbols. When the males bugled ancient calls that sounded like rusty creaky gates, the sound signaled the start of a duel, known as the rut. Two bulls would lock antlers to determine who got first choice of the prime female cows for his harem. The strongest bull gathered the biggest harem.

When someone at the ranch where we were staying told me about a meadow close to the Black Butte Trail where we could see the rut, I said to myself, "Let's do it." He said the meadow was close to the road. All I had to do was convince the group. How could we

Corned Beef on Rye

be in any danger from a bear when we would be less than a mile from a well-traveled highway? The man had said, "You can see them just before dark. You have to sneak up, because if the elk sense you are there, they disappear."

Most of the group agreed that it sounded like a fine plan. We would take sandwiches, wine, and cookies, and sit on a knoll that overlooked the meadow to watch the show. I hoped everyone had forgotten about cowboy Bruce and his griz, because this was our once-in-a-lifetime opportunity. We'd have a front-row balcony seat to see elk rut, a chance to witness something primordial, nature's way of ensuring that the strongest will sire the next generation. How could I let common sense get in the way of adventure? I put bear thoughts out of my head.

Six out of ten said "yes." Dave and Jean declined, as did Ken and Louise from Colorado, saying they saw elk from their windows and it wasn't a big deal for them. The rest of us drove to the deli at Big Sky and picked up corned beef on rye with extra mayo and double Swiss for the picnic. I added a dozen chocolate chip cookies to my backpack and two bottles of Merlot.

We'd barely started the hike when two men stopped to ask if we'd seen their wives. "My wife has dementia," the older one said. "Sometimes she wanders off the trail."

The younger one, who looked like his son, added, "They got ahead of us. Said they were following some tracks." My antennae went up. Sure hope it's not the griz.

"Where are you all going?" the older man asked.

"We're going to see the rut," Susan said. "We'll keep an eye out for them." She was ahead, racing up the trail, filled with enthusiasm and excitement for our adventure.

I asked if the men had a flashlight. "You'll need one. I have one you can borrow. You can return it to the Rainbow Ranch." I dug an

137

extra flashlight from my pack and handed it to him. "Good luck. We'll be out before dark."

By that time, our shadows stretched in front of us. We needed to hurry to see the elk while there was still some afterglow from the sunset.

After we crossed an open field and started to climb up a small knoll, I whispered to the six who followed close behind, "We're almost there. No more talking." I pointed to the trail that had started to disappear. "We'll sneak up on them."

"Cari, wait, I stepped in something." Sandy stopped to clean off her boots. "Oh, yuk, it's full of berries and ick—it looks fresh."

We were close to the meadow and the elk. I would not tell Sandy that she had stepped in fresh bear shit and what that meant.

"Keep moving, we're almost there." I hoped they didn't think about our corned beef sandwiches and a bear's sense of smell.

"I hear a bugle," Susan whispered. We tiptoed around an aspen grove, climbed a grassy knoll, and sat down to watch the show. Through an opening in the trees, we saw a pack of gorgeous bull elk with massive, branched, shiny antlers. Occasionally one bugled, but mostly they milled around as if to size each other up before the duels began. We could barely see them.

Every time one of them bugled, it raised its head and let it rip. We sensed their pride in their magnificent manhood on display for the girls, soon to be herded into separate harems. But there were no females in sight.

Fran pulled out her binoculars. "I'll share if you want. It's hard to see."

"Can we eat our sandwiches now, Cari? How about opening the wine?" Jill opened her paper bag. It crackled in the evening silence.

"Shhh. We don't want them to know we're here."

It was too late. As she bit into her corned beef on rye, every bull ready to duel raised his head, sniffed the air, took a few steps into the middle of the meadow, and disappeared into the surrounding trees.

"Show's over. They know we're here." I spoke quietly, not wanting to spoil the evening's magic despite the sudden disappearance of the main event. "It's too dark to wait. We can eat back at the ranch." It was time to get out of there. "Let's get moving."

Now I felt the danger. If the elk sensed our presence, so did the bears. We had lost the chance to see the rut, and worse yet, my enthusiasm had buried my common sense. I had broken three rules of bear avoidance. We had arrived in their territory at twilight, we came in silence, and we had brought food.

"Everyone get out your flashlights and make lots of noise. We want the bears to know we're here."

"Bears, Cari?" You didn't tell us we might attract a bear." Susan sounded angry. She glared at me, "We're not supposed to be here. Tiptoeing in with corned beef in our backpacks was really stupid."

"I know. I wanted you to see the rut." I was outed. That was a dumb thing to do in griz country. "Let's get out of here."

In less than fifteen minutes, we were back on the main trail where we had left the husbands looking for their wives. As we approached the highway, we came upon a group of people standing next to the trail. We heard sirens in the distance. Several of the group held the reins of their horses.

"Looks like an accident," someone behind me said.

"What happened?" Lois asked. She was ahead of us. Her voice shook. "I don't like this. I want to be safe in my own room."

A woman holding the reins of two horses answered. "Bill's horse bolted and threw him. He can't even move his fingers." She started to cry. "Sounds like the ambulance is here. We'd better get out of the way." She walked over to Bill, lying motionless under a blanket, knelt down to touch his face, picked up his limp hand, and held it close to her.

"We've been married forty-eight years," she said. "He is a good rider."

We waited with the others as the emergency team brought a stretcher for the injured man. Their evening ride had been cut short by tragedy. For no reason, a healthy person thrown to the ground, and in a nanosecond, a life altered forever.

Bill had done nothing wrong. It was a random accident. But I had led six people who trusted me to a place where a dangerous bear had recently been sighted. Did I deserve to be a guide?

Our adventure ended at the ranch. As we sipped Merlot, we wondered, did the husbands find their wives? Would Bill walk again? Did Cowboy Bruce find the griz?

We had a lot to talk about.

Chapter Thirteen

Breaking Rules

2000 Venture West Catalog

What makes Venture West special? The convenience of airport pickups, well-researched itineraries that leave space for reflection, leisurely yet challenging hikes that account for individual abilities, a relaxed guide with a sense of humor, and always, an emphasis on fine dining in unpretentious restaurants.

Backpacking trips don't require permission slips from doctors or fitness certificates from a gym. Maybe they should. Maybe the catalog description should read, "Only the fit need apply" or "Strenuous steep hikes require perseverance" or "Stoic hikers welcome." When people signed up for a trip, I assumed they had considered their abilities. This was supposed to be a self-selecting process, but then we all exaggerate our strengths when we sit on the couch and dream. It's easy to see yourself climbing a mountain when you're safe at home.

I've never put anyone in a place where they could get hurt, although I've applied a few nudges that pushed people out of their comfort zones and into situations where they said, "Oh, my God, I can't do that."

I figured they could always push harder and exceed their expectations, like clients at a gym with personal trainers. It was always easier to say, "Keep going. You can do it. Don't give up," if it was someone else, not me. Dozens of times, I encouraged people to keep moving. It was my job. Many times, conversation diverted an unhappy hiker's attention. I'd bring up some reality TV show and they'd forget about their pain. *The Biggest Loser* always worked. I had to keep them moving. Occasionally I resorted to discussions that involved *American Idol* or *Dancing with the Stars*.

I used to say, "If I can do it, you can do it," but that's not true, because I had to follow through whether or not my legs had turned into spaghetti, or I was desperately thirsty, or completely exhausted. I had to be stoic, set an example of strength for people who struggled. I'd say, "This is a tough hike. You can do it." If I let on how much my legs ached, I'd lose my guide credibility, so I faked it more times than I care to remember.

Over the years, many people thanked me for encouraging them when they were ready to collapse, said the experience built confidence for other challenges. This validated my early philosophy for Venture West—that the trips were more than mini-vacations. The idea I could initiate personal growth gradually eroded as I figured out why most people signed up for a trip. They wanted the experience, to commune with wilderness, but more importantly, they wanted to have fun. I tried to give them confidence-building sweat equity along with laughter, camaraderie, and, of course, memorable meals, but to be honest, for most people, Venture West trips were mini-vacations. That was fine with me. Even though I worked hard, I had, at the least, as much fun as anyone else.

Once in a while someone who wasn't quite fit enough slipped through.

Broken Rule #1: Don't walk behind a horse.
Her name was Jane. She said, "I'm tired. I can't walk anymore." In her mid-fifties, overweight, out of shape, she told me later she

expected something more like a three-mile walk in a park, not an eight-mile schlep up and down a mountain, her idea of a death march. Always a good sport, she never complained, hiked with a smile, and told stories about her grandchildren.

I tried to be clear in the catalog description about elevation gain and distance, but not everyone bothered to read it. And people who hadn't hiked in the mountains couldn't relate to the stamina needed to hike up fifteen-hundred feet in two miles.

We were more than three miles from our camp at Walnut Bottoms in the Smokies. We'd climbed up and down several ridges on our way to an overlook, then descended to a place where we needed to climb one more ridge to get to camp.

"Jane," I said quietly in my patient voice, "You have to keep going. We can't stop here." I took her hand and pulled her up from a stout log. "It will be dark in two hours."

"Cari, please. I need to sit for five more minutes." She sat down. There was no moving her until she rested.

"Eat chocolate," Cindy suggested. "You'll get an energy hit."

"Good idea. Why didn't I think of that?" I wondered out loud.

I heard voices on the trail and two horses and their riders came up behind us and stopped. "How you all doin?" one of them asked. They looked like city guys out for a trail ride. Their jeans and cowboy hats were new, as if they had outfitted themselves for the day.

"Pretty good, but we're pooped. We have a long walk back to camp." I nodded toward Jane. "She doesn't want to leave her log. Right, Jane?"

She shrugged and ate another piece of chocolate.

We had two hours until dark, in the woods, on a moonless night. I'd noticed a sliver of new moon the night before, not enough to light our way. In this rugged terrain, we needed flood lights, not pocket flashlights.

"What if she holds on to my horse's tail and lets him pull her up the mountain?" One of the cowboys had a smile as wide as the Mississippi. He had a great idea if it worked.

"Cari, I can't do that. He'll kick me." Jane stood up, picked up her daypack. "What if he bolts? What if he drags me? What if he poops?" She sighed. "I'll walk."

"Miss, you insult my horse. Grab his tail and hold on tight." The horse stood motionless as if waiting for Jane to make up her mind. "We'll give you a fast ride to the top of that ridge."

"Go on. He knows his horse." I would try anything to get her back to camp. If she didn't move, we would have to hike in the dark. "You can do it," She walked behind the horse, stood there as if waiting for him to kick her in the face, then reached for his tail.

They started up the trail, Jane half walking, half running, called back, "It feels like I'm going up an escalator. See you at the top."

We were the ones who lagged behind. At the top, Jane stood, waiting for us. "So, what took you so long?" She looked over at the horse, gave it two thumbs up, and started down the trail. We followed Jane, our new leader.

Broken Rule #2: Bring enough water.

Everyone needs a shove once in a while, but on a backpacking trip in Olympic National Park on the High Divide Trail, someone in the group needed more than "You can do it." She needed my water.

This time, we carried forty-pound backpacks on a ninety-degree day. Mary sat down in the shade and said, "I'm out of water and my head hurts. I quit." She wasn't thinking clearly, which is often the first sign of more trouble to come. I had told her before we left in the morning to bring at least two quarts of water; she didn't want the extra weight.

Sometimes I back off. "It's your choice. You will want that extra quart later." She was a big-boned woman, stubborn, uncomfortable with my leadership. She often resisted my suggestions.

I wanted to kick her. Everyone was hot and thirsty, crabby. Through a clenched jaw, I said in a tight voice, "Here, take my water." What I wanted to say was, "You lumbering idiot. Pick up your ass and walk." She emptied my bottle, picked up her pack, and trudged on.

On a hot, sunny day, lack of hydration can put a person at risk for hyperthermia, a life-threatening situation when the body overheats and its cooling system shuts down. If that happened, she could die. I needed that water as much as she did, but of course, I was the guide.

Broken Rule #3: Respect limits.

Once I encouraged an overweight woman down a four-hundred-foot sand dune. Sally and I stood at the edge of a former log slide and looked down to Lake Superior, a lovely presence that called us to come, play, and hunt for pretty rocks to take home. The rest of the group had started down, but Sally wanted me to tell her she could do it.

I've learned not to say, "This is easy." I needed to confirm Sally's fear, not deny it. At times like that, I walked that fine line between letting her give up, and giving encouragement when I believed she could do it. These situations took me back to my original premise: give a person like Sally a challenge, and she will find a way to rise to the occasion.

"Oh, you can climb back up. It just looks like a long way to the bottom. Follow me." I spoke with impunity, because people who paid to take a trip believed me when I said, "You can do this."

I grew up scrambling up and down sand dunes at Sleeping Bear Dunes National Lakeshore in Michigan, where the return climb was a small price to pay for the thrill of flying down the dune.

Sally followed, testing each step as if she thought she might pitch forward and roll to the bottom. I wanted to holler, "Enjoy the ride" but bit my tongue. She was too far away to hear me, her body rigid, as she concentrated on staying upright. A tiny warning tingled in the back of my head. This was the easy part; she didn't know that yet.

There were ten of us. We hung out, hunted for chain coral rocks and Petosky stones; then it was time to go back to the van. Eight people started the climb taking two steps forward and one sliding step backward, tedious, but easy for everyone except Sally.

Eight people made it to the top; one stayed at the bottom. I ran back down to the beach, pasted a smile on my face, and repeated to Sally, "You can do it. Follow me."

She didn't smile. Her taut body and grim face said no. "I can't," she said.

"You can." She didn't answer. "Step in my footsteps. That will help keep the sand from sliding under your feet and give you traction."

She stared at the sand.

"Don't look up." I said, hoping to distract her attention from the tiny figures waving at the top. I looked at her. Her eyes behind her sunglasses were teary. One rolled down her cheek.

I remembered the time I pulled someone up the last mile in the Smoky Mountains when she couldn't take another step and she meant it. That time we were five hundred vertical feet from our destination, the cabins on the top of Mount Le Conte. It had started to snow. I found a stout stick alongside the trail and used it to pull her up the last mile.

This time, I didn't have a stick, only words of encouragement. "You can do it." I repeated. "This is hard for everyone. Me, too."

"I have to breathe," she gasped. "My heart's pounding so hard, it feels like I'm going to explode." She took another step. "I can't get my breath."

"It's okay. I'm here." As we climbed, her face got redder, her voice weaker. She struggled to breathe, but she kept moving. When she crawled on all fours over the edge at the top, she spread-eagled on the sand to the sound of applause from a gathering crowd.

When she could speak, she said, "I didn't think I could do it. Just wanted to roll back to the bottom and stay there."

She stood up and hugged me. "I'm so proud."

"Me, too," I said. I wanted to cry. What had I done? I had encouraged someone who was out of shape to go down that sand dune. What if she had collapsed? She could have had a heart attack, a stroke. Sally's story had a happy ending, but the fact remains, this lovely, albeit overweight, woman, had spent her money to end up in a panic situation I created.

Broken Rule #4: Always tell someone where you are going.
AND
Absolute Rule# 5: What goes up must come down.

It seemed like a good idea, a solo backpacking trip in the Gros Vente Wilderness Area across the valley from the Tetons. A free airline ticket and a ride to and from the trailhead fit my budget. On this scouting trip, I would check out campsites, trails, and available water.

Life on the Loose

I arrived in Jackson at 1:00 in the afternoon and called a friend who said he was busy, but he'd come by in an hour to give me a ride to the trailhead. I took my backpack outside, leaned it against the terminal, and sat on the sidewalk.

As I watched people leave the airport, everyone looked young and fit, with tight quads and muscular calves. This description did not fit the man who smiled at me from across the street. After he stamped out his cigarette, he walked to where I sat on the ground.

Middle aged, like me, paunchy, an ordinary-looking fellow with a lined face, he started a conversation. "I'm visiting my son. He works for Exum Mountain Guides." I'd often seen their guides, working with novice climbers on a boulder close to the Cascade Canyon Trail. "We've been hiking for a week, and I've been looking around for some property to buy. Think I'd like to live close to these mountains."

"Me, too. I come here every year to hike." We chatted, talked about our favorite Teton trails. When I mentioned I planned to trek in Nepal in November, he handed me his business card. "My wife travels there often and I've been in the Himalayas myself. Give us a call. Maybe we can help you plan your trip."

Of course I would. I'd never met anyone who had been to Nepal.

I told him about my backpacking trip in the Gros Vente and where I wanted to set up camp the first night.

He said, "As long as you'll be at Goodwin Lake, why not climb Jackson Peak. Walk about a mile and a half on the trail past the lake, and you'll see the mountain." He didn't look like a climber. "The route is obvious. It's an easy climb to the top."

We talked until they called his flight. I walked with him to the gate. "Have a great trip. You'll love the view of the valley from the peak, and don't forget to call me." And off he went to catch his plane to Washington, D.C., where he said he worked for a magazine.

After he left, I looked at the card he'd handed me. It read, "Barry Bishop, Vice President Explorations, National Geographic Magazine.

"I work for a magazine," he said. That's all he said.

When my friend John picked me up later to give me a lift to the trailhead, he said, "I'm leaving tomorrow for a ten-day canoe trip on the Missouri River."

"What? I gave my family your phone number. I always leave them an emergency contact." I was in trouble. "Now I don't have anyone to tell where I'm going. I can't do that." John steered around a boulder on this remote two-track that led to the trailhead. "I'm not leaving a car. No one will know where I am."

"That's right. You'll disappear without a trace." He steered around a pothole with one hand, looked at me, and laughed.

"That's not funny. What am I going to do?" I should have known better than to assume John would be parked in Jackson while I went off to the wilderness.

"Can we go back to the Forest Service Campground? I'll give the ranger an itinerary." I always told someone where I would be and, if I could, left a detailed itinerary, a contact person, and a phone number with my family.

"The campground closed the end of August. You're out of luck."

"Oh, well, I'll be extra careful," I said to John as we bumped up the primitive road to where I would start my journey. "By the way, have you ever heard of Barry Bishop? He gave me his card at the airport."

"Are you serious? He's famous." John almost ran off the road. "You met him? He climbed with Sir Edmund Hillary on Mount Everest." Geez, now we just missed a tree. "He turned back because of frostbite, lost part of his toes. He doesn't climb anymore, but he's beloved in the climbing community."

"He looked so ordinary. Not like a climber." I remembered the cigarette he dropped. "He smokes. All he said was, 'I've been in the Himalayas myself.'"

"Do I look like a climber?" John climbs often. His middle-age paunch hid his impressive climbing skill.

"Not really. Do I look like a backpacker?"

"Nah. You're too old."

At the trail head, I put my travel clothes in a plastic bag, hid them in the woods, and started up the trail. After four easy miles, I set up camp behind a boulder in a secluded site in the woods, close to Goodwin Lake.

The next day, I packed a lunch and headed for the "obvious route," the "easy climb," according to Barry Bishop, who had climbed with Sir Edmund Hillary.

A short walk took me to the base of Jackson Peak, where there was no obvious trail to the top. I figured Barry saw the same steep slope leading to a summit somewhere out of sight. He saw a trail and called it easy. I saw rock.

I started up, climbing on scree, rocks that varied in size from pebbles to tennis balls. They rolled under my feet, kept me off balance. I started to crawl. There was nothing to hold onto. Blood ran down my leg. I progressed, two steps forward, one sliding step backward as I groveled toward the summit. Every rock I grabbed gave way.

I looked down. That was a mistake. Crawling up a mountain on my hands and knees was doable, the reverse impossible. My bloody knee started to shake. Somewhere, there was an easy route. This wasn't it. I leaned into the mountain, drank some water, ate a candy bar, and started up again, still on my knees.

At the top, I found the route, a barely discernible path in the rocks, the one obvious to a seasoned climber. Using mini-white-bark pine trees for hand holds, I skidded to safety, one tree at a time. Maybe Barry Bishop had come down on his feet; I came down on my ass.

Barry was right about one thing: the view from the top was lovely.

More Stories

151

Chapter Fourteen

The Chauffeur

2011 Venture West Catalog

**Lush canyons, red cliffs, blue skies; Zion's colors
are spectacular. Add red, brown, and gold from aspen,
oak, and maple, and you have an artists' view of Zion.
On this trip you will see sculptured red rock walls, finger
canyons, vistas from above, and intimate nooks below.
You won't know whether to look up or down as we
traverse trails in the canyon and in the
Kolab section of the park.**

No one told me how many hats I would have to wear when I
started Venture West. I didn't know how to run a business,
I just knew how to run a trip, or so I thought, until something went wrong. I bumbled through each crisis and smiled a lot.
Somehow it worked. I got to play and spend time in the wilderness
with smart people who read good books. I traveled with people
who had interesting things to say. What better way to live a life
than by doing what I loved and calling it a business.

I learned to keep the books, set budgets, design and write the
annual trip catalog, market the business, scout the trips, plan the
meals, buy the groceries, cook the camp food, and organize the files.
In other words, I was a one-person band, running in place, patching
a business together, raising a family, and eating beans and rice
at home because after the divorce, we were poor. At least the

emotional lows that plagued me during the years we struggled with our marriage had ended.

My least favorite Venture West hat—chauffeur: Here's how that worked. If a trip originated in Milwaukee, I met people at a Park-and-Ride and chauffeured them to the trailhead. For trips in the West, I arrived a day early, picked up a fifteen-passenger van, and met the group the next day at the airport. All meals, lodging, and transportation were included in the price of every trip.

In the beginning, I used my own car to transport groups to and from trailheads. With no money, few customers, an old car, and youthful optimism, I didn't think about aging clutches, soot-filled catalytic converters, leaky mufflers, exhausted timing belts, broken radiators, dead batteries, and flat tires. If I filled the tank, changed the oil, and washed the car, it would run. Right? Everyone knows a clean car behaves better than a dirty car. If we feed it and change the oil regularly, it will perform. Then my red Dodge Aries popped that theory on a cross-country ski trip to the Sylvania Wilderness Area in Michigan's Upper Peninsula.

We'd had a perfect trip, sun every day, temperatures in the thirties, pristine fresh snow, an idyllic weekend. While four exhausted women slept, I drove home in the dark. Something wasn't right in the clutch, a little slippage, not a crisis. I knew my car and every burp that came from its engine. At 9:00 p.m., we traveled south on Highway 45 at sixty miles per hour. At 9:01, I stepped on the gas pedal and nothing happened. I pushed harder. Nothing. We came to a complete stop in the middle of the highway between Appleton and Oshkosh, Wisconsin.

The women in the back seat woke up, "Cari, what happened? Why did you stop?" Marie was the group worrywart, likeable but tense, always apprehensive when we skied in the woods.

I hoped no one heard me say the "F word" as we glided to our final resting place.

"I could use some help. We need to move this thing out of the middle of the road."

Now everyone was awake. We shoved the car off the highway onto the shoulder, what there was of it, a narrow strip barely wide enough for my car. No one said what we all knew: this was not a safe parking place on a moonless winter night.

Mary's voice quivered, "It's almost midnight. What are we going to do?" She looked out at the dark highway and shuddered.

"The clutch died. I see some lights, maybe a farmhouse." My casual, smiley demeanor didn't reveal how I felt—terrified. "You all wait here while I walk up the road. If there's someone home, we can call 911." I used my cheerful voice. "This won't take long."

There is always that moment when something goes wrong, when it seems hopeless, before I remember that things always work out. One has to trust that help will arrive in some form, but at the moment of crisis, it's hard to visualize how the rescue will play out.

"I want to come with you," Marie said. "I don't want to stay here in the dark." No one else said a word.

"I can go faster by myself. If I leave the engine running, you'll stay warm." It was my guide job to look at the bright side. "Things could be worse. It could be really cold."

My brain raced ahead to possible scenarios. Was a large, angry dog guarding the farmhouse? It's late; no one will hear me scream. What if there's no one home? (This happened before people had cell phones.)

"I'll be back soon. We'll be fine."

About two hundred yards up the highway, I saw lights in a farmhouse, pounded on the door, and woke up an elderly gentle-man who let me use the phone to call 911. I ran back to the group, where I found the car toasty, windows steamed from chatter and laughter, because apparently, they figured someone else was in charge and a rescue would soon take them on their merry way. That someone was me.

Within an hour, a tow truck arrived. He pulled the car on to the flatbed, jammed five of us in his cab, and delivered the car to the local Dodge dealer. Then he took us to a nearby airport where I rented a car, and in less two hours after the clutch died, we were headed again to Milwaukee.

This business, the one with the on-the-job-training, reminded me of Girl Scout camping trips. Many times, with one "mother-helper," I took twenty-five preteen girls on overnight trips. Each experience was like getting on a tunnel slide at a water park. I did a big one once, came out stunned and dizzy, ready to toss my cookies from the ride that threw me from side to side in a black tunnel. It was the absolute loss of control that terrified me.

That's how I felt on those camping trips, I started fresh, hopeful, optimistic, that this time we would have a smooth ride, but it never happened. Something always went wrong, something out of my control. Emily would get her feelings hurt and cry. Laura would fall down and cry, or Jane would be homesick for her mom and cry. There were always tears and I, the adult in charge, the fixer-upper, did my best, soothed hurt feelings, bandaged skinned knees, but homesick can't be fixed by the leader. When it was over, I crawled into bed on Sunday night, battered, bruised, and exhausted, a spent weekend warrior.

* * * * *

That Dodge Aries with its new clutch misbehaved two years in a row on trips to the Smoky Mountains. The first time, the starter quit. That's not death for a car if it has a functioning clutch, just an issue that comes up when you want to drive somewhere. We had a choice. We could leave it with a mechanic and miss a day in the mountains, or when we needed it, we could park it facing downhill, put it in gear, get it rolling, and pop the clutch. I let the group decide; this was their trip, they had paid for it. I was the chauffeur, the hired help, albeit one with the unreliable car.

The group voted. We hiked. We were in the mountains. There was no shortage of downhill places to leave the car. However, driving back to Milwaukee posed a few problems. Most of the time, the group pushed. When four women get behind a small car, they can move it. I'd sit behind the wheel; put it in first gear, and holler, "Go." Who needs a starter? We moved it enough to pop the clutch even when we parked at a restaurant and had to push it uphill. They loved the challenge. I'd look in the rearview mirror and see four women doubled over with laughter.

It was not the first time I owned a car with a problem. When I lived in San Francisco, my Volkswagen needed to roll down a hill before it started. For three years, that was business as usual. Then again, we were a couple, my car and I, not a group who had paid for a hiking trip.

The year the starter died was also a prom year. My oldest daughter Cathy was to attend her first high school dance, and I wouldn't be there. She had looked lovely, poised and confident, beautiful in her dress when she modeled it for me. I pushed back tears of frustration as I looked at my oldest daughter, who would dance at her first prom while I hiked in the Smokies. That was a high price to pay for following my passion. For me, regrets last forever, especially the ones that involve my children.

* * * * *

Life on the Loose

I took the aging Dodge to the Smokies again the next year. I still had no money, few customers, and the same blind optimism that kept getting me in trouble. This time the catalytic converter malfunctioned on Interstate 65 just outside Lebanon, Indiana.

When we left the mountains, we traveled at seventy like everyone else except the trucks. They passed us going eighty, an annoying distraction when I noticed that my foot on the gas didn't generate any momentum. When I floored it, the car had no pick-up. It was dying, but I pressed on, determined to ignore the problem. Always the Pollyanna, I decided we must have been going uphill despite the cornfields that surrounded us. We had traveled four hundred miles before I asked, "Does anyone smell anything?" I couldn't continue to ignore the gassy smell that had seeped into the car.

"Fumes?" said Janet. "Wonder what's wrong?" She took her bandana off her neck and held it over her nose and mouth.

"Well, if we can smell it, we won't die from carbon monoxide," Julie added. She was also the first person to say a year ago, "Who needs a starter? Let's hike." Every group needs a Julie, someone besides me to maintain good humor when things start to fall apart.

"Oh, we won't worry about that. I have a new muffler; that can't be the problem. I wonder why it's slowing down. Guess we're going uphill."

"Looks flat to me," Sandy said. "Did you not notice the corn-fields? This is Indiana, remember." She opened a window.

Janet chimed in again. "I think you better get out of the fast lane. We have a truck on our tail." I should have done that an hour ago. "That smell is getting really strong."

"I'm sure it will be fine." I said, using my optimistic voice. "Someone open a window. We need some fresh air in here."

"I already did," Sandy grumbled from the back seat.

I punched the flasher button and watched the speedometer drop to forty, thirty, twenty-five. Trucks honked as they sped by. When we saw a sign for a rest area in five miles, I floored the gas and prayed. We slowed to twenty.

"Can you find a mechanic on a Sunday?" Susan asked. "I have to be at work Monday morning. I don't want to spend the night in Indiana."

"You're not the only one," someone muttered, probably Sandy.

"You watch the road, Cari," Julie said. "Don't worry about us. We'll be fine."

By the time we coasted into the rest area, I could have walked those five miles and gotten there first. I called 911, and a tow truck packed us in his cab, put my car on the flatbed, delivered it to a muffler shop, and drove us to a nearby motel. It had bars on the windows and a sign that read "Sleep Cheep." This would not be the Four Seasons.

"Welcome to Lebanon," I said. "It's not fancy, but we're stuck. I'm really sorry." I still didn't know what was wrong with the car. "We'll get out of here in the morning."

At 8:00 a.m., we walked to the muffler shop and waited for the owner to install a new catalytic converter because he said the other one had filled up with soot.

"Enough," I said. "From now on, I call Avis."

* * * * *

Rental cars and vans have issues, too, like the time I showed up in Las Vegas with a group of eleven headed for Bryce National Park and the Budget man said, "I'm sorry. The van you reserved didn't come back from California yet." He didn't look sorry. It wasn't his problem.

"What? I reserved this van six months ago." He couldn't be serious. "You have to have a van for me. What's the point of a reservation?"

"According to Budget policy, there's no penalty if you keep a vehicle past the original reservation." He used his authoritative, bored-with-the-public-voice." Most people return vans on time, but sometimes this happens." I wanted to stuff his paperwork down his white collared shirt.

Ten people stared at me as if they thought I could solve this with a few well-chosen words. I heard mumbling in the group, then from Nancy, "Cari, if you get two mini-vans, I'm willing to drive." She'd taken several Venture West trips and was a strong hiker who always helped me keep track of people who fell behind.

"That's a really nice offer. I'm tempted to take you up on it, but just so you know, this is a liability issue." What was I thinking? I couldn't let a customer drive a van. "Oh, well, we'll be careful. Why not?" Did I say that? "You came to hike. Let's do it."

That was not a wise decision on my part, as the most dangerous part of running a trip was driving the van. I knew that. I also knew my liability insurance would not cover Nancy if something happened. I wasn't even sure it would cover me.

I turned to Mr. Budget, "Can you get us two mini-vans?" Just then, a fifteen-passenger van rolled into the lot. Other than the fact that it lacked a side-view mirror on the passenger side, it appeared to be a fine van. With a little help from the passenger in the front seat, I drove the damn thing without the mirror.

The following morning, after Eggs Benedict at Flannigan's Inn and Restaurant in Springdale, Utah, eleven hikers climbed into the van to drive to our first hike. I turned the key. Nothing happened. We had driven to Springdale from Las Vegas, and the van had started with no problem after we stopped on the way to buy groceries for our lunches. I tried again. Nothing.

All the men had an opinion.

"Did you leave it in park? John asked.

Bill walked in front of the van and tried to open the hood. "Maybe the spark plugs are loose?"

"Try to start it again, and this time step hard on the gas. Be careful you don't flood the engine." Dave owned a van and thought he knew about possible idiosyncrasies.

The women stayed out of the way while the men fussed with the key, checked under the hood, and crawled under the van to look for whatever lurked under there that might be relevant to our problem. We called the local mechanic. He couldn't figure it out.

Finally I called the Budget office in Las Vegas. "Didn't someone tell you? There's a small button in the car you have to activate before the key will start the engine."

"Oh," said John. "I noticed a tiny red light on the dash. Maybe that's the button." No one blamed me. If four men and a mechanic couldn't figure it out, how could I decode the problem?

While everyone was poking at the van, I had picked up a local paper. Just for fun, I checked my horoscope to see what was happening that day in the life of a Taurus. It read, "*You're not likely to get to your destination in an orderly linear fashion. It may seem that every direction you take leads to a detour-nothing personal. Persevere and you'll get there.*"

What else could go wrong?

On the way back to Las Vegas, we stopped for coffee and pie in Hurricane. I needed to comb my matted hat-hair after a day of hiking in the canyons. In the woman's room, I took a comb out of my purse, set it on the back of the toilet next to the key to the van, used the facilities, and flushed the toilet. As I reached for the comb, one of its teeth caught on the key ring and flipped the van key into the toilet. Sucked into the downward swirling water, the key—the only key to the van—disappeared. I jammed my right arm into the toilet and with the tip of the fingernail on my ring finger, caught the edge of the key before it disappeared down the neck of the bowl and on to the sewer.

It took a few minutes to regain my composure. My left sleeve was soaked to the shoulder, my hair still matted.

I met Bill coming out of the men's room. He was one of the wannabe mechanics with an opinion. He had crawled under the van to check something. I don't know what.

"Cari, what's wrong? You look like you saw a ghost." He put an arm around my shoulder and gave me a half hug.

"Why are you so pale? You look terrible," asked Judy, his wife. "Did something happen?"

"Why is your sleeve wet?" asked Jill. "Are you okay?"

"Everything's fine. I'll have some coffee and cherry pie. Maybe I got too much sun this week."

I would never tell about the key and the toilet.

"I forgot to comb my hair. I'll be right back."

Chapter Fifteen

Crash Landing

2007 Venture West Catalog

Welcome to Pictured Rocks National Lakeshore on the shores of Lake Superior in Michigan's Upper Peninsula. Towering cliffs, pristine beaches, sand dunes, sparkling cascades, spring flowers, and dense green forests beckon you to come and explore.

O n a sunny day in October, we were day hikers. We set out each morning with food, water, rain gear, and a plan to explore a section of a forty-five mile trail from Munising to Grand Marais, Michigan.

On the third day of a five-day trip, I planned a twelve-mile hike. We would walk to a backcountry camp site at Mosquito River, follow three-hundred-foot bluffs to Chapel Beach, and return on a wooded trail that skirted Chapel Falls. I'd done this a dozen times with groups. It was everyone's favorite hike.

Six women and two men stuffed themselves with bacon and eggs at a breakfast buffet and headed out. "It's a perfect day. Look at that sky," said Lucille, a strong hiker.

Lucille's husband John smiled, "I wonder what the rest of the world is doing." He took off his jacket and tied it around his waist. Lucille and John would be in front of the group, while I brought up the rear.

Life on the Loose

A quiet, little voice said, "Cari, I don't know if I can keep up." This was Julie, a novice hiker, full of enthusiasm, but apprehensive, with good reason. A slow hiker, she looked tense, nervous, and uncertain of her balance when she walked downhill.

"Don't worry, I'll be behind you. Remember to watch for rocks and roots." That's the usual warning before I remind them they can hike at their own pace. "It's easy to stumble if you don't look where you're going." Then I give myself permission to saunter.

We had eleven hours until dark, a generous estimate for a twelve-mile hike. I ask people to take off their watches to keep them focused on the hike and not the time, but I keep one hidden, especially in late October when days are short.

As we hiked through a maple beech forest alongside a stream, Julie said, "I love being here in September when the black flies are gone. I hate it when the bugs get in my ears." Only the sound of our footsteps completed her thought. Maple leaves, backlit by the early morning sun, gave everything a golden glow.

When we got to Lake Superior, its color matched the sky, and we could see the bottom from our trail high above the lake. The cool, crisp air kept us moving but not too fast, as everyone wanted to savor the perfection of the hike. We traveled slowly, separately, lost in our thoughts. At Mosquito River, we spread a jar of peanut butter, cheese, crackers, fruit, and Snickers bars on the warm rocks and lay in the sun, relaxed.

"I can see forever. Life is good," John said from his front row seat on the sun-warmed rocks. He'd taken off his boots and sprawled like the rest of us, facing the lake, soaking up the last of the autumn sun.

"Look at the clouds over the lake. It seems like they're coming our way," said Chris, Julie's friend. She tightened the laces on her boots. "Should we get going?"

Lucille looked at me, "It looks kind of gray out there. Is there a storm coming?" Her voice quivered. She stood up and looked at John. "Let's get moving. I'm ready."

"Don't worry. We'll beat it." I stepped away from the group to check my watch. It was noon. We had seven and a half hours of daylight left. No problem.

On this perfect day to hike at Pictured Rocks National Lakeshore, I was in a good mood. With a divorce behind me, a growing business, and dozens, if not hundreds, of satisfied customers, life was good. My two youngest children and I had recently moved from Whitefish Bay to a duplex on the other side of town as my "family maintenance" after the divorce had ended and I felt the pinch of two mortgages in Whitefish Bay. After I sold the family home, I was able to pay cash for the duplex. No more double mortgage stress for me.

Only a storm threatened to mar the day. However, we'd be safe in our motel before the wind and rain arrived.

I felt confident that I could deal with problems. I'd paid my dues, survived a few mistakes such as a wrong turn in Utah, a missed turn in Montana, and the unfortunate incident in the Smokies when I split the group. Those learning experiences grew my confidence, made me realize that I'm fallible and need to pay attention to my surroundings. I wouldn't make those mistakes again

If I could only get over the "kid guilt" I felt every time I left, life would be perfect. The year before I'd missed another prom, this time Wendy's. She looked young, vulnerable in her dress when she modeled it for me. But I missed the big night. No doubt I cared more than she did; missing the prom hurt. How could I be super-Mom and outdoor guide? I tried. By that time, I'd missed three proms. I rationalized that my ex-husband was there for them, but that didn't dispel the guilt. Nothing ever could.

As I admired the view and the red bunchberries that lined the trail, I heard a panicky voice. A scream.

"Cari, help. Julie's down."

I raced down the trail, heart pounding, fearful of what lay ahead.

"She's hurt," someone said. The group stood in a circle looking down at Julie.

"What happened?" Everyone stepped back so I could see her, a miserable lump in the middle of the trail.

"She was talking, looked back, and didn't see where she was supposed to step," Chris said.

I could see she hadn't fallen far, but she had landed hard on her knee when she missed the root meant to be used as a step down to a broad, sandy ledge.

"I can't move," she said. She lay where she had fallen, close to the drop-off that plunged to the lake.

"Can you stand up?" I asked and reached down for her hand. "I'll help you. Hold on to me and let's see if you can walk"

"I can't put any weight on it," she whispered.

When I pulled her to her feet, she slumped to the ground. Her kneecap slipped sideways and her leg buckled. It looked bad, like a misplaced link on a bicycle chain that's come off the track.

The lovely sandy ledge no longer felt hospitable. I glanced at the lake, now gray instead of sparkling blue. Waves had started, and a wind from the north brought a nasty chill to our perch on the sand. Her knee useless, Julie rolled on to her side and stared at me.

I pulled out my cell phone. No signal. No surprise. This had happened before when there was no nearby tower.

Everyone talked at once.

"The group has to stay together," whispered Lucille. She was right. An impossible request, but one that was absolutely correct. Again, I thought about the time I had split a group in the Smokies and our close call in the dark.

"No. Cari should leave us here and go for help." John pointed to the black clouds coming from the lake. "There's a storm coming." He was right, too. We all saw the ominous clouds coming from the north. There would be no right answer.

"No. Cari should stay with Julie," someone behind me said.

"She can't." Lucille grabbed John's arm as if to steady herself. "We can't go without her. We don't know the way."

"What about a boat?" Susan asked. Did she not see the cliff and the rocks?

"What about a helicopter?" John had been a pilot in Vietnam, had told me about some kamikaze rescues.

There was an edge of hysteria coming at me.

"What about the storm? It's not safe here." I heard panic in Susan's voice.

"We can't leave her." The words hung in the air because they were true.

From our location close to a well-known landmark, the Indianhead, we were exactly halfway to the parking lot. A cold wind started to blow off the lake. Everyone put on a sweater or a jacket. Help was six miles in either direction. My watch read 2:30. Five hours to darkness. In the storm, it would come on fast.

Time was short. Which would come first, the rescue or the rain? Even with raingear, Julie would be wet—no, soaked. People die under those conditions. She could become hypothermic, a condition where the body's heating system shuts down after prolonged exposure to cold. With the rain coming, she would be especially vulnerable if she couldn't move to keep herself warm.

Life on the Loose

There was no time to waste. "Chris, you stay with Julie. The rest of us will start walking. Don't leave the bluff." I put the phone in my pocket. "I'll find a place where I can call 911. Stay warm and you'll be fine."

I handed Julie my extra shirt and jacket and said to the other five, "We're going to walk as fast as we can. Follow me."

A couple hundred yards down the trail, we came to an opening where the edge of the bank jutted out toward the lake. "I'll try the phone again. This looks hopeful."

I stepped away from the group, pushed the "on" button. The screen came to life. I dialed 911 and heard "Hello."

"I need help. There's been an accident." I yelled into the phone as if that would make things happen faster. "I have a hiker who's hurt, needs to be carried out."

"Can she walk? Can you describe her injuries?" She sounded unconcerned.

"Her knee is out of the joint. She can't walk." I could barely understand the woman's monotone, as if she were watching TV and I was interrupting her favorite show. "She has to be carried." Surely she heard the panic in my voice.

"Okay, I hear you. We have a volunteer rescue squad. I'll contact them as fast as I can and they'll come with an ambulance. Where are you?"

"She's on the bluff just before the Indianhead between Mosquito and Chapel Beach. I'll meet the squad on the trail from the parking lot." I paused, remembered there were two trails. "I'll be on the one that leaves from the east end of the campground. I can tell them where she is." I hoped she was paying attention to my directions. "Please hurry. There's a storm coming."

"I'll do the best I can. They're volunteers." Oh, fine. It's Saturday afternoon. No one stays home on Saturday. "I have to find them. This will take a few minutes."

The dispatcher sounded barely engaged, as if she were planning dinner. Why should she worry? This was business as usual for her. She's safe in her office. What's a storm if you're not in it?

"Let's boogy," I said to the rest of the group. They lined up behind me, let me set the pace. I had to keep them upright while we raced across rocks and roots, over sandy ridges, up and down the undulating bluffs. If someone fell, we'd be in serious trouble. It took ninety minutes to get to Chapel Beach. I looked at my watch. Now there were three hours of light left.

I gave the group directions to the parking lot at a trail junction just past Chapel Beach, took two Advil, and jogged the final three miles in thirty-six minutes. Our volunteer rescuers had arrived with an ambulance. They stood in a bunch, smoking, as if they had hours before the storm, before darkness. Didn't they know the object of their rescue was six miles away? I watched them put the stretcher back in the ambulance and said, "Take it. She can't walk."

"We don't need it. We have blankets." Did they know how far six miles can be when you're carrying someone, the trail is uneven, and you can't see your feet, or the three-hundred-foot-drop-off to the lake? Did they know about the storm?

"I think you need the board," I repeated in a loud voice as they started down the trail. They ignored me, disappeared into the woods.

"At least there are four of them," I said to the group who rejoined me about the same time the rescue team sauntered off. "They'll have to figure it out. We have to trust they know what they are doing." My group of five had collapsed on logs and rocks. We'd walked nine miles on rough terrain with three to go. "It's time for a glass of wine and some food. It's out of my hands now."

My concern for Julie had trumped my other concern—liability. I had set up a corporation for Venture West, and everyone who took a trip signed a liability release. However, the release was not airtight. I could be sued for negligence. If she stumbled, was I at fault? I didn't think so. I had reminded her, along with the others, to watch her feet. I would worry about that later.

* * * * *

After dinner with the group at the Dog Patch in Munising, I dropped everyone off at the motel, where I saw a note on my door from the owner.

Come to the office. I have news for you. Carmen.

I put on my rain jacket for the walk to the office. It had started to sprinkle, and waves crashed against the breakwater in front of the motel.

The note didn't say good news. Did she know what happened? My mind raced with possibilities, none of them comforting. When Carmen greeted me with a smile, the lump in my stomach loosened.

"What's up?"

"My dad's the sheriff. He called to tell me what's happening because he knows I have a group of hikers here." The phone rang. I could tell from her conversation it was about the rescue. "There's a National Park Service boat fifty yards off Chapel Beach. They can't land because the waves are too big, but they think they can figure out a way to pick her up."

"Oh," I said, not sure if that was good news or bad news. "Is she there yet?"

"I don't know. Hope she gets there soon." The door blew open. Carmen slammed it shut. "That should do it. This is going to be a nasty one. Gonna be ten-foot waves by midnight."

I thanked her for the update and walked into the weather. I'd done everything I could. Now it was a waiting game. I walked to the breakwater and looked out at the storm. It had intensified while I talked with Carmen. Rain pummeled my face and soaked my legs as the wind pushed me away from the edge.

After I changed into dry clothes, I drove to the hospital. There's not much happening at Munising Memorial on a Saturday night. The parking lot looked eerie, well lit, like a stage before the curtain rises. The emergency room staff was nowhere in sight. In the cubicle they called the waiting room, I stared at white walls from 9:00 p.m. to 2:00 a.m., worrying, wondering, what could take so long? There was no news coming from the rescue. There were voices in the hall, but no one came to talk to me.

At 2:05 a.m., they wheeled Julie in to the emergency room. She looked like a ghost—pale, wrapped in blankets, with one leg raised in front of her. Chris told the rest of the story.

"I was terrified. They didn't get to us until after dark." Chris looked like hell, her legs scratched and bleeding, boots covered with mud, hair in her face. "Then they didn't know what to do with Julie because she couldn't walk."

I explained, "They didn't want to bother with the stretcher. Said they left it behind because it would slow them down."

I remembered the scene in the parking lot when they put it back in the van and took blankets instead.

"They made a sling out of the blanket, but that didn't work. They dropped her twice. It was dark. They didn't wait for me. I couldn't see where I was going. Julie kept crying, so they cut down four trees to make a stretcher with the blanket. That worked, but they had to keep setting her down because they got tired."

Chris talked so fast I barely understood her. She sat on a bench, took a breath, and kept going.

"One of the guys used a radio to call the rescue boat. I heard him say, 'Use your bull horn to get help from people at the campground.' I guess he did, because when we got close to Chapel Beach, we saw flashlights coming at us." She started to cry. "A bunch of campers came to help. Everyone took turns carrying Julie, and someone with a headlamp stayed with me."

I sat down next to her and gave her a hug and a Kleenex.

"What happened when you got to the gully?" I remembered it from other hikes, a gash in the land where a spring creek drains from the north, making a steep hike down and up even in good conditions.

"We crossed it. No one could see where they were going. It was steep and scary, especially going down. I guess they didn't drop Julie anymore after they fixed the blanket. I was too far behind. I didn't know what was going on."

She looked at Julie and said, "You were brave."

"It was awful. I was freezing." Now Julie started to cry. "Rain got on my face and ran down my neck. At the beach, they put me on a real stretcher and walked into the lake." Julie's teeth chattered when she talked. Her lips were blue. "I thought they would float me, but they were still wading when we got to the boat. Didn't matter. I was soaked anyhow."

"The water was chest deep," Chris said. "They lifted her above their heads and slid her on to the deck. When they hauled me onto the boat, I knew everything would be okay"

"So that's what took so long. They had to cut down trees so they could get her out of there. What a nightmare."

I told them about the phone call to 911, and how the rescue squad decided to leave the stretcher in the parking lot. "By the way, did you see the tour boat? We did. I heard him point out the Indian."

"Oh, yes. We certainly did," Chris said. "I heard them coming, so I took my red jacket, stood on the edge, and waved and waved and waved. Thought maybe I could get us some help. Everyone on the boat waved back, but they kept going." She laughed at the irony of the friendly waves from the passengers. "We thought we'd lost our only chance."

"When they passed us coming back the other way, the announcer said, 'We are in contact with the Park Service. Help is on the way.' That's when we knew we'd be rescued."

* * * * *

The storm raged for three days with gale-force winds, temperatures in the low forties, and driving rain. It didn't matter how Julie was rescued or if the volunteers listened when I insisted she wasn't going to walk no matter how many shoulders they offered. Everyone was safe. That's what counted.

Later, I learned she had torn a ligament. A month after she returned home, she had the knee surgically repaired.

Accidents happen. I'd rather they didn't happen on my trips, and if they must, I'd prefer to have an emergency room around the corner and a waiting team of specialists. Life should be neat, orderly, with uncertainty banished, especially in the wilderness.

But it isn't.

Chapter Sixteen

Food

1996 Venture West Catalog
Join a Venture West group to backpack in the stunning world of Olympic National Park. We'll explore a fog-shrouded coast with booming surf, alpine country with sparkling lakes, mountain meadows, towering peaks, and the lush Hoh rainforest. Three distinct environments; we'll explore all three.

Years ago, I planned to save the world as I replaced animal flesh with plant food. Converts, dozens of them, would go forth and proclaim my wisdom to their world. The mention of a New York strip with red wine sauce turned my stomach. Give me mung beans and brown rice topped with cheddar cheese or sautéed, tamari-flavored tofu and I was a happy camper.

The book *Diet for a Small Planet* fed this smug idealism. It dominated the food choices of the committed as we followed author Francis Moore Lappe's deadly dull recipes. We combined incomplete proteins, often beans, and rice to satisfy our bodies while our taste buds suffered. We ate the corn rather than feed it to pigs. If we craved bacon with our whole-grain waffles, we replaced it with fruit, and for Thanksgiving, we stuffed our pumpkins with grains and greens.

175

Life on the Loose

My family did not appreciate those vegetarian dinners. When I served couscous with cheesy broccoli sauce, or brown rice with green beans and almonds, dinner turned into a battlefield.

"Take one bite," I'd say. "You might like it. It won't poison you."

My ex-husband complained, told me privately I should go back to meat and potatoes because I cooked veggie dinners to please one person—me. Full disclosure: there was some truth to that.

Those healthy dinners were a lot of work: planning, shopping, and driving to the other side of town for special ingredients. I felt proud of those meals, and my efforts to promote healthful eating at home through vegetables and grains. Maybe it was the Mung Bean Stew that drove the final coffin nail in the marriage.

This passion ended for me and for Venture West the night I made soy-based beef stew.

After a four-day backpacking trip, five women looked forward to the final banquet, a meal they would love, something different, unique, and an appropriate finale to their wilderness adventure. We'd carried packs nine miles daily, and survived rain, wind, mud, and overweight, out-of-shape Louise, the group's self-designated complainer. When the sun finally came out, we anticipated a glowing end to a long day as we pitched the tents close to the edge of a bluff overlooking a wide sandy beach.

A friend had recommended a soy product that tasted like steak, even though the round, brown things in the bag at the natural food store looked like dog pellets. Had I bought Fido's dinner by mistake?

"It looks awful," Louise said. She always stayed in character. I could count on her to say something negative about the obvious, the thing I didn't want to talk about.

Food

I shrugged, dumped the stuff in the cooking pot, and told them what the skinny man at the store said, "Add hot water and simmer for ten minutes. It will taste like your mom's beef stew."

Louise sniffed the pot, held her nose, and said, "It smells like dog food."

Tricia disappeared into her tent. She loved to eat, and thought my camp meals were exceptional, or at least that's what she said. I could count on her to say, "Cari, thanks for a great dinner. I don't know how you come up with these meals when we're in the wilderness."

I lit the backpacking stove, put enough water in the pot to cover "Mom's Beef Stew," and brought it to a boil. Those little brown things immediately sucked up all the water in the pot. I added more. They doubled their size. They had an insatiable thirst as they puffed up until they looked like something we deposit in the bathroom, and finally overflowed all over the stove. They didn't need more water; they needed a landfill, or better yet, a flush.

"Do we have to eat it?" someone asked.

I looked at Tricia, hoping she would say something nice about the mess. "It looks kind of weird." That was the best she could do?

"I'm not all that hungry. I think I'll skip dinner and watch the sunset from the beach." Jane left the group.

Everyone followed except Louise, who couldn't resist a final shot. "I was right. This is awful." She stood up and lumbered to her tent. "I'm still hungry. I want this trip to be over."

I agreed. Those brown things didn't look like meat, didn't smell like meat, didn't smell like anything except maybe wet wool socks. We ate cheese and crackers, and carried "Mom's Beef Stew" out in our packs with the rest of the garbage.

At home, it was back to meat and potatoes. My children thanked me.

Life on the Loose

* * * * *

Post veggie, I made impressive camp meals given the challenges of a tiny backpacking stove and just one pot. Prepackaged dinners, the ones they sell in outdoor stores that advertise "add water and wait three minutes" were not part of the repertoire. In my opinion, those gas-producing meals tasted like wallpaper paste mixed with salt and sawdust, something like the unfortunate stew.

Because I love to eat, we dined well in the backcountry. We feasted on noodles with toasted almonds in a béchamel sauce, Chicken Curry, Pasta with Pesto and Pine Nuts, Creamed Dried Beef on Couscous, and a favorite, Cashew Calvado, layers of avocado and rice smothered with cheese sauce and topped with raw cashews. We ate as well on wilderness trips, as we did at the end of the trip at a fancy restaurant. There's nothing better than a soul-satisfying meal when you've canoed, hiked, or hauled a forty-five pound pack up a mountain. Everything tastes better in the wilderness.

We sat on the ground, but we sat in style. We had ambiance, even though no one offered to carry my lovely wedding gift, an elegant, three-pronged silver candelabra. That would have added a nice touch on a wilderness backpacking trip, but after we weighed every ounce, and left our deodorant behind, it wasn't coming with. We didn't need the silver. We added pizzazz with centerpieces made of sticks and stones and a single candle.

* * * * *

One year in the Smoky Mountains, dinner came with entertainment when two men who were camped nearby invited us to join them. They came into their camp with horses and a wagon from the "hollers," or backwoods coves, where they drank raw whiskey and pissed in the fire. "Turn around," one of them would say and we'd hear a hissing sound as they wet the flames.

They looked old, beaten down, rock-bottom-poor mountain men with matted hair, ragged jeans, and ripped jackets. As we walked by their camp, the older one said, "Hey, Joe, maybe these ladies would like to stay for dinner." He sat on a stump, drinking a beer with a shot glass next to him.

"How 'bout it?" Joe replied. "Wanna have some grub with us, we have plenty." He took a straw out of his mouth, tossed it in the fire, and picked up a half-full Jim Beam bottle. "We brought it in on our horses, not like you all, on your backs. What are ya, mules?"

Everyone looked at me.

"Let's do it," I whispered. "We'll worry about indigestion tomorrow. Everyone agree?"

"You're in charge," Jean said. "It will be an adventure."

When Joe and his buddy walked away to find extra plates, we looked for somewhere to sit close to the fire. The day had turned chilly, and our jackets were back at camp, half a mile away. We huddled by the fire and ate their grits and greens and home-cured hog. It tasted okay, gamey, edible, if you didn't mind pork fat oozing from every bite.

They dumped garbage and grease from the cooking pan right where they stood. It dribbled down their pants and stuck on their boots. They threw the trash in the fire—tin cans, foil, ham bones, and empty bottles.

After dinner, the older man stood up, rubbed his hairy belly, and said, "Hey, Joe, how 'bout you and me entertain the ladies. How 'bout showin' 'em some clog dancin'?"

We sat in a line on the edge of their wagon and watched the show. This wasn't a country music extravaganza at Branson, this was the Smoky Mountains, and we were the honored guests. We sat by the fire, the mountains barely visible in the evening light, and watched them kick their heels and stomp their feet.

* * * * *

In the Tetons, we had another post-dinner show: homemade ice cream served at sunset on a sandy bank by the Snake River. I had hired Kim Fadiman, wilderness guide and ice cream aficionado, who said he could make ice cream anywhere, anytime. On the canoe outing, he brought one thermos filled with cream, sugar, sweetened condensed milk, and Kahlua, and a second thermos filled with liquid nitrogen.

He said, "You won't find this at the grocery store. I buy it at the local sperm bank, where they keep it at minus 321 degrees Fahrenheit to maintain the frozen sperm."

Everyone looked up at the mention of a sperm bank, an unusual place to shop for ingredients to make ice cream.

"The first time I came to the bank with my one-quart thermos, the receptionist looked at me, looked at the thermos, and said, 'My, what a donation.'"

When the time came to make the ice cream, I held the bowl while Kim poured the nitrogen into the creamy mixture.

"Don't move," he said. "Hold it steady. If you spill it on your skin, it will burn you."

"Well, then, how can we eat the ice cream?" I envisioned our mouths bursting with blisters from the nitrogen. My liability paranoia escalated. Would someone sue me for disfigured lips? I could see them getting on the plane after the trip with bandages covering the lower half of their faces. That would be hard to explain.

"Don't worry about the ice cream. The nitrogen evaporates instantly as it freezes"

Food

"This makes me really nervous. I'm afraid to breathe." My hand shook no matter how hard I tried to hold it firm. What if I dropped the bowl?

Everyone stared at the hissing, bubbling mess. How could we eat anything that came out of that bowl? It did not look promising.

"How do you know when it's done?" Susan asked. "It looks weird, a funny color. Are you sure we can eat it?" She stepped away from the pot. "I don't want to eat nitrogen. I have to get on a plane tomorrow."

"Bring your cup over here and I'll show you," Kim said, as he pulled an old-fashioned ice cream scoop from his day pack. He served his masterpiece and yes, it was smooth, creamy, Kahlua-flavored, rich, a delicious finale to a week spent hiking in the Tetons.

We took tiny bites, like children trying to make it last, while we sat by the Snake River and watched the sun sink behind Mount Moran. A flock of sandhill cranes flew across the river in the dim light, adding their primordial call to the golden evening.

＊ ＊ ＊ ＊ ＊

The year of the late snow melt in the Three Sisters Wilderness Area in Oregon, I almost ruined dessert. On the sixth night of an August trip, camped by Squaw Creek, we pitched our tents above the cascading river with the Middle Sister in the foreground and the North Sister behind her. After dinner, my co-guide Ann said, "Cari, did you read the instructions for the Crème Caramel, the part where it says *refrigerate for an hour and then unmold?*"

"Whoops. We'll figure something out tomorrow. Good thing we have cheesecake for tonight." I walked to a place where the snow had drifted and pointed to it. "Look. It's four feet deep here. I think I see our fridge."

The next morning, I lined a bowl with caramel sauce, poured in the custard, the part that needed to chill, covered it with a red bandana, buried the bowl in the snow bank, and took the group on an all-day hike.

When we returned, our snowbank, slightly diminished, still surrounded the bowl. "Hope it didn't leak into the flan," Agnes said. She had a sweet tooth, and always looked forward to dessert.

"There's one way to find out." I slid the lid off the pot and jiggled it. "Perfect."

I took a makeshift plate, our Frisbee, turned the flan upside down, and waited for it to unmold. "I can't look. Someone tell me."

At first, it wouldn't slide out.

"It's stuck," some pessimist said.

"Trust me."

I said that a lot on my trips.

"I'm going to blow on it. My hot air should release it."

Suddenly it dropped, a picture-perfect crème caramel flan.

We camped at Squaw creek for three nights. On the third day, the snow disappeared. Our freezer left no trace of its serendipity.

* * * * *

Those tasty, sometimes upscale, occasionally creative, wilderness meals brought from Milwaukee to the West required more than a modest effort. I measured portions for each meal, ripped open grocery store packages, repacked the food in double baggies, packed duffel bags, and dragged the duffels down my front steps to my car. This happened before the airlines charged extra for checked bags, before they put a fifty-pound limit on luggage. My duffels weighed the max, seventy pounds. Meal planning and hauling duffels felt like slave labor, but when satisfied customers raved about the food, I glowed, and of course, I like to eat well, too.

There were also failures, like the time I took ten trail lunches from Milwaukee to Yellowstone in February for a cross-country ski trip. I had a plan. We would sit alongside a geyser with the sun shining on glistening snow while we spread our three dips on cocktail rye and pumpernickel. The mountains, the elk, the bison, would pale in comparison to the lunch that traveled by air, car, snow coach, and cross-country skis. This lunch would bring words of exultation. Someone would say, "Cari, this is the best trail lunch we've ever had. You were so clever to bring this delicious food all the way from Milwaukee."

I would smile modestly and say, "Oh, it was nothing."

A trail lunch has to be something special when you stay at Yellowstone Lodge and sandwich it between Eggs Sardu in puff pastry with artichokes and spinach and Broiled Tournedos with Potatoes Anna. It has to fit in a daypack, be visually appealing, and out of the ordinary, something special.

In ten separate bags, I counted, weighed, and packed: dried apricots, dried apples, five kinds of bread (pita, pumpernickel, tortillas, cocktail rye, and bagels), bean dip, cream cheese with walnuts and olives, a fancy cheese spread, salami, trail mix, two plastic knives, ten paper plates, and ten dinner napkins.

There was a problem. I couldn't refrigerate the food because the indoor temperature never dropped below seventy-two, and the outside thermometer read minus ten at night. There were two choices—freeze it, or leave it in the warm room. There was no right answer. I kept it indoors.

The bean dip turned slimy and made some sort of methane gas, the cream cheese sprouted an intricate net of green mold, and all the bread products developed scary brown spots. We ate what was left: salami, dried fruit, trail mix and took pictures of the rest.

Life on the Loose

Sometimes I had a little help. On backpacking trips in Oregon, my co-guide's husband, Geoff, brought a final banquet. At the end of a nine-day trip, tired and unwashed, we wanted showers, clean clothes, wine, and dinner on a plate. We were sick of sitting on the ground and digging our food out of a metal cup. Someone would bring up the subject of home and we'd reminisce.

"I'd love hot fudge sundaes with chocolate mint-chip ice cream."

There was always someone beside me with a sweet tooth.

I'd say, "I'd love a cold beer and a fat, juicy cheeseburger, followed by a hot fudge and caramel sundae topped with real whipped cream."

"I want a veggie burger," from my co-guide Ann, a vegetarian.

Penny, or someone who loved wine with dinner, would sigh, "I'd settle for a glass of Merlot, and some brie with crackers and fruit."

About then, Geoff would stroll up the trail carrying a seventy-five pound pack he had carried five uphill miles from his car to our camp at Park Meadow.

"Ann, there's Geoff. What's he doing here?" someone always shouted.

Then the group stood around like hungry dogs, watching, drooling, as Geoff unloaded the pack, Ann and I spread the table-cloth, and we loaded it with veggies, dips, smoked salmon, crackers, cheese, artisan bread, fruit, and a five-liter box of red wine.

We gorged until everything disappeared. Some of us drank too much wine. We followed the feast with chocolate chip cookies and angel food cake dipped in chocolate fondue. In the morning, we nursed our hangovers with pancakes, blueberries, and Wisconsin maple syrup.

Food

On a backpacking trip in Olympic National Park, we had a guest my co-guide Ann and I would prefer to forget.

"Ann, I need you. We have a problem." I whispered when I crawled out of my tent to start coffee. "Come here. Fast. Look in the pot and don't say anything."

This was the dinner pot, the one we had filled with water after a pasta-pesto dinner. We were going to clean it before the group woke up.

"Cari, there's a dead mouse in it. Gross." She backed away from the corpse and looked at me as if I knew what to do.

" It's not like I can run over to Walmart and pick up a new pot." I laughed.

She covered her eyes. "You have a perverse sense of humor. This is not funny." I thought it was hilarious, another story for later, but not one to share with this group. "Do something and do it fast. Any minute someone is going to get up."

"I'll bury the mouse, scrub the pot, and cook the cereal. We'll keep our mouths shut and act normally."

We had to carry our packs several miles that day. Everyone needed a hearty breakfast. "No one will know, and if they find out, well, we have to eat. It's not like we're putting mouse turds in the cereal."

The mouse was a better jumper than swimmer. He died in mouse heaven, somewhere between bits of pesto-coated angel hair pasta and grated Romano cheese. I picked up the limp body by its tail, buried him under a log, scrubbed my hands, scrubbed the pot, and cooked breakfast. Everyone complimented me on the delicious, seven-grain cereal.

Chapter Seventeen

Adventures with Worms

2007 Venture West Catalog
This itinerary includes the best hikes in the Tetons with plenty of flexibility depending on the abilities of the group. You'll see more of Grand Teton National Park than people do who return year after year. We did our homework and planned hikes that include the best of the area and yet leave time for contemplation in this beautiful place.

W e're perched on the edge of the East Rim in Zion National Park in Utah in late October. It's half a vertical mile down to the Virgin River. We can see hundreds of miles in every direction, a fitting reward for the grueling, twenty-six -hundred feet we climbed in four miles. From here, the river looks inconsequential, a trickle, but it split Zion Canyon and it only took a few million years. And the canyon, a geological masterpiece, is bracketed by pink, white, and red cliffs.

We're weary; our feet throb, our calf muscles sting, our quads ache. For three hours, we plodded upward, then hiked through ankle-deep sand for the last half mile. We collapsed next to the rim at the end of the hike. No city sirens or car alarms insulted our senses, a cool breeze freshened our sweaty tee-shirts, and the smell of pine and juniper added to the sensory feast. We sat, silent, lost in our thoughts and gazed at the endless Utah landscape.

Life on the Loose

Then someone, usually me, asks, "Is this a worm moment?"

I started this tradition in the early days of Venture West. While some might call it silly, even childish, I've learned it's a creative way to add a playful touch to the hikes, and, the worm ceremony never failed to enhance group camaraderie.

I have a special talent for silly, which used to embarrass my children. Maybe that's why I couldn't live a conventional life in suburbia and drive a minivan. When I took others on a journey, I liked to share my joy with them, even it that meant taking a chance with something that could bring on eye rolls and disdain.

The worm, a gummi worm, measured about four inches, fat as a first grader's pinkie, and had alternating stripes of blue, orange, and green. It resembled a night crawler, albeit one with gaudy colors. It jiggled. The worms were often met with dubious smiles or, "I don't eat candy."

I know grown-ups don't eat fat pieces of sugar that taste like kindergarten paste held together with corn syrup and food coloring, but this kiddie candy forced us to pay attention. That was the point. It gave us permission to acknowledge pain, joy, sweat, appreciation, and pride in the trek to a memorable overlook. It was all sugar, no substance, but it took a long time to chew, and while we gnawed, we were present, alive, centered in the moment, aware that we were privileged to be where we had landed.

A "worm moment" had to be a group decision. No one would eat a solo gummy worm. If someone said, "Look at that view," or "Let's stay here forever," it was time to bring on the worms.

If I said, "Is this a good time for a 'worm moment'?" and if everyone agreed, and they always did, then we dug into our packs for the candy.

I would say, "When you're ready, take a deep breath and a big bite. You did it!" Then we chewed our gummies in unison, symbols of our accomplishment, a time for silent contemplation.

Sometimes I pulled out a book. On top of Cassidy Arch in Capitol Reef National Park, I read the children's book, *Everyone Needs a Rock* by Byrd Baylor and Peter Parnall. That forced our attention to the landscape, to our seats on the rock, to the massive arch in front of us. It's a kid's book, filled with artful illustrations that mirrored the front-row seats that overlooked a world of red rock and blue sky.

An unexpected guide skill I learned I needed was the art of building camaraderie. I'm quiet in a group, know how it feels to be left out of conversation. Once out, it's hard to jump in. Many times, I sat with strangers, afraid to speak for fear of sounding ignorant.

Armed with that self-awareness, I included everyone in conversation on Venture West trips. After a while it became second nature to notice the quiet ones. I asked questions or commented on something they'd done until they joined in. It worked almost every time.

* * * * *

The first worm event happened on a backpacking trip in the Three Sisters Wilderness in central Oregon. I had a co-guide on this trip, Ann Wheeler-Bartol, a good friend from my days as a volunteer naturalist at Riveredge Nature Centre, close to Milwaukee.

Ann and I were a team on all my backpacking trips in the West. When we prepared meals, I was the chef and Ann my sous-chef. She chopped, measured, and peeled, while I had the easy job, tending the stove and creating the meal. She had to peel the garlic and chop the onions.

Life on the Loose

At the trailhead in the Three Sisters, I gave everyone a multicolored gummi worm. "Put it with your gorp," I said. I'd given everyone a bag of chocolates, raisins, and peanuts, the traditional mix carried by people who hike in the wilderness. "I know this looks odd, but when we find a 'worm moment,' you'll get it."

One doesn't plan a worm moment—it happens. Perfection, unlike the Swiss rail system, doesn't run on a schedule. Nor does a backpacking trip.

On the first, day we hiked up the mountain to South Mathie Lake, three miles into the wilderness, where we spent a leisurely afternoon swimming, sunning on warm rocks, and settling on a place to watch the sunrise and the sunset. We had no schedule, no agenda, and, thanks to a tradition on Venture West trips, no watches. We ate when were hungry, slept when were tired or when it was dark, depending on which happened first.

The second day we set out mid-morning to hike to a pass, a high place where we could see where we'd been and where we were going. We carried water and lunch as we strolled through meadows decorated with blue lupine, sunny buttercups, and rose-colored Indian paintbrush. We ate peanut butter, dried apricots, crackers, and cheddar cheese by a rocky lava field, and filled our water bottles with nearby spring water.

On the third day, we hoisted forty-pound packs, tightened our waist straps, and set out on a nine-mile journey to Squaw Creek. It was a long, hot, ninety-degree day with stream crossings on tipsy logs, shiny black sand lava fields to cross, and long, steep switchbacks that took us closer and closer to the peaks.

When the afternoon temperature hit ninety-five, we cooked. People who backpack will tell you, if you want to leave the day hikers and the roads behind and experience pure wilderness, pain happens. This time, it came from the unrelenting sun.

"I'm hot and tired," said Jane, whose beet red face corroborated her misery. "And I'm crabby." She took off her pack and sat in the middle of the trail. "I need to cool off."

"Me, too. How much further, Cari?" Anna, young, strong, with muscular legs, looked like someone who could go on forever. She was at least twenty-five years younger than me. If she was tired, everyone else would be exhausted.

"I don't know. I've lost track of the distance."

I wilt in the heat. Anything over eighty degrees and I'm useless and miserable. "Maybe another hour. You'll love our campsite." This had been a tough day for me. I felt awful, but a guide must set an upbeat tone. It was my job, not easy when I wanted to whine and complain and sit by myself in the shade.

After nine miles in about that many hours, we arrived at Squaw Creek, our camp for two nights and a welcome layover. First we had to cross the creek, balanced on a log, ten feet above fast moving water that cascaded over pointy rocks. I chose not to mention this earlier, as I knew people would worry.

Everyone took off their packs and sat down. No one said anything until Anna spoke up.

"Do we have to cross? Why can't we camp on this side?" The group nodded their agreement in unison. "We can camp here." She pointed to a space, too small for five tents. We were a group of ten.

I answered slowly, hoping to calm their fears, "We don't have a choice. That's our campsite." I pointed across the creek. "The trail continues on that side. We can walk on the log." I didn't like this either. The creek looked nasty, swollen from the afternoon snow melt. "You can do it."

When I had scouted the trip, there had been a second log with branches to grab on to. Maybe it washed away in a spring flood.

Life on the Loose

This wasn't fair. After we had traversed black sand that felt like Death Valley in July, we shouldn't have to risk life and limb to cross a raging creek. Fortunately, there were two upright branches on the log that made the crossing look manageable—not easy, but relatively safe.

"I'll go first," my co-guide Ann said. "Then I can grab hands from the other side." I was glad she volunteered to go first. I'm not afraid of heights; ten feet didn't scare me, but balance had been an ongoing problem. I have flat feet, and I'm shorter on the left side, a combination that affects my balance, especially when I'm scared.

"I want to get it over with," Ann said, as she crawled on to the log, stood up with forty pounds on her back, and reached for a branch. "I can show everyone how to do it." She held on to the first branch, took a big step with her right foot, reached out, grabbed the second branch, and slowly made her way across.

"Okay, everyone. Tighten your waist straps so your pack won't jiggle and throw you off balance." I stood on the log at the start, grabbed a branch, and reached for the first brave person. "If you hold on to me, you can reach the first branch. You can get a hold of the next one from there, and Ann will guide you the rest of the way."

This maneuver was more than they bargained for when they'd signed up for a nine-day beginner's backpacking trip.

June stood up, her face still red from the hot climb on the black sand. "Good thing we didn't know this was coming. This is a really hard day for me."

"I know. We're all hot and tired. Me, too."

They needed to know their guide was beat, like the rest of them. "Tomorrow we rest."

This was a time for my Iron-Woman-Guide façade. I felt like hell—weak, exhausted, drained from the hot trek and the stress of that dangerous crossing.

One by one, they put on their packs on and shuffled across. Once on the other side, Jane said, "That's not as hard as it looks. Do we have to come back this way?" Now she smiled at me. Meeting a challenge guarantees an attitude adjustment.

"The good news is no. The trail goes on to Park Meadow from here. We stay on this side of the creek." I opened my pack and pulled out a gummi worm. "Get your worms out. It's time." We sat on the bank overlooking Squaw Creek and chewed. We were proud, ten grown-ups, eating candy. It was the first Venture West "worm moment," one of the best.

* * * * *

In the Tetons, a different worm species showed up. We were camped in the Gros Vente Campground alongside the river of the same name. Each day, we hiked into a different canyon. Everyone had a bag of gorp that I'd brought from Milwaukee, this time a healthful mix of nuts, seeds, yoghurt-covered raisins, and dried fruit.

I had a co-guide, Mary Eloranta, ten years younger than me, with a wicked sense of humor. Her stories kept us laughing at every meal. One morning, she pulled me aside and said, "Cari, I'm going to show you something, but you have to promise you won't say anything. Can you do that?" I didn't take her seriously. Why would I? She kidded about everything.

"Sure," I said with a smirk. She liked to surprise me when we ran trips together. Once, in late October, she brought a dozen pumpkins for a carving contest.

193

Life on the Loose

She uncurled her fist, and in her hand were nuts, seeds, and dried fruit—our gorp. It looked like an ordinary mix until I took off my sunglasses to get a closer look. At first I saw yoghurt-covered raisins. I put one in my hand. It looked like a half-cooked navy bean, white, crinkly, just what I expected. I stared at it. "What's the big deal?"

"Just wait." She said.

I clenched and unclenched my fist. Something tickled. The yoghurt-covered raisin had moved.

We'd been eating mealy worms for three days.

"Protein?" I whispered. "Do we tell them their gorp is alive? I bought it at a health food store."

"I'm clueless," Mary said. "I don't know what we should do."

"They'll be upset if we tell them. Let's not tell and hope they didn't notice." We had to make a decision and make it fast. "They're edible. I've eaten chocolate covered ants, crunchy bumblebees, even fried grasshoppers in Mexico when I could count their tiny legs."

I looked more closely at the thing in my hand. It was disgusting. "I've eaten live larvae from goldenrod galls at the nature center. It's all protein," and to prove my point, I grabbed a handful of gorp, including a mealy worm, and ate it.

There was no right answer.

"It's a special kind of worm moment," Mary said, and popped one in her mouth.

On the way to hike that day, we stopped in Jackson to buy more gorp. I used a resupply excuse and gave everyone a new bag. No one mentioned the uninvited protein.

Chapter Eighteen

Bear Scares

2005 Venture West Catalog

We meet at a motel in Knoxville the first night and you're on the Little River Trail by mid-morning the next day. Then it's time to settle into an elegant inn tucked into the mountains where you'll enjoy pre-dinner wine and snacks on the screened porch overlooking the mountains and a gourmet dinner just up the road.

The year I took my four children to the Smoky Mountains during their spring break, we watched a bear devour an entire Kentucky Fried Chicken dinner at the Chimneys Picnic Area. Every night, we packed a picnic supper and took it to a spot alongside the West Prong of the Little Pigeon River.

At precisely 5:05, as families sat down for their evening meals, a black bear bounced down the mountain, chose some victims, and ravaged their dinner. We noticed he preferred something fried, usually from a fast-food restaurant. Twice we watched him scarf down in seconds an entire dinner from Burger King, even the chocolate milk shakes. By the time someone hollered "bear coming," it was too late, as he was already gorging on his daily feast.

We knew the routine. When we saw the bear head in our direction, we outsmarted him. He arrived at 5:05 the night I had made burritos. When we heard "bear coming," we scooped the tortillas, the salsa, the avocado, and the refried beans, jumped in the Volkswagen van, rolled up the windows, locked the doors, and watched.

Through the window, we snapped photos of our uninvited guest while he sniffed the ground where food might have fallen, sat on our picnic table, and looked straight at five Carlsons huddling behind metal and glass. We could smell the bear from inside the van, a combination of dirty gym shoes and rotting garbage. He grunted, growled, and slobbered as he searched for food scraps.

In the rush, we had left my daughter Linda's camera on the table. When the bear lumbered on to the next family, we crept from our safe haven with our dinner intact. I heard Linda's eleven-year-old tone of disgust, "Look, Mom, he slimed on my camera."

That was the first of my five Smoky Mountains bear encounters.

* * * * *

Three years later, I took a group of backpackers to Walnut Bottoms in the eastern end of the park. I loved that camp: the sound of Big Creek at night, the giant tulip poplar trees that dropped huge yellow leaves in October, and the four trails that spun off close to the site. It offered seclusion, challenging hikes, giant rocks to sit on for water contemplation, and an almost-level seven-mile walk from the trailhead.

We felt mellow there, relaxed, removed from the traffic that clogged the park roads when the "leafers," people who viewed autumn colors from their cars, arrived for the fall viewing spectacle. We'd lie on our backs and watch leaves flutter, golden parachutes that tickled our faces.

That site, a well-known bear haunt, presented a dilemma. The bears came at night, and according to the ranger, never bothered the campers; they just wanted their food. Okay, so the bears were a problem, but on the other hand, how could I give up the best backcountry site I'd found in the park. I felt confident, competent, in my ability to guide a backpacking group in bear country. I'd done it many times in the West without even one bear encounter. I would outsmart them.

I packed each food item in two plastic baggies, then stored those bags in double garbage bags. A bear has to smell the food before he can find it, and if it's hung properly on the poles provided by the Park Service, he's not likely to bump into it. Toothpaste, shampoo, deodorant, anything that could possibly attract a bear by its odor, we placed inside the double garbage bags and strung the bags up the poles.

Despite my careful preparations, we had an uninvited guest.

"Cari, you won't believe this. The bears took our food." Helen's voice had a touch of hysteria. A newcomer to backpacking, not comfortable camped seven miles from the safety of our van, she had told me she was afraid of bears. My words of comfort fell by the wayside next to her fear. Of course she was afraid, so was I, even though I believed what the ranger had told us. Fear of a large animal in the wilderness, especially a bear, is a natural fear. To deny it is to deny the reality of the wilderness.

I stumbled from a deep sleep into the morning chill to find the group pawing through the remains of the double-bagged break-fasts, lunches, and dinners.

"There goes the pole theory," I said, more annoyed than frightened. "Why put up a pole if the bear can climb it?"

"Are you sure he's gone?" asked Joy. Her voice trembled.

"Let's assume he took what he wanted and now he's off to harass another group. He's gone." I walked to the pile the bear had left behind and started to sort through the mess. "If he comes back, we can scare him off by banging on the pots."

"If you're not worried, then I'm not worried," Brad said. Everyone nodded.

Our bear had strange dietary habits. He ate the honey, the butter, the crunchy peanut butter, and a small container of Vaseline. He left the rest for us.

"Maybe you'll get to see a bear. Wouldn't that be a treat, something to tell the folks back home?" I wanted them to see a bear, from a distance, a big black one crossing the trail ahead of them, an innocent, safe encounter, and one where food was not involved, and preferably not a sow with a cub. I did not want to see a bear in the dark because, despite my bravado, bears in the night frightened me.

I would never again knowingly take a group into grizzly territory. As I described in chapter twelve, I did it once in Yellowstone with corned beef and rye sandwiches in our packs and promised myself, "Never again." That was both negligent and irresponsible, as the griz has an unpredictable personality. Smoky Mountain bears are thieves, not killers.

The year before, I had backpacked solo in the Spanish Peaks Wilderness Area in Montana. Someone had told me there might be bears, but not to worry, they wouldn't bother me. At camp the first night, one lumbered by my tent. It was dark; I was awake, heard heavy breathing, and felt the ground shake. I lay rigid, afraid to move. I knew I'd hung the food, the toothpaste, the shampoo, and the clothes I'd cooked in far away from the tent. Logically, I should have been safe. By the time I found my glasses in the dark and peeked out the door, the bear had disappeared.

When I returned to town, a local told me I had camped in grizzly territory.

That was my first and last backpacking trip in the Peaks, another wilderness scratched from my list of bear-safe places to take backpackers.

I had to be careful about what I said to customers about bears. The perceived danger from a potential bear encounter can be more real than the actual danger. When I went solo, I mostly ignored bear warnings, and assumed nothing bad would happen. However, I would never do that with a group. I always acknowledged their fear, even where there were no bears.

For the rest of the week, the Smoky Mountains bear left us alone while we hiked and enjoyed autumn in the Smokies. The maples blazed red, the tulip poplars burned with shades of gold, and the creek reflected the colors of the surrounding peaks. The smell of wood smoke from our evening fire, the clear blue sky, the leisurely hikes up to ridges and the surrounding vistas made an idyllic week. But for that one incident, this had been a perfect autumn trip in the mountains.

* * * * *

I returned to Walnut Bottoms the following year, where I found a laminated sheet with "bear instructions" attached to the bridge that spanned Big Creek. The Park Service rangers had left us explicit directions for hanging our food underneath the bridge. They had screwed a metal bar across the bottom of the width of the bridge, then added a set of pulleys. We were supposed to tie the food bags to the pulleys and drag the bags to the center, which left them hanging, more or less four feet from the edges of the bridge and six feet above Big Creek.

Since this looked like an ingenious arrangement, I assured the group our food was safe. What could go wrong? We followed the directions, trusted that the rangers knew what they were doing, then promptly forgot about the bears.

This time we had come in April. Big Creek earned its name, flowing fast and deep, unlike the gentle creek we'd known in October. When we hung the bags, we didn't notice the mouse condos, a mini-village perched on the rafters that supported the bridge. Since mice are nocturnal, they were unlikely to show their little, whiskered faces as I hung the food before dark.

The next morning, I heard, "Cari, wake up. The food bags are gone. I mean gone, disappeared." Bill sounded amused. He was in his sixties, a seasoned backpacker, unflappable, a good person to have on a trip with beginners.

"What? That's impossible." I crawled from my tent to find the group, eight of them, on their hands and knees peering under the bridge. "We did everything right. They have to be there."

"You're not going to believe this. The food's gone!" Lucy stated the obvious. "Come over here and look." She lay on her stomach, head hanging down, peering under the bridge.

This couldn't be happening. Those bags were heavy, stuffed. This was the first of four days at Walnut Bottoms. We had to eat. Forty pounds of food can't disappear. I had this one nailed. So much for my enthusiastic optimism and the ranger's clever pulleys.

"Cari, guess what? Mice chewed through the rope. The bags fell in the river." Bill held up the remains of our rope and laughed. Everyone thought it was hilarious; I managed a smile. This was not their problem. People think guides work miracles, that magic powers come with the job. Guess they thought I'd jump in the creek and come up with the bags. Just like that; I'd be their miracle worker. All I could think about was the food. How would I feed them?

"I'll go look for the bags. Anyone want to come with me?" I crawled into my tent to find my boots. "I need some help getting them back to camp."

"Yeah, Cari. How much can a mouse eat?" Pat, fearful at first, joined the rest who found this a big joke.

A hundred yards down the river, we found our food, safe in the double bags. The mice had nibbled on the almonds, left tiny tooth marks on the toothpaste, and eaten all the M&Ms.

* * * * *

The next year, I brought stout ropes. This time I would win. I'd keep the food safe from the bears and the mice and any other critters that had a taste for meals that didn't belong to them. For some reason, I put the key to the van in the blue bag that held my toothpaste and shampoo, then hung it along with the food under the bridge.

In the morning, I heard, "Cari, come here, quick. The bear got our food." Like Bill the year before, Pat sounded amused. "It's all over the bridge. It's a mess, stuff everywhere." She was also an experienced outdoors person, used to camping in bear country

That was one of those moments when time stopped. I couldn't breathe. My body went rigid. Nothing mattered except the blue bag and the key. Was it on the bridge? What had I done? In a moment of carelessness, I might have lost the key to the van. How could I call myself a guide if I did something so stupid? Maybe I should go home to Whitefish Bay to clean the stove and polish furniture after all.

The van sat at a trailhead, two hours from a town, on a bumpy winding road. If the key had fallen in the creek or if the bear dropped it somewhere, we were in serious trouble.

Life on the Loose

I faked calm and walked to the bridge to survey the damage, a mess, obviously left by a bear. He had figured out the system, maneuvered our bags from underneath, then dumped our food. My blue bag was not on the bridge. I couldn't tell the group the van key was gone, though I suspected the look on my face, or my trembling hands, suggested something was amiss. If I told them I'd lost the key, they would panic, and rightly so.

From the mess, we knew the bear had eaten peanut butter, honey, and butter at the scene of the crime, then took the bags somewhere else to finish the rest.

I didn't know where to look. We were in the wilderness. The key could have been anywhere, and if he had ripped the blue bag and dropped the key, we'd never see it again.

"Let's go look for the rest of the food" I hoped no one would ask what would happen if we couldn't find the bags. "Everyone spread out, go in a different direction. We'll find it."

Normally, I go into the worst possible scenario mode to reassure myself that no matter what happens, we'll be fine. But this was different. There was no help at the trailhead. On foot, we could be as long as two days from civilization, a gas station, a phone, a locksmith. We had seen no other cars on the road when we drove to the start of the hike. We were in the middle of nowhere, in a remote section of the Smokies.

I heard someone call my name, "Cari, I found something. Looks like bears hang out here. I found old boxes and wrappers, and is this your blue bag?" Jane handed it to me. "Looks like we found your toothpaste."

"Oh, thank you. Yep. That's my bag." I tried to sound unconcerned. I'd sleep with the key in my underpants. It would never leave my body again, and I would never, ever tell.

Since the bear didn't have a taste for lentil chili, noodles almandine, chicken curry, or seven-grain cereal, we retrieved everything except the usual peanut butter, honey, and butter.

Those were the early years of Venture West. Being in charge was no fun when things fell apart, when people expected me to make everything right. But give up my favorite backcountry campsite at Walnut Bottoms. I couldn't do that. I'm not proud of that stubborn part of my personality, but it's who I am. Sometimes it works in my favor and sometimes it gets me in trouble. Sometimes I'm lucky.

* * * * *

The following year, I returned in October. Bad judgment? Probably. I loved that site. It was my job to give customers the best possible experience in the Smokies, and where better to take them on a backpacking trip but Walnut Bottoms? I didn't have to tell them about the bear climbing the pole, and mice chewing the rope, and the extra-smart bear that outsmarted my fat rope and pulled the food out from under the bridge.

For four days, we hiked to ridges and waterfalls and tunneled through the shiny green rhododendrons. Giant red maples blazed in the cove hardwood forests surrounded by silverbell, yellow birch, and those golden tulip poplar trees. We shuffled along trails littered with red, yellow, tan, green streaked leaves, an endless collage of autumn colors. We hung the food under the bridge, and every morning, I heard, "Cari, it's still here." Jeri, an early riser, liked to be the first to check on the food. She loved backpacking and had taken three other Venture West backpacking trips in the mountains.

On the last day, on the last hike, she picked up a Snickers wrapper on the trail and stuck it in her pack. Before the hike that morning, I had done some laundry and set it on a rock by the creek to dry. I washed my tee-shirt, some underwear, and a couple pairs of wool socks. That night, I forgot to get my laundry. Jeri forgot something, too.

The next morning, I heard, "Cari, my pack is gone." Jeri stood next to my tent in her pajamas. "Why would an animal take it away? I don't get it."

"Did you leave your lunch in it?" I didn't want to insult her, but there was no reason for a bear to steal a pack. Our food was still under the bridge, hung with those stout ropes.

I took a deep breath, crawled into the sunny morning, and sighed. What else could go wrong? "I thought we outsmarted them." The van key, safe in my pocket, meant one less thing to stress about. "Why would a bear take your pack? I'm clueless."

We followed a trail into the woods that looked fresh: footprints, broken branches, paper debris. Half a mile from camp, we found the pack. Lying next to it we saw the chewed remains of the Snickers wrapper.

"Looks like he wanted chocolate. Good thing you stuck it in your backpack and not in your tent."

The bear had done only minor damage to the backpack, ripping a hole in the bottom pocket in his quest for the candy wrapper.

"It's time to get out of here." I smiled at Jeri, relieved to see she wasn't upset, just puzzled.

She shrugged. "Guess I should have left the wrapper on the trail."

"I guess," I said. "Don't know what else you could do with it. We could have hung it with the food, but to be honest, I would have done the same thing." And I have, many times. It was trail litter.

I remembered my laundry from the day before, strolled to the creek to collect it, and gasped. The bear had eaten my underpants, everything but the elastic. That did it! It was time to leave Walnut Bottoms for good. We were unwelcome guests.

Chapter Nineteen

Off the List

1996 Venture West Catalog

Everyone has seen photos of the Grand Canyon but few have a chance to hike deep into its breathtaking walls. Horses will carry your gear while you walk, unencumbered, carrying only a small backpack into Havasu Canyon and Supai Village. We'll swim in turquoise-colored water and marvel at stunning waterfalls and deep travertine-rimmed pools. Here's time to swim and relax and let the peace of this magical place settle into your body and soul.

O n the third or fourth day, after a glass of wine, someone always asks, "Do you ever get people you don't like on your trips? Do you like everyone?" It's a question I'd rather not answer.

I wish I could have said that I liked everyone, but some people got on my nerves, made me edgy, uncomfortable. On Venture West trips, I pretended to like everyone. It was my job to be bighearted and accepting, but like most people, I'm flawed, sometimes compassionate and empathetic, and sometimes not.

"Only people who love the outdoors sign up. That makes it easy to like everyone," I say. "It's a self-selecting process." But of course, that's not always true. Maybe every fifteen years someone came along who was hard to like. Occasionally, even people who love traveling in the wilderness were a pain in the neck. Food fussers, whiners, complainers—they all showed up.

Drooling Diane

She came on a backpacking trip in the Smokies, a week-long hike into the heart of the mountains. Although the nickname "Drooling Diane" came from the group, I tried not to let them know that I thought she was weird as well. A nice person, a gentle soul, she carried a pack eight miles without a complaint. It fit her poorly, looked like a hand-me-down from a three-hundred-pound man. Fortyish, plump, clearly not fit, Diane wore baggy, soiled clothes and smelled unwashed, like cigarettes and old sweat. She reminded me of a street person, someone a little off.

She did not belong on that backpacking trip. At meals, she drooled. Food came out of her mouth and ran down her clothes. It wasn't that I disliked Diane; I just didn't know what to do with her.

The friend who had recommended her, the one who had told me she was a lovely, intelligent, interesting woman, forgot to mention Diane's most recent residence—the psych ward at a local hospital. "She's been through some hard times lately. It will be good for her to spend time in the mountains with you," my friend had said. "You'll like her. She's lots of fun, and I know she'll love backpacking." That was all she told me!

I wish she'd said more, given a hint of possible issues with Diane. I wish I had known ahead of time that she might get con-fused. If I had, I would have stuck closer to her on the trail.

Drooling Diane scared me when she left the group on a day hike, wandered off, and disappeared. Because she seemed disori-ented, I worried about decisions she might make if she got lost. If she walked off the trail and into the woods, she could end up a long way away from where we could find her. I didn't want anyone to get lost looking for Diane.

She reminded me of my younger brother, Guy, who had been brain damaged at age two from encephalitis. Like Guy, her mealtime manners set her apart from people who chew their food and keep it off their clothes. Like Guy, Drooling Diane had a sweet personality, a naïve, childlike way of talking that drew people to her despite her limitations.

When Susan said, "Cari, where is Diane? Have you seen her lately?" I knew I'd been inattentive to the people behind me on the trail, daydreaming while sauntering alongside a beautiful stream. I did that occasionally, walked, lost in my world, oblivious to the group. I like to walk by myself. It's not that I'm a loner, or unsocial; I just don't need conversation when I hike.

"I don't know where she went; maybe she stepped off the trail to pee behind a tree." I walked back to the last bend to see if she was coming.

"She was with us at the last creek crossing," Sharon said. Sharon, the little mother on the trip, looked out for the slow walkers. A gray-haired grandmother, she stayed close to me, looked at flowers, and checked her book to learn their names. She showed me a painted trillium close to the trail, my first.

"She was eating chocolate. Half of it was on her chin and the rest on her tee shirt." Sharon looked worried.

I pulled a watch from my pack. "We have to find her. We only have a couple hours until dark." We'd passed an intersection an hour ago. That's where she could have wandered off the trail and into the woods. "She can't be far if you saw her at the last crossing."

Oh, yes, she could.

"She's always behind because she's slow," said Carole. "She doesn't hike, she lumbers." Carole, a personal trainer who took her own fitness seriously, expected everyone else to do likewise. She had no patience with Diane.

I made a quick plan. "Susan, you go back to the creek where you saw her eating chocolate. Carole, go with Susan but keep going back further than the creek in case she turned the wrong way." I did it again, divided the group, but it had to be done. "The rest of you come with me. We'll go back to camp."

"What if she wandered off in the woods?" asked Helen, an experienced backpacker and outdoors person. At seventy, she'd canoed solo on the Yukon River in Alaska. She knew what would happen to someone lost in the dark.

"Let's hope she stayed on the trail."

We gathered back at camp an hour later. Still no Diane. "Let's retrace our steps. Carole, you come with me." I checked the watch, an hour until sunset. "The rest of you wait here."

That's when we found her, casually strolling, in the wrong direction, a mile from where she had last been seen. She was a mess, chocolate down the front of her shirt, confused, going the wrong way on the trail.

"I stopped to eat my candy and went behind a tree to pee. When I looked up, everyone was gone." She fumbled in her pack as if looking for something. The map perhaps? "I sat on a log and ate some more chocolate. Did I do something wrong?"

I waited to respond. She needed a patient response, not the one I wanted to throw in her face. "It's okay, Diane, you found us. If you want to stop, next time, please tell someone."

She must have left her meds at home. Was she difficult? Not really. She just wasn't ready to backpack in the mountains. Drooling Diane came off the Venture West mailing list.

The Blind Woman and Her Dog

I should have known better than to take a blind woman down the Green River on a six-day canoe trip. We had a practice run, Cheri and I, a long weekend in the Sylvania Wilderness Area in northern Michigan. That's where I missed the clues, the subtle signs that pointed to the danger that would come later on the Green in Utah.

She had a guide dog, Visa, a beautifully trained animal that knew how to guide her up and down curbs and across busy streets. But Visa wasn't trained in the nuances of wilderness travel in a rocky canyon. When she let Cheri lose her footing and tumble down a steep hill in Sylvania, Cheri jumped up and said, "I'm okay. I forgot to tell you, Visa doesn't do edges, like drop-offs or hills."

That didn't seem like a big deal a year later when she signed up to canoe the Green River and said, "Cari, I really want to do this. I go to the gym every day to work on my upper body strength." She had told me she lost twenty pounds and worked out daily. "I can paddle; I'll be a strong partner. Visa will watch out for me. Remember how she took care of me in Sylvania?"

Yes, I remember. Like the hill you rolled down when Visa stepped out of your way.

I looked at her and saw a blind person, slightly overweight, about thirty, filled with passion and determined to follow her dream of a wilderness canoe trip. How could I say no? I thought about all the people who lack the courage to follow their dreams, who only read about other adventurers. I couldn't turn her down. I'd been a "doll in a jar" in Whitefish Bay, wanting adventure, but unsure how to jump in. "Sure, you can do it. We'll all help you."

My co-guide Tom and I spent six days on the river saving Cheri from sudden death. At every camp, at every lunch stop, on every hike, she faced treacherous drop-offs, not sweet, little grassy mounds like Sylvania, but canyons with sharp rocks at the base of sheer cliffs.

Visa, the city dog, might as well have stayed home, her guide dog instincts useless in Labyrinth Canyon. Every time we intervened to save Cheri from potentially damaging falls, Visa threw herself between us and her client. We needed a way to explain to the dog the difference between a canyon and a city curb. Again and again, we shoved Visa aside so we could grab Cheri before she hurt herself.

If that wasn't bad enough, the dog threw up every night in the tent. According to Cheri's tent mate Dawn, it went something like this. "Visa, no….No, bad dog … Stop that … Oh, yuck … Dawn, wake up … We have a problem."

Dawn would climb out of the tent, get the towel they saved for the nightly crisis, mop up the mess, then try to go back to sleep.

"It smells in our tent," she said, "and that damn towel stinks. I wash it in the river, but nothing helps." She glared at Visa. Cheri sat nearby, held out her plate with leftover pancakes, and pushed it in front of Visa.

"I'm sorry. Let's switch canoes. I'll paddle with Cheri and Visa." I should have done that right from the start. "You don't need to spend all day with them, too."

Tom, standing a few steps away, listened to me trying to make things better for Dawn. "Dawn, how about you and I paddle together? I'll drag the smelly towel behind our canoe. Maybe that will help."

I felt sorry for Visa, an eighty-five pound German Shepherd who did not appreciate her seat in the center of the canoe. As she shifted back and forth, so went the canoe. This was a tedious voyage for a dog, fifty-five miles from Crystal Geyser to Mineral Bottoms.

Cheri loved the trip, especially the physical part. If I'd been more relaxed about the danger to her, perhaps I could have said the same.

Diet Diatriber

On a backpacking trip on the backside of the Tetons, Carolyn talked non-top about diets while admonishing me for my body fat. A scrawny stick herself, she worked for Jenny Craig, one of those diet places. She brought her job to the mountains, where she viewed me as a work in progress and felt compelled to lecture on the benefits of her diet philosophy.

Carolyn had that anorexic look: sunken cheeks, an unhealthy pallor, and expensive Patagonia clothes that hung on her skinny body the way they would hang on a scarecrow. With no muscle tone, she struggled to carry her backpack. To keep her moving, my co-guide Ann and I talked to her about her diet plan, good fat, bad fat, nasty carbs, too much protein, and whatever else popped into our minds about unhealthy eating. Then she would she forget to complain about her backpack and the rigors of the trail. So it went for nine days. She knew a lot about food. I love to eat, but not the way she ate. I didn't confess my obsessions about ice cream, bacon cheeseburgers, and pepperoni pizza with extra cheese.

I had nothing close to an attractive curvy body and never wore a bathing suit unless absolutely necessary. I hated the varicose veins on my right leg that had remained with me after my fourth child, but those veins were there to stay. I didn't like to wear shorts, but no one does, unless they have perfect legs.

I hated my thick, albeit fat waist, chose not to wear tight-fitting clothes, and hid my figure inside baggy shirts. Despite its imperfections, I had a healthy relationship with my body. That didn't mean I liked it. I'd come to terms with it and accepted what I had been given. If I obsessed about my body, I'd never leave the house. But diet? Never.

We worked hard to get Carolyn to the campsite at the end of every day. I'd say, "Oh, Carolyn, you have such a nice, slender figure," and then Ann would follow with something like, "Carolyn, what did you tell us about counting calories?"

Fifteen minutes later, after she finished her lecture about the benefits of staying slim and paying attention to every bite, she slowed down, again.

Then it would be my turn, "Carolyn, how much weight did you say I need to lose before I meet the Jenny Craig ideal weight?" We did this for six days, fifty-five miles of diet diatribe.

I scratched Carolyn from the list.

The Tank

Meryl, "The Tank," took two backpacking trips. The first time, on Isle Royale, she complained about the food.

"There isn't enough," she'd say every night halfway through dinner. "I'm hungry. I need second helpings."

In her fifties, unattractive, chunky with gray, frizzy hair and a too-tight black tee shirt, Meryl had attitude. We had plenty of food; she just liked to complain.

"Here, Meryl," I said every night. "Take some of mine. I'm not all that hungry." I lied.

When she signed up for a second backpacking trip a year later, I remembered her complaints, but this time, I was ready. I packed enough food for everyone to have thirds. That meant our packs were heavy with the extra chow, but on the other hand, no one wants to listen to someone complain every night. She'd gain ten pounds; I'd be a hero, the perfect guide, the one who exceeds expectations, the guide who brought extra food.

Over the winter, Meryl had lost fifty pounds, quit eating, and took up pacing. She fidgeted continually at camp, never sat down, never relaxed, moved constantly. She drove us crazy, and the worst of it, she had no interest in my hearty dinners. I think she chowed on amphetamines while we ate chicken curry.

Every night, we stuffed ourselves because we didn't like the alternative, carrying out our leftovers. If we left food in our tin cups, it turned into garbage. We had to carry that garbage in our packs until the trip was over and we got back to the mainland. While The Tank paced, we added her extra food weight to our hips.

She refused to drink water. "I don't like warm water," she said. "I only drink water with ice."

She paid for that obsession at the end of the trip with a painful bladder infection. I hid my smile and kept my smug comments to myself. At the first gas station on the drive home, she bought two large boxes of Hostess Ho Ho's, Fritos, potato chips and two Mars bars. She ate every last crumb.

I erased The Tank from the Venture West mailing list.

Beenie Baby

I took Penny to Havasu Canyon in the Grand Canyon. She arrived wearing a yellow beenie topped with something that looked like it had come off a toy wind-up helicopter. It matched the rest of her outfit: purple tights and a Goodwill reject, an orange striped tee that hung to her knees. We teased her about her beenie, called her "Beenie Baby." But the truth is, I like people who dress themselves with unconventional color combinations; this shows character, an unwillingness to conform. I do that, too.

After several day hikes to gorgeous waterfalls, I noticed Beenie Baby becoming cranky. How could she not appreciate the grandeur of the red rock canyon walls, the deliciously warm, seventy-two-degree water in the swimming holes under the waterfalls, and the pure white, sacred datura blooms. Most people, myself included, find Havasu Canyon a paradise.

She said things like, "I'm not sure I should have come on this trip," or "I don't need to see any more waterfalls," or the martyr, "Leave me alone, I'll stay here. I'll be fine by myself."

She seemed to enjoy the imaginary conversations she had with her husband Sal, who had told her he wanted her to come on the trip. I could see why. This gave him a vacation from Penny, who muttered to herself, occasionally getting red in the face, and turning around as if someone behind her was part of the conversation.

I once heard her say, "I wish I was at the mall. Sal, let's go shopping when I get home, if I ever get out of here."

I found her strange, rich, and entitled. When she asked me to carry her daypack on hikes, she expected my doting attention. She'd say, "Cari, can you fill my water bottle and carry my pack?" Or, "I'm too tired to walk to dinner. Bring me something from the café."

She often had twenty-dollar bills falling out of her pockets.

When I'd say, "Penny, you need to keep your money in a safe place," she'd reply, "Oh, Sal doesn't care if I lose his money. He has plenty."

That made me crazy. I'd pinched pennies as long as I could remember, and this person threw twenty-dollar bills around as if they were discarded candy wrappers.

When the time came to plan the hike out of the canyon, twenty-six-hundred feet uphill in nine miles, she said, "I won't do it. I'm not having fun." She had the look I'd seen every time she wanted something: the raised eyebrow, the smug smile that said "I'm accustomed to getting my way."

"Penny, this isn't about having fun; we have to get you out of here." She glared at me as if I had done something wrong. "You can do it." I kept the snarl out of my voice.

"I won't walk. You didn't tell me how hard it is. It's your fault. I'll hire a helicopter. I don't care how much it costs."

I knew the price, $300 for a one-way ride from the village to the hilltop. Penny had watched the Native Americans bringing supplies in a helicopter that landed every morning at ten and left immediately afterwards. That's how she knew she could get a ride no matter how much it cost. I don't know how she came up with $300 in cash, maybe the $20s added up, but she did, and when she climbed into the helicopter wearing her yellow beenie, I suppressed a giggle and waved good bye.

The rest of us enjoyed a lovely stroll to the top. Beenie Baby wouldn't be taking another Venture West trip.

* * * * *

So it goes in the adventure travel business. Years passed quickly, good years, wonderful people, and to keep it challenging, a few onions tucked among the petunias. If I were clairvoyant, I would have sorted them out, but then, no one had promised me that life on the trail would be perfect.

I'd like to believe that traveling with these interesting, albeit challenging, personalities gave me insights into myself. I'm not sure about that. Many times, I clenched my jaw, shut my mouth, and carried on. At the end of the day, a glass of whatever wine was available tasted especially good when my patience had been tested.

We're still pouring wine when someone asks, "Are we the best group you've ever had?"

I smile. "Of course."

Chapter Twenty

Twin Miracles

2002 Venture West Catalog
Late October is the best time to be on the Green River in Utah. Sunny seventy degree days and cool nights, few if any other canoes, clear skies, and very little wind. The river flows three-mile-per-hour; the only paddling necessary is when you need to avoid a sandbar. We've done this trip ten times and just can't stay away from the river and these scenic canyons.

When I started down the Green River with a group, we paddled away from safety, human contact, and a possible rescue. There's no cell phone service in Labyrinth Canyon, and the river is too shallow for motorized boats-only rafts, canoes, and kayaks float the Green. We were in true wilderness. There wasn't even a flat place for a helicopter to land, a last resort in case of an emergency.

On the first day, my co-guide Denise and I floated behind our group of eight. That was one of the things I loved about Venture West river trips—the chance to lean back in a camp chair in the stern of a canoe, count clouds, and call it work.

I'd met Denise when she took a Venture West backpacking trip in Oregon. We became good friends, and since she too loved rivers, I asked her to co-guide the Green. My former co-guide, Tom, had moved on to other adventures, and I needed help on this wilderness trip. Denise and I made a good team. She was a strong paddler and loved the canyon country.

This year, the Green had an odd color, brown with hints of green stuff floating in it, which suggested recent activity, perhaps as far north as Wyoming's Green Lakes, the headwaters for the river. Whenever it stormed upriver, the water changed color from brackish green to dirty brown. When this happened, it had an earthy smell, like freshly turned soil in early spring. That's when the river deposited several inches of mud on the sandbars.

For the first two nights of our six-day trip, we camped at a favorite site, Trin Alcove, a place where three canyons cut into the red rock, leaving nooks and crannies to explore. We landed our canoes on the remnant of a narrow spit of sand, formerly a sun-bather's delight. This year, we found the rest of the sand smothered, hidden under eight inches of river mud, liquid clay that sucked moisture from exposed skin and left our calf muscles looking like prunes.

"Sure hope this doesn't mean all the good places are buried," Denise said. Covered with muck up to her shorts, she grabbed the bow of the canoe to drag it closer to the sand. "I think I know why the river looks brown."

"Yeah. Looks like a recent storm. We know what that means—muck, muck, and more muck." I dipped my hand into the river and grabbed a piece of burned wood. "This floating stuff could have come all the way from Wyoming."

"I hope the mud lets up in the next couple days or this will be a long trip." Denise's usual optimism had waned.

"Remember last year when we found a sandbar every time we needed a campsite? Maybe it's payback time." I didn't believe that. Things would work out; we'd find campsites. No problem.

Denise smiled at the memories of our idyllic trip the previous year, when we'd found sandbars big enough for several tents around every bend.

"Right. And we didn't have to beat our way through the damn tamarisk that the Corps of Engineers planted to stabilize the banks. That sure backfired."

That tamarisk, a fast-growing tree, dominated the banks of the river, forming a nasty, impenetrable thicket.

"We need the sandbars," I said. "Whatever happens, we'll manage, just have to work harder." That was my job, to make things look easy. After seven trips down the Green, I felt confident, competent, happy, because no matter what the river threw at me, I could handle it.

The third day we left Trin Alcove and floated between three-hundred-million-year-old sandstone walls decorated with red and grey, colors leached from minerals in the rock. Even the ubiquitous tamarisk looked almost pretty, its feathery green silhouetted against the glowing red rock. If an occasional shallow riffle or tiny wave changed our directional line, we dipped a paddle, but mostly we relaxed on the way to Two Mile Canyon, our camp-site for night number three.

Then it started. "Denise, look over to the right, quick, before it's too late. I think that's Two Mile Canyon."

Yikes! We'd almost missed it. "Doesn't that swamp look like the place where there used to be a stream? Remember? We paddled up that stream to get in to the canyon." This marshy spot did not look anything like the Two-Mile I remembered. "Something's wrong. We'd better stop."

"Holy crap. I don't recognize anything." Denise grabbed her paddle and we headed for the edge. "Where's the stream? How are we going to get into the canyon?"

Life on the Loose

Last October, we'd paddled up an inlet at the opening of Two Mile Canyon, tied the canoes, and scrambled up a low bank to a campsite. We had pitched the tents in a wide open space that had a perfect shelter for the camp kitchen and broad rock shelves that jutted out over the river. It was our favorite campsite. That was last year.

I hollered to the four canoes ahead of us to turn around. "You have to paddle upstream," I yelled. "Pull hard and follow me."

When the other canoes got close, I said, "You all wait here, out of the current, Denise and I will figure out how to get into our campsite."

"You want us to sit and wait?" asked Duane. "Are you kidding?" He and his wife Marilyn, strong paddlers, were used to working hard on a river. "Why don't we keep going? We can find another place to camp."

"Because this is my favorite camp. We'll be right back." There it was, the stubborn part of me that always popped up at the wrong time. The part of me that said, *Obstacles, what obstacles? I can make this happen.*

We tied our canoe to a tree root and scrambled up the fifteen-foot bank. I stood behind Denise and shoved her butt until she grabbed a root and hauled herself over the top. Then she gripped my forearms and pulled me up until I found a foothold and a sturdy root for support.

I looked down at the mud and the drop-off. "We can't go back that way. Someone will break a leg."

"You know, Cari, I had a premonition about this trip. I thought it was about Claudine." We both worried about Claudine, a cancer survivor who brought her diabetes medications with her in a cooler, an ineffective container that lost its cool on the second day.

As it turned out, Claudine was the least of our problems. She took care of herself.

We beat our way through tamarisk, a tangle that left us disoriented. We needed a machete, something to hack through branches that left bloody scratches on our arms and legs.

"Sure wish we hadn't left our shoes in the canoe. My feet hurt." Denise was not a complainer. "The sand is hot."

"I have a thorn in my foot. They're everywhere," I said. "What were we thinking?"

By this point, we had left the canoes, including our canoe, far behind.

"We'd better mark a trail or we'll never find our way back. We could be going around in circles." Denise turned around, looked back. "I don't know where we've been."

"Okay," I said. "I'll tie my pink bandana to a tree. We'll pretend we're Hansel and Gretel."

We forced our way through more tamarisk, came out to an opening in the brush, and looked back. The bandana had disappeared. I put my favorite green Patagonia river hat on a piece of dry juniper. We were in open desert. Nothing looked familiar.

"Where the hell are we?" Denise looked back. "Now your hat's gone, too." She set her hat on the sand and walked away. "This is stupid. We don't know where we came from, and we don't know where we're going."

I checked my watch. We'd been gone more than an hour. We were hot, tired, disoriented, lost. "We should have stayed on the river. My fault." Sweat rolled down my face in the ninety-degree heat. "I wanted to camp here, damn it."

Eventually we stumbled into the former campsite. A lot of good that did. We couldn't stay because we couldn't get to it from the river. There was no going back. We'd accomplished nothing. Forget the hats, the bandana, and the green tee Denise donated. They were gone. We needed to get back to our group. I checked the watch. We'd been gone two hours.

I felt fear, the familiar feeling when my mouth gets dry and my legs want to fold under me. I sat down hard on a rock.

"We have to stay calm."

Just as I said that, Denise spotted an opening in the brush, a tiny path that led down a steep rocky slope to the river. "If we slide down that bank, we can try to get to the rock that sticks out." She sat down and looked at the Green. "From there, we can wave to the group. They can paddle down the river and meet us."

"It's worth a try." I thought it looked dangerous. If one of us lost control, we'd end up in the water. "I'll go first." I hung onto the tamarisk roots to slow my fall, ripped my pants, and landed safely on the rock.

Now we had a new problem. We were two hundred yards down river from our canoe. I shivered in the waning sunlight. It was late fall, a lovely sunny day, but nevertheless, a short October day. Eight people waited for us to tell them what to do. This was one of those times when I wanted someone else to tell me what to do. I didn't want to be in charge. I wanted to be rescued.

From our slippery perch on the rock, we waved and shouted. We saw dots on the landscape, dwarfed by Navaho sandstone walls that towered a thousand feet above them. We hoped someone would see us and understand that they were supposed to paddle to where we were standing on the ledge—and bring our canoe. We figured they were confused. Why not? They didn't know what was going on.

They expected us to come back, to tell them we had a campsite, and we were set for the night. Soon we would open the wine. Instead, we were barely in sight, frantically waving at them. We watched Duane and Marilyn take charge, tie our canoe to the back of their canoe, and slowly make their way toward us. The others followed, a welcome sight, five canoes headed our way.

When we were all together, I asked them to gather at the side of the river for a briefing on the plan Denise and I had made in haste. It wasn't much, but we had to give them something to assure them of our leadership.

"Before we start, I want everyone to eat chocolate. I have a bag I save for special occasions." The idea for chocolate saved for an emergency came from a sea kayaking trip I had co-guided in the Canadian Gulf Islands. When we faced a rough crossing with a dangerous riptide, the lead guide, Jack, had everyone pull their kayaks on to a sheltered beach, where he gave directions and fed us dark chocolate.

"The chocolate will give you quick energy to power the kayak through the rough waters," he said. Maybe the chocolate worked, or maybe sheer terror pulled us across that channel, but everyone made it. Jack put away the rescue ropes.

On the Green, we were looking at a twenty-plus-mile day, and a possible overnight in the canoes on the river. We needed more than energy—we needed a miracle.

I remembered why I had started Venture West. I wanted adventure. I didn't want to read about John Doe's trip down the Green. I wanted to be there, feel the passion, the awe, and occasion-ally, the raw fear that accompanied wilderness travel. Right then, I could have done without the drama.

"Stay behind," I said. "Denise and I will go down the left side of the river, and Duane and Marilyn will stay close to the right. The rest of you stay in the middle." I didn't mention the obvious. It would be dark in less than half an hour, and every sandbar we'd passed for the last fifteen miles was covered with muck. "Watch us closely. We'll wave if we see something. We'll find a sandbar or an island soon."

My brain went into survival mode. What was the worst scenario? We'd spend a long, cold, night sitting upright in our canoes, tied together like a giant raft in the middle of the river. We wouldn't go anywhere because the river was shallow with a current less than three miles per hour. No one would die. No one would starve. We'd be together, safe, uncomfortable, and miserable. An overnight in a canoe wasn't in the trip description for this leisurely float down the Green, but it would make a great story back home.

I heard Duane holler from the other side, "Cari, we found a sandbar. Easy landing. We can stay here."

In the dark, we pulled five canoes onto the perfect campsite, a large, sandy island in the middle of the river. We whooped, we cavorted, and we danced with relief and joy. Then we went about our evening rituals, drank some wine from a box, ate dinner, and fell in bed, exhausted.

The next morning, we drank coffee, ate apple-pecan pancakes, organized the gear, emptied the pee bucket, and dragged the canoes across the sand to the water for the start of another day. Denise and I sent the group ahead while we finished the last of the camp chores. Because this was a perfect Utah day—cloudless, no wind—we planned a short paddle to a canyon a few miles downriver where we would set up early, leaving the afternoon to hike or read, or to do nothing.

We started down the river, relieved, smug, because we'd escaped a miserable floating overnight. A burst of wind, a powerful gust, suddenly spun our loaded canoe in a circle. A wave splashed over the bow and ran down my legs. I felt a chill and shivered in the cool late October morning. The tamarisks on the riverbanks bent low in the wind, their branches chattering against each other. I remembered Denise's premonition about the trip. Was that yesterday? Something was wrong.

When we looked back to give a last word of thanks to the river gods for our unexpected island, we could barely see it. It was almost gone. The gust that had twirled our canoe had turned into a steady hard blow.

Instead of the former campsite, our private island in the middle of the river, we saw blowing sand, sand that irritated our eyes, obscured our vision, sand that used to be an island, our safe landing. We felt a force, something in the wind we didn't under-stand. We had been safe in the night, but now what?

"Something strange is going on, and I don't like it," I said. "This wind is weird."

"You're right there. Look, the island is gone, disappeared." Denise struggled to keep the canoe from spinning again. "What the hell happened? I'm worried. Feels like the river gods are taunting us."

The red rock walls, yesterday's source of inspiration and awe, felt like a prison. They left no escape, for we could go in only one direction, down the river. A tickle of fear nudged the back of my neck. Denise and I looked at each other, afraid to voice our thoughts, to say out loud the fear we felt for the safety of the group. It was time to join them.

By the time we caught up, waves washed over the bows of the canoes. We struggled to stay close together, but the real challenge was staying upright. Waves pushed the canoes from side to side. Gusts of wind came at us from every direction. The wind roared, it swirled, and it controlled our boats.

"Keep your bow pointed into the waves," I hollered. "Don't let your canoe get sideways or you'll tip." I hoped everyone heard me over the sound of the water banging against the metal canoes. They battled the river and the wind with beginner's erratic strokes, their canoes zig-zagging, tipping from side to side in the increasingly powerful waves.

"Cari, I can't do this. I can't steer."

From my canoe, I saw Paula's hands shake as she gripped the paddle. We had paired her with Mable, thinking she would be the stronger partner, and she was. But Mable was a liability, a "lily dipper" in canoe lingo, someone who dipped her paddle, but had no power behind it.

When Duane and Marilyn took their paddles out of the water for a quick break, their canoe teetered on its side. Duane hollered at his wife, "Get that damn paddle in and pull. We're going over."

"Everyone paddle. Don't stop." With grim faces, tight bodies, paddles flailing, the canoes moved haphazardly down the river. "You can rest later. Pull as hard as you can."

Then Glenice yelled, "Cari, is the wind supposed to blow like this in the morning?" She was a hiker, someone who explored wild places in boots, but was out of her comfort zone in a canoe.

"I don't know what's going on. The river's supposed to be calm in the morning." That had been my experience; no reason to think otherwise except for the blasts of wind that came from every direction. It made no sense.

"Let's get off the river," called Duane.

"We can't. There's no place to land." Things were out of control. They counted on me to take care of them. But I get scared, too. Damn. I had launched my new life on the Green. That year, not a riffle disturbed the placid, calm river. Now look at it: waves almost as high as our canoes, disaster threatening around every bend, and I was supposed to keep them safe. Their canoes wobbled and tipped sideways in the churning water.

A quiet voice said, "I'm cold and wet. I don't want to do this anymore." Claudine, the diabetic, didn't have a surplus of extra strength for fighting waves.

"I don't know what to do," I whispered to Denise. "We have to keep going."

When we left the island, the wind was strong enough to spin our canoe, but not strong enough to raise these eighteen-inch waves. Now it felt like a personal assault, a private storm, a storm to remind us of our powerlessness on a wilderness river.

Suddenly, the wind storm ended. The waves disappeared as the benign river I remembered from past trips reappeared. Everyone stopped paddling. "I don't know where that came from. You all were great. Good job." *Saved again*, I said to myself, blessed by the river gods. "Time to go down the river instead of in circles."

Everyone smiled, chuckled, relaxed. I heard them talking, laughing, relieved to feel some control in their boats.

"I don't want to do that again," Paula said. "I was scared, sure we'd go over." She had done a great job. Paddled for two in the stern. Mable tried, but her ineffective stroke in the bow did nothing to control the canoe.

"You know what,. I was scared, too." I wanted to let them know guides are not invincible, but feel fear like everyone else. I don't care how much experience someone has had on a river, canoes tip. Someone could have drowned. Was I negligent, liable, if a canoe went over? I pushed that from my mind. There were more important things to think about, like getting off the river.

Without the wind, the five canoes moved in a straight line. This would be a perfect day after all. A calm river stretched ahead of us, like an endless sea of chocolate pudding. Denise and I floated behind, relaxed, certain of a safe return.

Life on the Loose

Suddenly the wind came back, not a breeze, but a gale. What was happening? Were we too relaxed? Had we insulted the river gods—again? It felt personal. The wind doesn't blow before noon on the Green. This had never happened before. In the middle of the afternoon, it often blew for an hour or more, but that only happened when the desert heated up on top of the canyon. The cooler air on the river would be drawn upward, creating a vacuum, and a draft. We expected that wind. When we could, we'd get off the river, or find our evening camp before it started.

But this mid-morning gale puzzled me. Twice, I maneuvered the group to the river's edge to rest. Paula and Mable barely controlled their canoe. Glenice and Claudine didn't do much better, while Carol and Maggie, the youngsters in the group, alternately laughed and cried as they went round and round in the waves.

As we came around a bend, I saw a familiar sandbar, an open sandy beach that stretched for more than half a mile. "Oh, my gawd! How did we get here so fast? This is the end." The wind must have blown us downriver, and now we were at the canoe landing, albeit on the wrong side of the river, a day early.

I waved to the group. "The river's too wide here to cross until the wind quits. Those waves will swamp us if we go out in the open water."

"You mean this is it?" Duane looked confused.

"Yeah, we got pushed down the river by the wind."

"I'm glad to be done," Paula said.

Everyone nodded.

"We'll eat lunch here and wait for the wind to die down, hopefully soon. This is the end, Mineral Bottoms. We get off on the other side. We're a day early."

There was no place to get the canoes off the river thanks to the tamarisk, so I delivered lunch.

"We love the personal service, Cari," Mable said. She never missed a meal.

I waded in mud up to my thighs, used a paddle as a tray, set out lunch as best I could from my precarious perch in the river, and served it with style. The improvisation worked. I delivered apples, cheese, salami, Triscuits, and chocolate to each canoe, one at a time.

We had a few minutes of peace. The waves subsided, the water calmed, yet, above my head, I still felt powerful gusts of wind. How could this be? Was a greater power playing with us, teasing us? Either the wind blows, or it doesn't. It doesn't blow three feet above the river without raising a riffle on the surface. Was this the same force that loaned us our evening sandbar then, took it away in the morning? I didn't trust it.

Midway through lunch, my intuition kicked in. Something told me that we needed to get out of there, fast. "We don't have time to finish lunch. We have to go. Now." I said. "Drop everything. Pick up your paddles. Tighten the straps on your life jackets. We're leaving." We had to cross before the big waves started. "Paddle hard. Don't let up, even for one stroke." We had a brief window of opportunity before the waves started to batter us again.. If we lingered, it would be too late. We'd be trapped.

"Should we point our bow into the waves like before? I don't know if I'm strong enough," said Paula. She knew she'd have to be strong to pull Mable's share, too. "My arm muscles are tired."

Mable joined in, "I'll paddle as hard as I can. I know I'm not very good."

From another canoe, I heard a faint, "I'm scared."

"You can do it. Concentrate, pull, hard, and you'll be fine." This would be a hard crossing for me, too. If I felt fear, how did they feel? Or did they trust me enough to be certain they would be safe? "Don't stop. Keep your bow pointed into the waves."

Life on the Loose

I hoped they overlooked the quiver in my voice. This was a dangerous crossing.

As we started across, the wind told us who was boss. There was a power present on the river that morning. I felt it; I honored it; I feared it. There was no logical way to explain that strange wind that followed us down the river.

My intuition came too late. First riffles, then waves, waves that threatened to dump us.

"Remember where to point the bow," I called out again and again. If they lost control, the deep water in the middle would push them too far around the bend, past the road at the landing at Mineral Bottoms. We'd be in serious trouble. The next place to get picked up and ferried back to town was fifty miles down river at the confluence with the Colorado. If that happened, we would run out of food and water. That would take about a day. I blocked that thought—too scary. The canoes teetered between the waves.

We couldn't go back to where we had eaten lunch. We were fully committed when we pulled into the current. I wondered, *Should I have waited?* It took maybe fifteen minutes to cross; it felt like hours.

After we pulled the canoes up the embankment, we looked back at the Green. We watched three-foot waves smash against our shore. Paula and Glenice burst into tears, Carol and Maggie sat, silent, numb. The rest of us hugged. No one spoke except Denise. "Cari, I think the river gods were playing with us. I don't like it."

"I know. Now I feel like I'm in *Grapes of Wrath* in the middle of a dust storm, except I'm eating sand. That damn wind just won't quit."

Everyone nodded. Mable said, "Well, anyway, thanks for getting us across. I was terrified."

230

As tension drained from my body, my legs quivered. Weak with relief, I looked for a place to sit before they collapsed. I needed time to think, to regroup. We needed a new plan or another miracle. Yes, we were off the river, in the middle of nowhere, in a blizzard-like sandstorm. It stuck to our bodies, got in our eyes, and covered our skin. The outfitter would come in twenty-four hours as per my instructions, a long time to wait with no shelter, no shade.

"We can't pitch the tents in this wind," Claudine said. She sat down in the road, took off her hat, and threw a rock in the river. She probably wanted to throw me in the river.

"I know. Try to find some shelter, maybe behind a rock or a tree." This would be a long afternoon. When would the wind let up? Who knew? Not me. "Do the best you can. We can't do anything until the wind dies down."

Then we heard something that sounded like a truck. I looked up the side of the canyon, up the switchbacks, and saw a bus with Tex's Riverways painted on its side, our outfitter, pulling a trailer with six kayaks on it.

"Oh, shit, another miracle." That was too much to ask, a ride to town, a nice dinner, and a bed, not a tent, in a god-forsaken place in a sandstorm. "Look who's coming. We can get out of here today."

"Hey, Cari, what are you doing here? We're supposed to come back to get you tomorrow," Dirk climbed out of the bus and started walking toward my sad little group.

"Look at the river. The waves almost swamped us. Why did you think we're here?"

"Yah, it's a little bumpy." Dirk wasn't impressed.

'Bumpy? It's kamikaze dangerous and we're damned glad to be safe." Denise and I looked at each other and exchanged high fives. "Yah, safe."

"Let me get these people and their kayaks on the river. Then I can load you all up and head back to town." Dirk's nonchalance made my blood boil. How could he be so dismissive of our near-death experience?

"You're putting them on the river in the middle of this hurricane? Are you crazy?"

We whooped, hollered, and got to work sorting the gear for Dirk to load. Everyone jumped up to help, their energy revived with our amazing good fortune. Soon we would be out of the sandstorm and on our way to a hot shower.

We loaded the canoes onto the rack, put the life jackets and the paddles in the back, collected our personal stuff, and jumped in the bus. Two hours later, we sauntered into Restaurant Rio in Moab, where we savored hot sandwiches and cold beer.

What was that about? I couldn't explain the strange wind that had chased us down the river. Some things are better left a mystery.

Chapter Twenty-One

Good Enough?

2005 Venture West Catalog
The Spanish Peaks in Montana offer some of the best scenery in the Rockies. We'll hike and backpack above 10,000' where this geological showcase of ancient rocks, glaciation, and snowmelt erosion will awe even the most experienced mountain hikers. The first day is an easy five-mile hike to the confluence of three mountain streams. The following day we hike to Hell Roaring Lake, where we'll settle for three nights and explore the rocky world above timberline.

On my way to start a solo backpacking trip in the Spanish Peaks Wilderness in Montana, my taxi passed the scene of a recent fatal accident. There was an overturned, badly smashed car next to the highway, and a semi pulled over fifty yards farther down the road.

My driver explained what had happened earlier that morning. "Someone told me a car going about fifty swerved to miss a deer, right into the path of the semi." She pointed to the wrecked car, "Three people died, a couple and a child."

The accident reminded me of the many times I had said to family and friends, "You have more to worry about when you drive on a freeway than I do when I hike in the mountains." They assumed, as most do, that traveling alone in the wilderness, far from help, a hospital, or a ready EMT squad, equaled danger. I never convinced anyone there will always be more accidents on highways than fatalities above timberline. Whenever I pointed out the danger inherent in traveling seventy in rush-hour traffic, people shrugged and rolled their eyes. But, of course, I was right.

The accident dampened my excitement. Things can turn sour in the wilderness. I would be alone in the mountains for seven days. Despite my confidence and experience as a solo backpacker, three deaths on the highway reminded me that I too was vulnerable.

After the cab driver dropped me at the trailhead and promised to return in a week, I headed into the mountains in search of the perfect base camp. I planned to set up for a few days and enjoy nearby hikes. My ideal base camp had to have space for my tent, preferably with a view of the mountains, water nearby, and at least three trails that invited exploration.

I took this solo trip into the Peaks after I'd been a back country guide for twenty-five years. I had a successful business and confidence earned from surviving the unexpected: hazardous stream crossings, gale-force winds on the Green River, and a terrifying hitch in the Virgin Islands when I got in a car with a Bob Marley look-alike at midnight. I'd also survived my own bad judgment and learned the hard way not to cut the hike too close to darkness in the woods. After a few wrong turns, I checked the map twice, then checked it again. Bad timing, mistaken directions, and misinformed optimism about peoples' stamina, had taught me lessons about life on the trail. I also learned to temper my enthusiasm for potentially dangerous situations, like hiking at dusk in bear country.

Just ahead was the start of the recession in 2008. I didn't know then that Venture West was on the downhill side of the curve, not that I was about to give it up. I ran trips for another five years after the dip in the business.

Good Enough?

At the same time, I cut the mailing list to two thousand from six thousand to avoid the hassle with bulk mailings at the post office. I put a first-class stamp on each catalog, but the reduced mailing meant fewer customers. It also rescued my sanity as the rules for bulk mail became increasingly complex.

Competition from big travel companies like Elderhostel, now Road Scholar, didn't help, nor did the Internet, which encouraged potential customers to research their own trips.

I couldn't have anticipated the storm ahead for the business, but I knew how to negotiate in the wilderness when weather threw a curve. I smiled through unexpected rain, sleet, snow, wind, and whatever else the weather gods sent me. I also set high expectations for myself. If my legs ached, I ignored the pain and pushed forward. I wanted to be the strongest hiker, though not the fastest, so my customers saw an invincible guide, someone who didn't get tired. I wanted to be a person who never had sore muscles or an aching back at the end of the day. I had to be superwoman. Truth was, I never felt good enough, needed to prove to myself that I was worthy of my guide job. I loved my job, and despite the glitches in the early years, I had thirty-plus years of idyllic trips. If my legs ached, and sometimes they did, I faked a bounce in my step and carried on.

The first night in the Peaks, shortly after dark, I heard heavy breathing. This wasn't a small mammal having a nightly rendezvous but more like a hyperventilating, seasick passenger in a small boat on a rolling sea. Something large stood nearby, perhaps because the tent sat in the only available open space, too close to an animal trail. It paused, made slurpy sounds like a bear enjoying a delicious morsel, and left. The tent and the ground vibrated as if someone worked nearby with a jackhammer.

235

Life on the Loose

I held my breath, lying frozen on the floor of the tent. By the time I found my glasses and a flashlight, the thing was gone. A lot of good it did me to bring a whistle. I couldn't find it in the dark. I'd taken every precaution, hung the food a hundred yards from the tent, cooked a hundred yards in another direction, and taken off clothes that could have smelled like dinner.

It happened so fast I didn't have time to register the terror that glued me to the floor of the tent as the thing lumbered down the trail. The bear knew I was there. He smelled me; he sensed my body heat; he chose to ignore me. I was alone in the mountains. What could I do? Where could I run? I needed time to calm my thumping heart. Sleep that night was a long time in coming.

The next morning, before daylight, before I could get out of the tent, first lightening, then thunder, and then the storm arrived. The temperature dropped into the forties, and the tent shivered in the icy wind, no longer a warm morning breeze. Golf-ball-sized chunks of hail that sounded like artillery bounced off the fragile layer of nylon that separated me from them. I felt a second frisson of fear. This had started to look like a long week in the mountains, my personal week, the time I took from a busy life, just for me.

What next? A dead stove? A collapsed tent? Snow? And stuck in my head, the possible return of the bear. I had done my research and knew bears will travel many miles in the mountains looking for food, especially close to timberline where I planned to find a base camp for the week. Yet, I had always pretended bears didn't scare me, but if one came into camp, I'd crawl under the tent. If he wanted food, I'd give him everything—that is, everything except my tiny bottle of Jack Daniels.

As suddenly as it started, the storm ended. The sun came out and melted the hailstones. I brewed a cup of strong coffee, ate three Michigan cherries, six white gum drops, and a handful of M&Ms. Life was good again.

Good Enough?

For the next two days, I congratulated myself on my fearless competence every time I picked up my backpack and set off on a mountain trail. To protect myself from surprising a bear, each time I rounded a blind corner, I hollered, "Hey, bear!" to announce my coming. My announcement shocked a moose from its resting place by the creek, and the bears—they disappeared.

Without warning, my legs quit. They throbbed from exhaustion and the rigors of climbing up and down steep trails. It felt like ten-pound weights had attached themselves to my ankles. What had happened? Even at sixty-eight, I thought my legs were still strong enough to carry forty pounds in the mountains. A tear rolled down my cheek when a cramp attacked my right calf muscle, shortly after crossing Hell Roaring Creek in water up to my under-wear. The leg hurt like hell, but at least it happened at the edge of a meadow, a perfect campsite with a mountain view.

Was this the end of the line? Was I getting old? What would I tell people back home? That I had quit? Only hiked half the distance I'd planned to cover? A ten-year-old could do that blindfolded before breakfast. I wanted to rip the pack off my back and call a helicopter rescue.

Pride, hubris, pure grit couldn't get this aging body moving again. I'd crossed into my sixties, gained wrinkles and grandchil-dren, and found myself increasingly exhausted. Why was I surprised?

Vulnerable was not a role I wanted to play. People thought I was Iron Woman, or at least that's what they said. If I quit, or slowed down, I would destroy my image.

I peeled off wet clothes and lay naked in the sun, waiting for my legs to unclench. An eagle soared against the clear blue sky, a warm breeze rustled the sparse aspens, a feeling of pure joy washed over me and relaxed my body into a nest of grass. This was good enough. I could turn around. Instead of feeling exposed, I felt content, satisfied, happy to be there, despite my aches and pains. I wanted to jump up and dance, but my legs wouldn't let me.

I loved my role model as a guide, but more than that, I loved the peace, solitude, and happiness I found in the wilderness.

Friends admired me, or said they did, for my solo adventures. I needed the attention, the looks people gave me that validated my backcountry expertise. I felt proud, different from the regular people I'd left behind in suburbia. I had taken the doll out of the jar twenty-five years ago and never looked back. There was no quiet desperation in my world, it overflowed with adventures.

Maybe I wasn't a perfect mother, but despite my travels, my four children survived, graduated with degrees, and moved on to marriage, successful careers, and children.

Chris married Cindy. He's an actuary and has a daughter named Lily. Wendy joined an accounting firm as a partner, married Gary, and they have two children, Andy and Caroline. Linda worked for several years for Outward Bound, married Eric, another outdoors person, and they have one daughter, Etta. Cathy joined BLM Technology as a vice-president, and with her husband Bob, has two children, Audrey and Bobby.

The hell with my Iron Woman image. What if I quit, turned around, cut my losses, cut thirty miles from the planned route? Would anyone care?

I put on the last pair of clean wool socks and went to bed.

It took three days to hike back to the highway. Three days filled with sore legs, a stiff knee, aching shoulders, and low energy. Despite the shortened itinerary, I came out at the exact time of the arranged meeting.

As for my tarnished image, no one noticed. It was time to let down the bar, to trash my expectations, to acknowledge my age. It wasn't time, yet, to give up the business, but it was time to relax.

Chapter Twenty-Two

The Annapurna Trek

2011 Venture West Catalog

Picture yourself awakened each morning in your tent by a cheerful 'Namaste' and a cup of tea. This is camping at its best, a hikers' dream, a trek into the heart of Nepal to the basecamp of the women's group who climbed Annapurna I in 1978. This trek takes you to 13,500 feet as you walk through villages, rice terraces, and up to the basecamp where you will find yourself in the center of a ring of 25,000-foot, snow-covered peaks.

D espite my epiphany in the Spanish Peaks, I wasn't ready to quit, but I knew with absolute certainty that I would have to slow down. My legs no longer had the spring they had when I was forty. I also knew I had to return to Nepal one more time.

* * * * *

After thirty hours in the air and layovers in Chicago, Los Angeles, Osaka, and Bangkok, the three-hour flight to Kathmandu was a pleasure. As we approached the city, the pilot announced we could see the Himalayas from the right side of the plane. Excitement lit up the cabin as everyone left of the aisle jumped from their seats to compete for a corner of a window and a glimpse of the famous peaks. Often they're obscured by the yellow-grey smog that hangs in the Kathmandu valley, but that day they sparkled in the afternoon sun. From a distance, only the blurry mass of snow around the peaks hinted of the hundred-miles-per-hour winds that continually batter them.

When we deplaned at the airport in Kathmandu, chaos erupted. Hundreds of international travelers mingled with masses of Nepalese as arriving passengers attempted to find the best, the shortest, the fastest line.

"Do they take travelers checks?"

"Anyone seen the Visa forms?"

"Oh, shit, I'm in the wrong line."

As this was my seventh trip to Nepal, I knew the routine, breezed through immigration in less than an hour, and exited into a sunny, sixty-degree November afternoon. My long-time guide, Saila Tamang, placed a lei of marigolds around my neck, a traditional good luck and safe journey greeting for trekkers, people who travel the ancient footpaths in Nepal. Then we were off to the Kathmandu Guest House, a hotel favored by trekkers who liked to gather on the patio to share stories from past treks while they enjoyed the local Turberg beer. The Guest House, not to be confused with the Yak and Yeti, Kathmandu's well-known upscale hotel, had flush toilets, but you had to stand back or get sprayed when you pushed the lever.

As we plowed through traffic in Kathmandu, our taxi driver swerved around cows, goats, motorcycles, gas-powered tuk-tuks—small, three-wheeled, open-air vehicles—and hundreds of garishly decorated trucks and busses. The entire route was a nonstop traffic jam.

I always felt the most dangerous part of trekking was the pedestrian-beware drivers in Kathmandu where young men, hundreds, thousands of them raced down narrow streets riding motorcycles, rickshaws, and bicycles. To them, we were no different than the cows and goats: obstacles to the drivers. Everyone with a horn used it. This cacophony assaulted us as we avoided piles of rotting garbage.

I had met my guide Saila several years earlier when my daughter, Cathy, and her friend Julie and I trekked to the Langjung Base Camp. Julie had found him when she lived in Kathmandu and had time to interview potential guides for our trek. On that trip, she also booked Cathy and me into Hotel Mona for our first night in the city. Our $2.00 room lacked essential amenities, including sheets, toilet paper, towels, and a lock on the door. We didn't care. We had brought sleeping bags, toilet paper, and towels from home, and as for the lock, we were too tired from the journey from Wisconsin to fuss about minor details.

Saila and I formed an instant friendship. Over the next sixteen years, we trekked together six more times on treks that ranged from nine to sixteen days. On the highest trek, we crossed the Laurebina La, a pass, in snow, at 16,500 feet, while the Ghorka to Pokhara treks never went above 10,000 feet. There were no casual outings in Nepal. Even the "low" treks demanded endurance and good physical conditioning. I never called a trek easy; I pushed myself beyond what I thought I could do every time.

On this seventh trek, I would travel to the Annapurna Base Camp (ABC), a fifteen-day journey from Dhampu, a small village two-hundred-fifty kilometers from Kathmandu. The trekking route we would follow crossed several river gorges on the way to the camp at 13,500 feet.

Footpaths through ancient villages, a common description of trekking in Nepal, suggests fascinating places populated by exotic people. Perhaps, but picture instead uneven, downward-slanted, crooked stone steps climbing straight up or straight down, stretching endlessly in the blazing sun until they disappeared around a bend. Was there an end to the ridges? There was always another and another, a vertical parade that gave trekkers false hope at every fake summit. Somewhere in the clouds was an ancient village and a cup of Nepalese tea, black tea made with sugar and water buffalo milk. There was one way to get to that tea, one step at a time, all day, usually up, occasionally down, but never, ever, a stroll in the park. This was a small price to pay for the privilege of arriving exhausted at a camp in a rice paddy near a village framed by snow-covered peaks, giant piles of whipped cream that towered above us in every direction.

But first, details to attend to in Kathmandu. Saila and I met the Venture West group the day after my arrival and escorted them to the Kathmandu Guest House, home for two nights, before we departed for Dhampu and the fifteen-day trek. Supplies had to be purchased, warm clothes checked, and official permits obtained from the Trekking Office. Saila had the hard job. He purchased, packed, and organized food and gear for five trekkers plus the entourage of Sherpas, porters, and kitchen staff. It was my job to suppress anxiety, and to reassure everyone in my group that this would be their adventure of a lifetime.

First-time trekkers fretted about details such as food, climate, safety, and hygiene. Reasonable concerns. Someone always asked, "Will there be enough food?" or "Is Nepalese food mostly rice and veggies?"

Cathy from Wisconsin had trained hard for the trek. She had hired a personal trainer, lost fifty pounds, and took up running up and down the hills in her neighborhood. She was the first to ask about food.

"Yes," I answer, "There's always too much food and yes, I promise you'll love the meals. Everyone does." That was true. Our

Nepalese cook took pride in feeding us three delicious meals every day. "Sometimes we have chicken."

Andrew worried about money, credit cards, and passports. "What should I do with my valuables on the trek?"

"Leave them at the Guest House. You don't need money on the trek."

I reassured the trekkers that their things would be totally safe in a locked room. They just had to hold on to the key.

"How many jackets should I bring?"

Karen, from California, worried about getting cold, and with good reason. It would be below freezing at the higher elevations.

"Bring everything. You don't have to carry it."

I could have brought more warm clothes for the trek, but I didn't know it then. I always tried to be a minimalist when I camped. If I got cold or wet, I dug in and never admitted my discomfort.

"Can I wash my hair?"

Maureen, my good friend, didn't need to worry. She rinsed her short hair every time we passed a waterfall and always looked good.

"No. Don't bring a mirror." My thin, fine hair never looked good, even on my best days when I used a blow dryer.

"How much toilet paper should I bring?"

This question from Andrew, and a concern for all of us.

"Twice as much as you think you'll need."

I answered that one honestly, from experience.

Their anxiety revolved around the details and the unfamiliar culture everyone fell into the minute they left the airport and dove into the clogged streets of Kathmandu. Words soothed part of the tension; the rest disappeared when they started climbing. Sore muscles quickly replaced worries about clean hair and wrinkled clothes. Trekkers learn how to do one thing at a time, walk, all day, every day, vanity and fussy hygiene forgotten.

For dinner, I took them to Tashi Deleg, a Tibetan restaurant. That's where I learned to pee in a hole that I couldn't see in a bathroom the size of a telephone booth. When Kathmandu's "load shedding," designed to conserve electricity, happened at dinner-time, all the lights went out, and candles lit the kitchen and the tables, but not the bathroom. That's when I learned the wisdom of carrying a flashlight everywhere, as well as toilet paper, and to place my feet carefully in the latrine.

For the group, I ordered momo, steamed bundles of dough stuffed with meat or veggies served with tomato sauce, and potato burgers with mushroom sauce. That way, first-time trekkers got a taste of what was coming on the trek, thus discouraging fantasies of American cuisine: hot dogs, hamburgers, and potato chips.

The following morning, we walked to Mike's Breakfast. Mike Frame, an ex-pat from Northfield, Minnesota, came to Kathmandu in the sixties and stayed. At his restaurant, we sat in a garden where classical music played as we dined on spinach omelets and home-made muffins. This was gracious living in Kathmandu, a stark contrast to the rest of the city, and to the trek to the base camp.

* * * * *

The next day, before daylight, we walked on deserted streets to our private bus. Reed-woven porter's baskets piled high with cauli-flower, cabbage, potatoes, canned stuff, and rice defied gravity on the roof of the bus. Every corner bulged with food and gear for twenty porters and Sherpas and five trekkers. On the trek Saila supplemented our supplies with an occasional live chicken and fresh veggies.

We jammed into the remaining seats as I called the front seat to protect my delicate stomach. It's unprofessional for a guide to puke on the ride to Pokhara, but then I had a history of passing my cookies at inopportune times. As I looked out the bus window at the peaks lit by the early morning sun, I glanced back at this band of adventurers and wished us well.

Once settled in the bus, no one said anything. It was too late to turn back.

The ride to Dhampu took ten hours. Karen emptied her stomach out the window and surprised Maureen, next to an open window behind her. I handed them diaper wipes, then practiced deep breathing to stay calm as the bus lurched around kamikaze curves on the narrow, truck-crowded road above the Trisuli River. We held tightly onto our seats each time the top-heavy bus swerved around a slow-moving truck and flirted with the two-thousand foot drop-off leading down to the river.

We camped that night next to the highway on a small, grassy space in front of a one-room store with a disgusting shed they called the toilet. Not a great way to start "The Grand Tour." If we rated toilets on a scale of one to ten, with a one being a full hole in a stall with a door that wouldn't close, then we found number one on the first night.

The trekkers had varying responses. "This is unacceptable." "It's filthy." "I'm going behind the bushes." "So what if someone see me." Cathy, who had never camped, took her roll of toilet paper and disappeared. She wasn't the only one to use the bushes.

We left at dawn the next day, ready to forget the first camp. As always, our porters left ahead of us. Each carried the legal load, sixty-six pounds of food, stoves, gear, fuel, and our duffels, all loaded into baskets they carried on their backs. They secured their baskets with tumplines, a wide straps that crossed their foreheads.

245

Life on the Loose

They wore common Nepalese footwear, flip flops, and carried no fat on lean, muscular bodies. In addition to the group supplies, they added their personal bedrolls and clothes to the load.

We lined up on the trail according to our abilities. Cathy, the strongest hiker, led the pack, followed by Andrew, a runner, and Karen, tall, not yet forty, and fit. Maureen and I fell behind. She had a sore knee, struggled going down the steep steps. I struggled going up and down, and my knees were just fine.

No one found the trek easy.

The first days in the heat and unrelenting sun, I didn't want to be there. Even in November, the temperature can hit ninety in the lower elevations, and that's what happened on day two. With my legs and lungs extended to their limits, I plodded up the Modi Khola River gorge cursing the hubris that had sent me, a "flatlander" from Wisconsin, to this place where my fitness was not up to the challenge. I hated the heat, my sore muscles, and the constant steps that led to a ridge, only to be followed by another, and yet another.

When we got to Chomgrong, a small village three thousand feet higher than where we started, Andrew challenged the decision to move our camp further down the mountain. It had been an especially grueling day. "We can't stay here," Saila said.

"Why not?" Andrew wanted an explanation.

"Too many rupees. I know a better place," Saila replied.

As we walked through Chomgrong, we heard the distant roar of a helicopter. "Twenty-four Americans," Saila said. "They ride up and walk down."

He always knew what was happening. Later, we passed some of this group having cocktails in front of a restaurant close to our trail. Unlike us, they smelled like soap and perfume.

Early the next day Maureen woke me up. "Cathy threw up in the tent. Says she thinks the curry last night made her sick."

By midmorning, three people were sick, Cathy, Andrew, and Maureen. Saila said they had altitude sickness and needed a layover day to rest and acclimatize. I ministered to them, handed out diaper wipes, and delivered weak tea to their tents. "You'll be fine tomorrow," I'd say as I handed them tea and cookies. "We all need a day of rest. Me, too."

The rest day was my favorite day on the trek. While Cathy stayed in the tent, Maureen popped out before noon and said she felt better. I sat in the sun and read Driftless by David Rhodes, a beautiful book about a small town in Wisconsin that took me far away from the discomforts of the trek.

After the unplanned layover, we set out again, the young, the sick, and the philosophically slow, to climb the endless steps toward the ABC. The sick ones enjoyed a quick recovery; we thanked them for the day of rest.

Conversation revolved around three subjects: the scenery, the toilets, the food.

We ate well. Pushpa, the cook, produced delicious Indian and Nepalese cuisine in a makeshift kitchen that he set up and dismantled twice a day. Occasionally he made a special treat, fried chicken. When he needed a bird, Saila disappeared for an hour or so in the village, where he bargained with the locals. Then Pushpa carried the bag with live chickens to camp where he used every scrap, including the neck and the feet to make soup and dinner. When that happened, we named the birds. We affectionately called our favorites Clucker and Coo—and then ate them for dinner.

We drank a lot of tea, a good way to get liquid into our bodies when we tired of the boiled water we drank as we hiked. Every morning a kitchen porter greeted us with wake-up tea, followed by tea at breakfast, tea at lunch, tea and cookies après trek, and post-dinner tea.

Life on the Loose

The tea rituals added stress to the toilet issues. The best solution was our own toilet tent, a brown tent the size of a small closet set over a freshly dug hole, within fifty yards of our camp. But on the ABC trek, most nights we were forced to use public toilets because it was a heavily used route and there was no place for our toilet tent. There were other trekking groups in the villages, and we all shared the same holes. That detail had not been in the Venture West trip description. As soon as we arrived in camp, someone checked the facilities and said something like, "I can't use this toilet. It's disgusting."

We'd have the usual conversation that ended with my, "I'm sorry. We don't have a choice." Indoor toilet holes set in tiny, damp, dark, smelly sheds were filthy, but that's what we found on the way to the base camp.

We weren't too far into this "adventure of a lifetime" before everyone knew there were compromises in the world of adventure travel. There were cold nights, aching muscles, long painful days, too many steps, blisters, strange food, and constipation, with its unfortunate twin. Worse yet, our egos suffered, as everyone except Andrew and Cathy needed a helping hand coming down the steep steps, while porters ran past in their flip flops carrying sixty-six pound loads.

We were rewarded with the magnificent Himalayas, exotic villages, and, every day, three delicious meals. We were also rewarded with occasional millet wine and dancing after dinner. The Nepalese love to sing and dance, and we were a willing audience. Sometimes we danced, encouraged by the camaraderie and a bit of the wine.

The last night before the final push to the base camp, we slept close to the sacred mountain Machupachare, or "Fishtail." Surrounded by a ring of peaks over 26,000 feet, we watched the evening alpenglow set them on fire, one by one. They glowed as if lit from inside, showing all the rainbow colors from purple to red to yellow to orange as a blur of snow swirled around each peak, making a fuzzy rainbow from the sunset colors.

Now we were in snow. Porters pitched the tents on the few remaining patches of bare ground. We knew this would be a cold night. Even the gurgling stream that ran past the camp had a layer of ice over the moving water that sparkled in the light from the late afternoon sun, like diamonds reflecting back to their source.

In the morning, we bundled. Even though I layered long underwear, fleece pants, and a pair of coated nylon rain pants on my legs, still they were cold. We walked quickly to stay warm. Soon we would arrive at the Annapurna Base Camp, the reason I chose this trek, to see where twelve women, led by Arlene Blum, an American, had been based before they climbed Annapurna II thirty years ago. Getting to the base camp had been my dream ever since I read about their accomplishment.

I'd read the book, *Annapurna: A Woman's Place*, and I saw the video the women made about the climb. Two climbers died on the final push to the summit. When I read the part where they disappeared before they fell to their deaths, I felt like I had lost two good friends.

Those twelve women were my heroes.

This was the hardest thing I'd ever done. My legs throbbed, my joints ached, and my brain no longer knew how to tell my feet where to step. Even Aleve and Advil couldn't dull the pain or calm my legs on the rocky path.

We didn't linger at the base camp. It turned out to be ordinary, a flat area the size of three football fields, albeit surrounded by 26,000-foot peaks. Despite the sun, the air remained bitterly cold.

Life on the Loose

I felt the spirits of the women who risked their lives to climb the mountain, sensed their presence at the camp, where they had spent many days acclimatizing to the thin air and planning their route to the summit. Despite my struggle with the trek, the endless steps, the cold nights in the higher elevations, and the blistering hot days in the lower elevations, it had been worth the effort and the pain.

We took photos, congratulated ourselves, and started the long walk back to Dhampu.

As we descended, the temperature rose and so did the spirits of the group. Everyone anticipated clean hair, clean clothes, potable water from a faucet, flush toilets, and a long, hot shower.

Back in Kathmandu, I remembered the backpacking trip in Montana where my age forced me to lower my expectations. At sixty-nine, I was no longer the forty-two-year-old woman who had started Venture West with a basket full of dreams and a youthful, strong body. I had barely survived the trek to the base camp. That would be something to think about another day. It was time for a glass of wine.

Chapter Twenty-Three

Awe

2005 Venture West Catalog

Each day you'll visit a different area of the Wind River Range in Wyoming, leaving from our bed and breakfast in Pinedale where we'll eat, sleep, and drink. Each hike measures approximately 8-10 miles with more or less 1500' elevation gain and loss. This is a moderately challenging trip because of elevations over 10,000' but doable for anyone who loves to hike in the mountains.

I love empty beaches, grizzled forests, and Lake Superior. After many years of taking backpackers along the forty-five mile Lakeshore Trail at Pictured Rocks National Lakeshore, the trip needed a makeover. I gathered my camping gear and headed north on a sweltering June day in Milwaukee under the guise of reorganizing the trip in order to bring variety to the day hikes. I couldn't miss with a group at Pictured Rocks: every trail holds surprises for hikers. There are no loser hikes, but since I look for variety, I wanted to bump up the diversity. That's what my customers expected.

I didn't have to live in a tent for a week to do this-I just needed a reason to play. I smiled all the way from Milwaukee to Beaver Lake, where a wind-driven cold front had arrived about ten minutes ahead of me. I threw up the tent in the rain, washed a peanut butter sandwich down with a glass of Merlot, and dove into a lightweight summer sleeping bag. The oppressively hot, steamy day left behind in Milwaukee was quickly forgotten in the rain and the drenched, fifty-five-degree campground.

I recalled a favorite quote from Anne LaBastille's *Woodswoman*: "Regardless of how miserable or splendid the circumstances, the sheer experience of camping seems a total justification for doing it." Good for her. Cold, wet, cranky, I wondered, what the heck was I doing there? Then a river appeared next to me in the tent.

This was neither fun nor character building. That's what I always told people on Venture West trips when we were challenged by cold, wet, rotten weather. "The rain will stop soon. You'll be stronger, a survivor," followed by something like, "You'll be so proud of yourself. Tomorrow will be perfect." Hopefully, someone bought that happy talk, but it had to be said even if no one listened, because they needed something positive when everyone, including me, was weather depressed. It's the number-one guide rule: smile through adversity. I smiled often.

I ignored the widening stream in the tent, rolled over, slept soundly, and awoke to a perfect Lake Superior day. The Lake Superior Merry Maids Cleaning Service had worked all night, scrubbing, polishing, and making the world shiny and new again.

The rain seemed trivial in the morning sunshine. I forgave the soggy tent, the wet boots, and the mud that crept up my jeans. The unpaid bills, the unanswered phone messages, the complications of a busy life evaporated into the misty morning. The unfinished business would stay in Milwaukee where it belonged, on the shelf in the office. I wanted strong coffee, scrambled eggs, and the trail that led to Lake Superior.

Awe

I had told myself this vacation from the work of Venture West was about choosing the best trails, but that wasn't why I had come to the woods. I came to restart my engine, to rediscover a waning sense of awe. Confidence in my guide role gave me peace of mind, but I needed more. The excitement and enthusiasm that drove me to start Venture West had gone missing. After taking paying customers to beautiful places for more than twenty-five years, I'd started to feel jaded. "Oh, look. Isn't that a beautiful view?" Sometimes the words were just words. "Aren't we lucky to be here? This place (fill in the blank) is so special." I'd say to myself, so what. Okay, it was lovely, but I'm tired, my feet hurt, and my knees are stiff. I wanted to sit down, be an observer, not the guide.

The guide had to focus on being in charge, keeping the structure of a trip together, instead of letting go and sinking into the loveliness of the place. What I wanted to do was lean against a log on the beach and watch waves make patterns on the sand. Instead, I worried about the time, the group, the next meal, and how far to the end of the hike. Were they having fun? Were they getting tired? Why hadn't Judy or Jane or what's-her-name shown up at the appointed trail junction? Did they like the hike?

I remembered the time I took a group on a day hike in the Wind River Range in Wyoming. Each day had been different: a waterfall, a lake, a vista, something special to place exclamation points along the trail. Most hikers wanted more than a pretty walk-they wanted a climax, something that gave them bragging rights back home. They wanted what they had paid for, excitement, drama, a well-scouted trip that justified the money they'd spent. That's what I gave them on those well-scouted trips, beautiful hikes with memorable destinations.

On the last day in the Winds, I'd planned a surprise. The group, tired from four days of hiking in the sun, had to be convinced. "It's

253

an easy hike in the shade with no elevation gain, just a few ups and downs." After all, folks, we are in the mountains I said to myself, but didn't dare say out loud. "It's less than two miles. You'll be there in an hour." Three from our group of eight joined me.

When we came to my surprise destination, a perch on a rocky ledge that faced a vertical drop to a grassy meadow, I expected expressions of undiluted rapture. After they glanced at the snow-covered peaks and the three-hundred-sixty-degree view, no one said a word. They responded all right-they shrugged. Finally Alice said, "This is it?" Without a single "wow," they turned and trudged back to the van.

Did they want to hang out, sit on the rocks, look at the mountains, and feel the breeze and the sun on their faces? No. They wanted to go back to town.

I hiked behind, disappointed by the lack of enthusiasm. Their blasé attitude compromised my joy and my sense of awe.

Why was everyone in a hurry? Couldn't they slow down, pay attention, be "present?" I wanted to scream Gandhi's famous quote at them, "There is more to life than increasing its speed." This wasn't a fitness test; we weren't at the gym, we were in the mountains surrounded by breathtakingly spectacular snow-covered peaks. Did they notice the Indian paintbrush along the trail, the waterfall across the valley, and the pointy peaks that bracketed our view in every direction?

This reminded me of something my mother said often, "You can lead a horse to water, but you can't make it drink." No matter how badly I wanted them to share my sense of wonder, I could only step aside and let them do it their way. If they wanted to hurry back to town, I could only follow. They owned the trip; they'd paid for it.

I wondered what they thought about me. Did they think I was the slow hiker who couldn't keep up, or the lazy hiker who liked to sit on rocks and do nothing? They could have been right about the lazy part.

When I traveled solo, I did it my way: no watch, no schedule, and time to do nothing. That's when magic grew in my gut, when I gasped with surprise and felt my heart throb and my fingertips tingle. Stop! Someone freeze this moment. I loved to sit, to absorb the ephemeral moment of undiluted joy. I loved that intensity, enhanced by the feeling of wind caressing my sweaty face.

The business of getting to the end of a trail shouldn't interfere with the importance of sniffing wildflowers and picking blueberries. Robert Pirsig wrote in *Zen and the Art of Motorcycle Maintenance*, "To live only for some future goal is shallow. It's the sides of the mountains that sustain life, not the top." I bet he knew how to sit on a rock halfway to the top.

I sipped coffee at the scarred picnic table at Beaver Lake Campground and pondered the significance of thoughts that wouldn't go away. Could a pokey tortoise lead nimble hares and still hold on to her passion for wild places? The morning sun warmed my bare neck while I planned the day.

A rose-breasted grosbeak belted its cheery song in the nearby woods, and far away the melodious notes of a thrush high did a ventriloquist's act with two simultaneous notes perfectly blended. It could almost fool a person into thinking there was a flutist hiding in the woods.

After I cooked scrambled eggs and muffins on my camp stove, a short hike to Lake Superior led me to a boardwalk and a spring swamp where I stopped and sprawled in the middle of the trail. Hundreds, thousands, maybe millions of golden marsh marigolds shimmered in the morning sunshine. If I held my breath, could I crystallize the moment? The world was too beautiful. If I closed my eyes, would it still be there?

Life on the Loose

In as much time as it takes to watch a shooting star complete its arc, I knew the answer to my quest at Pictured Rocks. I wasn't there to scout. I'd scouted the trip in my head, backpacked there almost every year since 1982. I needed a solo trip. This was recess, time to saunter, to watch the sun polish young leaves, and to lie on the sand and count the clouds.

I opened my eyes. The marigolds remained silent, nodding in the breeze. "Hey, guys, once in a while, I need to get away, to talk to you alone, to drink at the fountain of awe, and to recharge my passion for wild places." A sunbeam lit a single marigold hidden under a small tree. Its yellow blossom swayed in the gentle breeze.

Chapter Twenty-Four

Memories...

1991 Venture West Catalog

The *Isle Royale Queen* takes us four-and-a-half hours across Lake Superior to Isle Royale National Park, where moose and wolves roam and we're the guests. We'll carry our backpacks three to eight miles each day along the coast and across the backbone of the island to MacCargoe Cove. The interior of the island is true wilderness and Isle Royale will be bug-free in September. No backpacking experience necessary-be reasonably fit with a spirit of adventure.

Some people dream about trips, buy guide books and coffee table books with magnificent photography, but don't take the next step and walk out the door. They say, "I'll (fill in the blank) when I retire," or " I'll hike in the Swiss Alps when I can afford to," then time and age take a toll and it's too late. I traveled with people who took the plunge, signed up for a Venture West trip, and didn't look back. We had wonderful adventures.

After I had recharged my passion at Pictured Rocks, I continued to guide for three years. Each time I saw my wrinkled face in the mirror, I knew the end was coming. I did not want to be the person about whom people said, "Is she still guiding? She's old." Nor did I want to be the elderly guide behind the group, not by choice, but because I couldn't keep up. When our roles reversed, the faster hikers would say, "Where's Cari? I hope she's okay." I had never planned to guide after I turned sixty and certainly not into my seventies.

* * * * *

On what I came to think of as the "Guinness" trip, we tramped through muddy woods for four days. Door County, Wisconsin, can be lovely in May, the wildflowers, the budding trees, the rocky ledges overlooking Lake Michigan, but we couldn't see any of that from underneath the brims of our rain hats. We had to watch our feet so we wouldn't unexpectedly plop in the mud.

I wondered, what had I done to offend the weather gods? Tired of wet clothes and muck, I pretended to love the challenge and the cold, wet, dreary hike. At least the people in the group liked each other. Thank goodness for camaraderie.

"Is anyone having fun?" I tried to add levity to the drippy day. I felt wilted too, tired of taking giant steps over the puddles that dominated the trail.

"I don't mind," Jane offered with a shrug. "It's a chance to test my new rain gear before we go out west in July. It works." She pranced ahead, loved the challenge, and didn't give a hoot about the rain.

"Okay, we're almost there. This beats hiking in the heat, and there aren't any bugs." That was my opinion. "Another mile and you'll be safe and warm in the van." Not everyone preferred rain to a sultry summer day, but I did. That was the reason I had quit offering Venture West trips in July and August. I'm a fair-weather hiker; I wilt in the heat and despise biting insects, especially flies, which make me crazy.

Julia stepped closer to me. "This is the last time I wear jeans on a hike. My legs are soaked." Yep, you're right about that. Guess she hadn't read the pre-trip information, the part about jeans and how they're no good when they get wet.

Then someone said, "Cari, give it up. We're tired, we're cold, and I'm wet." Ah yes, Molly. I tried to cut her some slack. "Where are we going for dinner? I'm ready to eat and drink." Recently divorced, Molly's life had fallen apart. She had come to relax, not slog in the rain.

"There's a place close to Egg Harbor where they do a good fish fry. You Illinois people need to experience a Wisconsin tradition."

An hour, later at the supper club, eleven women squeezed around a square table next to a wooden bar in a musty room straight out of the 1950s. The aroma of stale smoke, old whiskey, and the fancy-albeit-fake Tiffany chandeliers didn't jibe with the preppy crowd in the dining room.

"What does everyone want to drink? I'll buy since you were good sports in the rain." Normally Venture West bought dinner while the group paid for their own alcoholic drinks. "I'm having a Guinness. If that's what you want, raise your hand." Ten hands shot up.

The server laughed. "Just wait till the bartender sees this. He'll love it." And he did. Along with our beers he sent ten shots of Jaegermeister, a potent, anise-flavored liqueur and a note written on a napkin. "A round of shots for you. I've bartended twenty-one years and never saw a group of eleven women order Guinness. You made my night."

We puffed up like a bunch of prairie chickens about to do a mating dance. Everyone ordered the fish fry, cod with the works, another beer, and homemade lemon pie for dessert. Even Molly forgave the weather after her third Guinness. "I'll always remember this trip. Thank you for bringing us here."

I heard that more than a few times. People forgot the bad times when life was good and the beer flowed. Maybe that's the secret solution when I'm weather-challenged: beer, but not any ordinary lager, Guinness, or whatever it takes to make everyone smile.

When I asked for the check, our server laughed, "Oh, didn't you know? The men at the next table paid your bill, including a generous tip. They left. They didn't tell you?"

"What?" I said. "We were kidding around with them. They didn't know anything about us." We knew they were golfers from Illinois, having a weekend vacation away from wives and kids.

Everyone laughed. No one laughed harder than me; I saved $250 on the tab.

The next morning when we said our goodbyes, everyone forgot about the mud and the rain. Sometimes weather-challenged trips were the best ones. That's when stories were born, embellished, and repeated year after year.

* * * * *

In Grand Teton National Park in late August, I expected clear skies, seventy-degree days, and freedom from biting bugs. Instead, we found temperatures in the nineties, swarms of mosquitoes, and sticky humidity. According to plan, we hiked up the Granite Creek Trail until we came to shade at lunchtime. We settled on rocks next to a creek where a misty spray from the cascades kept us cool. When mosquitoes feasted on our sweaty bodies, I said, "Bring on the Off; they found us."

When we had started out that day, I told the group, "We're on "moose watch." Everyone, especially me, gets a thrill from a moose sighting, the closer the better. We scored on that hot buggy afternoon. "Cari, there's a moose behind a tree across the trail." Lucy gathered the lunch she'd spread in front of her and jammed it in her pack. "It's close."

"Cari, it's huge. Are we safe here?" Lisa stuffed her lunch in her pack and stood up, ready to run.

"We're fine. He knows we're here." I saw him put his head down to strip leaves from the lower branches, then turn to watch us.

I motioned to the others to come closer. "Everyone sit still. We don't want to startle it, or it might charge," I whispered. "A moose can be dangerous."

We sat motionless while first one moose, then two, then three, stood twenty feet from us and munched leaves as we watched in silence. We had front-row seats for their lunch break. Our fear melted, and in its place came the magical sense of wonder that transcended our discomfort and placed us squarely in the moment. Suddenly everyone knew why we were there.

* * * * *

A less ethereal moment happened one of the years we climbed the South Sister in Oregon. This was not a technical climb, just four-thousand-feet uphill, an arduous slog. Fifteen-hundred feet below the summit, my group came to an intersection where people from two different routes met before the final switchbacks that led to the top.

Hot, thirsty, and apprehensive, we looked at the narrow trail that zigzagged steeply in loose gravel. Dottie was not doing well. At sixty-two, she was the trip elder, an experienced backpacker, but her bird-like appetite often left her short of energy on long treks. I wanted to fatten her up, force-feed her at meals.

"I don't know if I can make it, Cari. I'm drained." The group had waited for her often as she slowly made her way up the trail. "I can't keep going. Look, that trail goes straight up."

She sat down, took off her pack, and looked for her water. She didn't look good, her skinny legs splayed in front of her like "Pick

Up Sticks." I marveled at her stoic endurance and her will to climb mountains. It took a lot to keep Dottie down.

"I'd kill for a Snickers bar," she said.

"Did someone say Snickers?" asked a woman sitting nearby. "Here, I have an extra. You want it?"

With a smile as wide as a North Dakota prairie, Dottie ate the candy, picked up her pack, and, without looking back, marched up the trail.

We found her at the summit.

* * * * *

On a trip to the Smoky Mountains in April, we had planned to see wildflowers. Instead we found snow. First rain, then sleet, then large flakes piled up and smothered the spunky little blooms. After a cold, wet hike, we ate dinner in Gatlinburg. I had planned dinner at camp, but no one, including me, wanted to eat in the snow. When we finished, half the group voted to stay in a motel in Gatlinburg. The rest of us went back to camp and crawled into cold, wet tents. I didn't care if they went to a motel. I just wanted the night to be over.

When we got back to camp, Tricia spoke up, "Cari, things will be better in the morning." I could count on Tricia. I could put her feet to the fire and when her shoes melted, she'd say, "That feels so nice and toasty warm."

In the morning, sun flooded our camp. Everything sparkled in the newly washed air. We built a snowman, cooked scrambled eggs and bacon, and wondered what we had been so worried about. The campers won't remember the long cold night, but they will remember tiny spring blooms that peeked out from under the snow. They won't remember wet clothes. They will remember the blue sky, the snow that clung to pine branches, and the snowball fight on the way to Grotto Falls.

* * * * *

The last time I took the *Isle Royale Queen* across Lake Superior to Isle Royale National Park, I threw up for four-and-a-half hours. Almost everyone did. Only Gail from Minneapolis escaped the nausea, but since she could watch the waves, she was terrified. The rest of us were too busy puking over the side of the boat. She had her own problems with hyperventilating and had to breathe into a bag. The rest of us hoped for death by drowning. Two people, not from my group, stayed inside and broke their wrists when waves slammed them against a table. Fourteen-footers crashed over the boat and tossed it like a bottle in the ocean. The waves also washed away the evidence of the breakfasts we deposited on the deck when we couldn't get to the side fast enough.

On the island, the weather gods rewarded us with six perfect, seventy-degree, bug-free days. I haven't been back. Why would I ever again risk that extreme discomfort? As I said to myself many times during that nightmare trip on Lake Superior, "If this is adventure travel, I prefer laundry."

* * * * *

In Utah, we arrived at Bryce National Park in a driving rainstorm with temperatures in the low forties. "We came to hike. Let's hike." I felt the group disdain, but what's a guide to do? I made an executive decision. We could drive two hours back to Zion National Park where we were camped and do nothing, or we could carry on.

Covered in rain gear, we started down the Fairyland Trail, an eight-mile loop that wandered among hoodoos, large rock forms usually admired on dry, sunny days. When the rain finally stopped, the temperature rose, and those hoodoos glowed in the mist. They looked like someone had lit giant candles inside them. They didn't look like rocks; they looked like temples in a holy place. Then a double rainbow appeared. Not what we came for- something better.

* * * * *

Sometimes weather interfered with dinner. When rain pounds the hard desert soil in southeastern Utah, it runs downhill to the bottom of the nearest canyon. A sudden storm on the Green River in Labyrinth Canyon brought an unexpected delight: fifteen waterfalls.

We'd set up camp on a bend in the river where we could see red rock walls for miles in two directions. After a long day in canoes, the group was ready for a well-deserved rest, wine, and a leisurely dinner. Then we heard thunder. "Grab your rain gear. It's coming," I called to the scattered group. An opaque curtain of rain splashed mud on our legs, the stove, and the pot that held dinner. It felt like someone had turned on a giant spigot and dumped billions of gallons of water on top of us. No one went back to their tents. We wanted to watch the storm.

Then we saw the waterfalls, trickles that turned into torrents, fifteen of them, cascading over the edges of the canyon, up and down both sides of the river. We stood, speechless, at the spectacle that unfolded in front of us.

I'd struggled so many times with nature as my partner/ opponent, but this felt almost spiritual, a quick glance at something powerful, a river spirit that demanded respect.

It ended as suddenly as it started. The waterfalls turned into trickles and disappeared. We washed the mud off the dinner pot, discarded our rain jackets, poured the wine, and carried on.

* * * * *

Memories

The third time I took a group on the High Divide Trail in Olympic National Park in Washington, we walked for five days and never saw the mountains. Every day rain, fog, and mud greeted us as we hauled backpacks up steep trails, hoping to see a glimpse of Mount Olympus. We didn't see anything except the trail, our feet, and each other.

"Cari," Janet said, "I'm not having fun." She was fifty-something and had worked hard to get in shape for this trip. She looked great, had a good attitude and a sense of humor.

"I know. I'm not either." This was one of those occasions when cheerful guide-speak wouldn't work. The fourth night, after another day in the rain, everyone including my co-guide and I, climbed into their two person tents. We were all cold and wet, and worse yet, they had paid for that misery.

Karen spoke for the group. She was the youngest, a stylish, outspoken, successful business owner from Chicago. "We want you to serve dinner in our tents. We want to stay in our bags where we're warm. We're not coming out to eat and we're hungry."

"I don't blame you. It's cold out there." By this time, I'd snuggled into my own sleeping bag. "I don't want to come out of my tent either, but I'm happy to serve you." They were the customers, and I, the willing wilderness worker bee, cooked dinner in the rain and they ate in their tents. In some odd, perverted way, I enjoyed stirring the pot while rain washed my face. When things got tough, I felt strong and happy when I rose to the occasion.

The next morning we left the mountains and headed to La Push, a log-strewn beach on the Pacific where we set up for two nights by the sea. After the sky cleared, my co-guide and I drove to town and bought salmon from a local fisherman. We built a driftwood fire, dried our clothes, and grilled the salmon.

Life on the Loose

"This is more like it, what I came for, luxury in the wilderness." Karen had forgotten the last five, cold, wet, miserable days on the trail. "Thanks for dinner. The salmon was delicious."

* * * * *

I created Venture West; I made the stories happen; I was there when things fell apart and when everything was perfect. Though I wanted to be the flawless leader, I wasn't. I was an observer like everyone else. I watched the hoodoos light up after the rain. I saw the moose stop by the creek, and I sat next to the Green River when fifteen waterfalls burst forth in a canyon. Each time I embraced the quiet joy of my rejuvenated spirit and shared that joy with my fellow travelers. That's why I started Venture West.

There were guilt-ridden times when I wanted to give up, be a full-time mom, but quitting wouldn't honor who I was, who I am. No one promised me that life would be perfect, that guilt would vanish, and that I would never look back and wonder if I should have stayed home.

I smiled through misadventures and carried on through unexpected challenges. I learned to build group camaraderie, to be secure in my guide role, and to project confidence when I was terrified. I'd like to think wisdom was part of the package, that I gained insights into human behaviors as I learned to accept others' frailties as well as my own.

There were many challenges because nature was the boss. When I released the doll from the jar, I knew life would be complicated. I also knew it would be good.

Epilogue

Venture West gave me opportunities far beyond my most optimistic fantasies. I traveled the world and made wonderful friends. I wish I could personally thank each person who signed up, showed up, and shared those trips. From them I received countless gifts, friendship, humor, courage, and laughter. They partnered with me on those journeys, trusted me, and shared their awe, their fears, and their joys as we explored the wilderness together.

Now I'm off to a new chapter of my life, but this much I know: when the weather's warm, I'll be in the woods with my morning coffee, sitting in my camp chair, planning my next adventure.

Acknowledgments

F riends, family, and fellow travelers, I owe you a blanket debt of gratitude for your support and patience as I stumbled and grew in my role as an outdoor guide. I owe a special thank you to everyone who guided or co-guided Venture West trips: Sue Ann McCotter, Becky Crawford, Mary Eloranta, Ann Wheeler-Bartol, Tom Swinford, Denise Goforth, Kim Fadiman, Eric Bjornstad, Paul Guerin, the kayaking guides at Island Escapades, Jack, Francie, and Martin, and most of all, Saila Tamang who kept us safe on seven treks in Nepal. I also want to thank the frequent travelers, the ones who returned year after year, (eight plus for most) and trusted me to bring them home safely: Paula O Neal, Nancy Ball, Dave and Jean Cronon, Sharon Suter, Pam Thiel, Nancy Torres, Betty White, Amy Randolph, Sue Gibson, Lucie Berte, Dean Rockstad, Abe Elliott and Jane Smith, Carol Hebbring, Tricia Mesarich, and Maureen Fitzgibbon.

I couldn't have kept Venture West going without help from my bulk mail crew and especially Lisa MacLaren who finessed the intricate postal system and kept me sane as we drank cheap wine and slapped labels on six thousand annual catalogs.

Thanks are in order to Denise Goforth who said "Yes," packed her bags, got on airplanes, and kept me company as I scouted new trips for the business.

My gratitude also extends to the wonderful doctors and interns who healed my broken body at Hospital del Sureste in Villa Hermosa in southern Mexico.

Thanks to Jo McReynolds who kickstarted my writing career when it was not on my bucket list; thanks to Carolyn Kott-Washburne, who fixed my second-grade grammar and moved my commas to their correct position on the page; a bucket of thanks to the Friday morning writers at Red Oak, my critique committee: Pam Parker, Carol Wobig, Judith Zuckerman, Emily Bertholf, Sharon Foley, Nancy Bauer-King, Eric Hanson, and especially our leader, Robert Vaughan.

None of this could have happened without the friendship and art direction from Lynne Bergschultz, who designed all the Venture West catalogs, the cover art, and the page art for *Life on the Loose*.

I also want to thank Andy Larsen, Director Emeritus, and all my Riveredge Nature Center friends. I came to Riveredge at age thirty-nine, just another suburban housewife, and left encouraged and empowered to start down the road to adventure travel guide.

And a big hug for Kira Henschel, who took on my mess and turned it into a real book.

About the Author

Cari Taylor-Carlson's former day jobs include assistant buyer at an upscale department store in San Francisco, environmental educator at the Schlitz Audubon Center, and children's horticulture educator at Boerner Botanical Gardens in Milwaukee, Wisconsin,

She combined her passion for walking and eating and has written six books: *Milwaukee Walks, Milwaukee Walks Again, The Food Lover's Guide to Milwaukee., Milwaukee's Best Cheap Eats*, and the *Upscale Outdoor Cookbook*. She also founded the former *Milwaukee Walking and Eating Society*, now called *Venturing Out*, a group dedicated to exploring Milwaukee's neighborhoods and ethnic restaurants.

Taylor-Carlson has written about food and restaurants for *M Magazine, Milwaukee Magazine*, and the *Milwaukee Journal Sentinel*. Currently she reviews restaurants for *Urban Milwaukee.com Arts and Entertainment* section and *Riverwest Currents*, and reads her essays on *Lake Effect* at WUWM-FM, Milwaukee's NPR station.

Cari prefers to travel with a tent and backpack, and continues to live on the loose, always checking around the bend for the next adventure.

Please visit her website at www.lifeontheloose.com

CPSIA information can be obtained
at www.ICGtesting.com
Printed in the USA
FFOW04n0406041016
28151FF

9 780962 945267